JOHN GALEN HOWARD
and the University
of California

The publisher gratefully acknowledges the generous
contribution toward the publication of this book
provided by the Director's Circle of the University
of California Press Associates, whose members are

Jeanne Falk Adams
Jola and John Anderson
Elaine Mitchell Attias
Janice and Thomas Boyce
Alice and Robert Bridges
Chambers Family Fund
June and Earl Cheit
Margit and Lloyd Cotsen
Camille Crittenden
Sonia Evers
Wilma and William Follette
Phyllis K. Friedman
August Frugé
Sheila and David Gardner
Harriett and Richard Gold
Ann and Bill Harmsen
Florence and Leo Helzel
Mrs. Charles Henri Hine
Marsha Rosenbaum and John Irwin
Beth and Fred Karren
Jeannie and Edmund Kaufman
Nancy Livingston and Fred Levin,
    The Shenson Foundation
Sally Lilienthal
Sheila and David Littlejohn
Sally and Peter McAndrew
Susan and James McClatchy
Hannah and Thormund Miller
Nancy and Tim Muller
Elvira Nishkian
Joan Palevsky
Mauree Jane and Mark Perry
Jennifer and Mark Richard
Bernat Rosner
Frances and Loren Rothschild
Shirley and Ralph Shapiro
Sharon and Barclay Simpson
Judith and William Timken

JOHN GALEN HOWARD
and the University
of California

The Design of a Great Public University Campus

Sally B. Woodbridge

University of California Press

Berkeley Los Angeles London

University of California Press
Berkeley and Los Angeles, California

University of California Press, Ltd.
London, England

© 2002 by the Regents of the University of California

Library of Congress Cataloging-in-Publication Data

Woodbridge, Sally Byrne.
    John Galen Howard and the University of California: the design of a
great public university campus / Sally B. Woodbridge.
        p.   cm.
    Includes bibliographical references and index.
    ISBN 0-520-22992-4 (alk. paper)
    1. Howard, John Galen, 1864–1931.   2. Architects—United
States—Biography.   3. University of California, Berkeley—Buildings.
4. Architecture—California—Berkeley—20th century.   I. Title.
NA737.H64 W66   2002

727'.3'092—dc21   2002004966

Manufactured in Canada

12   11   10   09   08   07   06   05   04   03

10   9   8   7   6   5   4   3   2   1

The paper used in this publication meets the minimum requirements of
ANSI/NISO Z39.48-1992 (R 1997) (*Permanence of Paper*). ⊗

Contents

Acknowledgments   *vii*

1   The Early Years to 1888   *1*

2   Paris and New York: 1889–1895   *11*

3   The University of California and the 1898–1899 International Competition for the Hearst Architectural Plan   *22*

4   Postcompetition Reversals: 1900–1901   *39*

5   Supervising Architect for the Hearst Architectural Plan: 1901–1903   *57*

6   The Move to California in 1902   *68*

7   The President's House, California Hall, and the Hearst Memorial Mining Building: 1901–1907   *74*

8   University Work, Private Practice, and the Alaska-Yukon-Pacific Exposition: 1904–1907   *89*

9   Doe Memorial Library, Boalt Hall, and Sather Gate: 1907–1917   *98*

10   Expositions in Seattle, San Francisco, and San Diego: 1909–1915   *112*

11   The San Francisco Civic Center and a Trial: 1911–1913   *121*

12   A Move and the Publication of *Brunelleschi:* 1912–1915   *129*

13   The College of Agriculture, Sather Tower, Hilgard, Wheeler, and Gilman Halls, and Campus Landscaping: 1910–1917   *134*

14   World War I and Postwar Changes at the University: 1917–1924   *152*

15   Dismissal as Supervising Architect and a Career as Educator: 1923–1931   *165*

Appendix: Buildings by John Galen Howard   *177*

Notes   *183*

Selected Bibliography   *195*

Illustration Credits   *201*

Index   *207*

Acknowledgments

I would like to acknowledge the following individuals, who provided invaluable assistance in the preparation of this book:

Elizabeth D. Byrne, Head, Environmental Design Library, UC Berkeley

Robert Gayle, Director of Project Management, UC Berkeley Capital Projects, and Project Manager for the Hearst Memorial Mining Building Seismic and Program Improvements Project

Daniel P. Gregory, Ph.D., Architectural Historian and Senior Editor of *Sunset* magazine and grandson of Warren and Sadie Gregory

Galen Howard Hilgard, daughter of Robert B. Howard and granddaughter of John Galen Howard

Brendan Kelly, Project Architect with NBBJ Architects for the Hearst Memorial Mining Building Seismic and Program Improvements Project

Waverly B. Lowell, Curator, and Carrie McDade, staff, Environmental Design Archives, Wurster Hall, UC Berkeley

Janet S. Parks, Curator of Drawings, Avery Architecture and Fine Arts Library, Columbia University, New York

William M. Roberts, University Archivist, UC Berkeley

Doug Robertson, Structural Engineer with Rutherford & Chekene, for the Hearst Memorial Mining Building Seismic and Program Improvements Project

The Early Years to 1888

"The streets are overrun with young, handsome, bright-eyed, well-dressed men, real estate agents, I imagine, rushing from one bargain to another.... Every other shop is a real estate office.... Land business is really gambling. Over a million dollars of real estate changes hands daily, and this in the 'dull season,' in a city which claims 60,000 but probably only has 40,000 persons. Beautiful orchards, gardens, and vineyards are cut up into city lots and allowed to peter out for want of care. Great avenues, which no one uses, are laid out across the now sterile lands."

The year is 1887; the writer is John Galen Howard, age twenty-three. He has just come to Los Angeles from Boston to take advantage of the boom times, which were providing an unprecedented amount of work for the small number of people with experience in the practice of architecture. Most people who called themselves architects at that time worked in construction, not design; they were better described as "carpetects." So-called pattern books, often published by companies that produced construction materials, provided the designs that builders used for most residential and some commercial buildings.

Howard's attendance at the Massachusetts Institute of Technology, which had the premier architectural program in the country, and his employment in the Boston office of Henry Hobson Richardson gave him a record that few who claimed to be architects in Los Angeles—even in California—could boast of. Among the other young men in Los Angeles of Howard's acquaintance who called themselves architects with some justification were Ernest Coxhead and Willis Polk, both of whom moved to San Francisco around 1890 and established successful practices. Howard was to renew his acquaintance with Coxhead and Polk in that city in the late 1890s.

Howard's impressions of Los Angeles, conveyed in letters to his mother and his Aunt Nette, were a mixture of admiration for the climate and the scenery and abhorrence of the crass materialism that ruled life there. "I am constantly shocked and disgusted with the low tone and degradation of thought and speech which is nearly universal," he wrote in September. Yet the driving force of moneymaking aside, Howard found that "man meets man much more freely and unreservedly here than in the deeply rooted, prejudiced East."

Howard's eastern roots were deep indeed. One of his paternal ancestors, also named John, crossed the Atlantic from England about 1630 and settled in Plymouth, Massachusetts, where he lived in Miles Standish's house. His descendants, among them Levi Howard, a doctor who made his home in Chelmsford, Massachusetts, settled around Boston. Levi had five children, two daughters and three sons, the youngest of whom was John Galen. John's brothers, Amasa and Edwin, with whom he maintained close contact throughout his life, became, respectively, a doctor and an actor. But the family member that John was closest to in his youth was his Aunt Nette—Antoinette—his mother's sister. It was she, not his parents, who encouraged his artistic bent. Indeed, Levi Howard appears to have had little sympathy for his son's artistic aspirations. His letters of 1882 to John, then eighteen and in his last year at the prestigious Boston Latin School, mainly concerned his son's inability to live within his means.

Boston's rich cultural life drew Howard. He enjoyed theater and opera as well as social events that required more money than he was allotted by his father. In answer to his father's questions about what he wished money for and whether much of it was not "spent needlessly on theater tickets," John wrote that he needed new clothes and a cane, haircuts, drawing materials, and books. Levi sent him funds, but was disappointed that John had not "kept his expenditures within reasonable limits." With birthday money from Aunt Nette, Howard was able to buy the books that he coveted: poetry by Wordsworth, Coleridge, and Keats; Isaac Walton's *Compleat Angler;* Longfellow's translation of *The Divine Comedy;* Meiklejohn's translation of Kant's *Critique of Pure Reason;* and Ruskin's *Seven Lamps of Architecture.*

Following his graduation from high school in 1882, Howard chose to enroll in the Massachusetts Institute of Technology, even though he had a certificate of admission to Harvard because of his high standing at the Boston Latin School. In addition to architecture, Howard's three-year stint at "the Institute" included such extracurricular activities as writing for *The Tech,* the school journal. Although no evidence exists that he considered a literary career, writing remained an avocation to which he devoted as much energy throughout his life as he did to his professional calling.

The tension between father and son over money came to a climax in 1883, when John announced that he would not return home after the end of his first term at MIT but instead would go to New York to find work. Anguished letters from his mother and his Aunt Nette followed. His older brother, Amasa, wrote that he understood John's anger but felt that his father, sorry for his lack of understanding, would meet him halfway. Although the relationship was patched up, subsequent letters from his mother expressing her sadness that John never wrote his father or asked about him reveal the real distance that existed between them. Now when Howard needed money, he addressed his requests to his mother and Aunt Nette.

Levi Howard died in 1885, leaving the family in financial straits. John left MIT, a premature departure that seems not to have troubled him. Although the institute's school of architecture was the oldest in the country, having been founded by William Robert Ware in 1865, the emphasis on engineering did not satisfy Howard's predilection for design. That summer he began work in Henry Hobson Richardson's office in Brookline, near Boston. He found the office, which employed twenty-one men on jobs being undertaken in Cincinnati, Albany, Chicago, and Washington, D.C., extremely pleasant, the work agreeable, and the other draftsmen likable. Yet even though Howard was learning a great deal and was content in his new job, office talk of boom times in Los Angeles intrigued him. He wrote his mother that a Mr. Saunders, who had had four years of architectural work in Los Angeles, had offered him $1,000 to go there, adding that Saunders had said that the opportunity "for a young architect with brains and push is very great." Evidently this offer did not work out, for in 1886 Howard was still working in Richardson's office and living in Brookline.

Richardson's death that year left the firm awaiting confirmation of a commission for Senator Leland Stanford's new university in California on the peninsula south of San Francisco. With the departure of Charles Coolidge, George Shepley, and the other partners for San Francisco to present drawings to Senator Stanford, Howard was left in charge of the office. Coolidge told him that if all went well Howard would be sent to San Francisco as head of design in the branch office that the firm intended to open there.

When this tantalizing offer, too, failed to materialize, Howard decided to go to California on his own. With money borrowed from his mother and Aunt Nette, he left the East Coast in August 1887 and traveled by train to Los Angeles. He found the city "bare and brown, the streets ankle deep in dust and sand." From his boardinghouse room he wrote, "The grounds about the better class of houses are beautifully kept with palms, orange trees and roses. I have seen bananas, pomegranates and oranges. No rain falls in summer—all is parched and sere. [Yet] I can imagine myself becoming passionately attached to the place and, indeed, with money I think it would be delightful to make a home here." Two minutes later his writing was interrupted by shouts of "fire" in the street below his window. The fire, which had started in a restaurant, was under control in half an hour. The bystanders' lack of concern prompted Howard to reflect on the day-to-day risks of living in a city of predominantly wooden buildings.

The Los Angeles that Howard encountered was experiencing an unprecedented surge of economic prosperity that had begun more or less in 1885 when the Santa Fe Railroad reached Los Angeles. For a short time a rate war between the Santa Fe and the Southern Pacific brought the price of a Kansas City–Los Angeles ticket down to $1, stimulating tourist and immigrant travels. The Southern Pacific had its own publicity bureau, staffed with writers who made southern California's Edenic image familiar not only in the Midwest and the East of the United States but also in Europe.

Yet the reality of the city was not as glamorous as advertised. In *Picturesque California and the Region West of the Rocky Mountains, from Alaska to Mexico,* edited by John Muir and published in 1888, the writer Jeanne C. Carr praised the fine business blocks that were replacing the older, smaller buildings on the "level streets" of San Pedro, Alameda, and Main. The more substantial, masonry-clad business blocks we know today, represented by the 1893 Bradbury Building on Broadway at Third Street, were yet to come. Notable residences were in progress on Bunker Hill and Boyle Heights, but many of these were not built until the 1890s. Angels Flight, the funicular railway that transported people from the business district up the steep side of Bunker Hill to their homes, was not built until 1901. In reality, the building boom that Howard had heard about in Boston was still in progress; it had not yet produced buildings of high quality in respect to either design or materials. Many buildings existed only as drawings on paper.

Howard's letters to his mother and Aunt Nette are filled with detailed observations of the landscape and vegetation of Los Angeles. An excursion on August 14 to Pasadena took Howard nearly as far as the Raymond Hotel, a famous resort that served visitors with its own rail system to Los Angeles. "We were in sight of the mountains all the way," he wrote. "Certainly the air was the most pleasant I have ever breathed. Everything is dry and brown but the scenery is lovely. Great groves of live oaks dark and green cover the hillsides and relieve the monotony of brown." Beautiful orange groves appeared and "long lines of bluish green eucalyptus."

Like many easterners, Howard was much impressed by California's

OPPOSITE
California houses drawn by Howard in 1888. In a letter to his mother from March 1888 about some adobe buildings he had seen, Howard wrote, "They attract little enough attention and interest, but to me they offer one of the greatest charms of the place. There is a naturalness about them, a frank acknowledgment of their limitations and an easy accomplishment of all possible effect within those limitations, a modest dignity in striking contrast to the 'loudness' of the smart, pretentious, vulgar loudness of the mansions being built now."

AN·OLD·TIME·
CALIFORNIA·HOME·

COVRT·OF·OLD·ADOBE·HOVSE·
LOS·ANGELES·

climate. In October he wrote that "every day seems finer than the last, cleaner, softer,…every evening seems brighter, more crystalline." Yet he noted that the climate was changing because the newcomers had tried to make the place more like home by planting trees, which had somewhat increased the humidity. Still, the dryness of the air made the summer heat much more tolerable than in the humid East.

Among the exotica that attracted Howard's attention were tarantulas. While on a ramble through the countryside with another architect he

Howard's pen-and-ink sketch of the Santa Barbara Mission, summer of 1888. Earlier in the year he had visited the San Fernando Mission, which he described in a letter of March 5: "Imagine a long, low, rambling pile of building of sturdy walls and naive distribution of voids and solids, once whitened but now stained and enriched with warm yellows and browns and greens and falling into an almost unkempt decay—and all crowned with the soft, deep red of the hillocked tile lichened and weather beatened…. Behold the Mission!"

had trapped one of these huge spiders, which he described in great detail, including the fact that it was reluctant to bite. He also took the trouble to excavate the nest of a trapdoor spider, which impressed him as a marvelous construction. A visit to an ostrich farm, a well-known local tourist attraction, reassured him that, contrary to what he had heard, the fashionable feathers were painlessly removed.

Sketching trips were favorite weekend activities, the colonial missions being favorite destinations. In San Gabriel, Howard found the "quaint and unfashionable, simple adobe houses in white or pale colors with wide, overhanging eaves, three-foot-thick walls" very satisfying. He identified these buildings with the simple, pastoral life the inhabitants had led until the greedy Americans overran them. However, this nostalgia for a vanished past did not prevent him from relishing the exciting pace of the present. In September 1887 he wrote home about the "new men from all over—Chicago, Dubuque, Boston—nice fellows, good class."

The firm he worked for, Caukin & Haas, was a little over a year old in 1887 and, in Howard's judgment, by far the city's best. The office was located at 14 N. Spring Street in the heart of downtown. But even though the work was better than he had expected it to be, Howard wrote that he had to "shut his eyes" to most of it. He described Caukin as a "very pleasant, slight, pallid man, gentlemanly—maybe 40 or 50." Although Caukin did not express approval of Howard's performance in words, he did increase his young employee's salary and treated him as the head designer in the office. Even so, Howard yearned to go into business on his own. He was confident that he could "do the work needed in Los Angeles better than almost anyone here because of training and sensitivity." Only the size of his financial debt to the family finally convinced him to remain at Caukin & Haas for the year he had originally intended to stay in Los Angeles. The projects being worked on—a new city hall, several competitions, and a house for which he noted the use of stone—were promising.

Cultural entertainment was not what it was in Boston, nor was church. In September, Howard wrote Aunt Nette that he had gone to a church service in the opera house, where he heard "a particularly stupid sermon." And when he asked his landlady where the churches were, she told him that she had never been to a church in Los Angeles, which seemed to be the case for most of the residents he spoke with.

In mid-November a rent increase caused Howard to move. Rents were exorbitant all over the city, he wrote, and an even greater influx of people was expected because the Atchison, Topeka, and Santa Fe Railroad was soon to begin its four-and-a-half-day run to New York. Fortunately, he was able to move into the house of a co-worker, where he had a room for $10 rent and $30 board, with French windows and a great view because of its location on the edge of a steep hill. This may have been Bunker Hill, which was being aggressively built up at the time. In previous letters, Howard had commented on the steepness of the city hills, which in many cases were accessed by stairways rather than streets.

Streetcar lines to outlying communities provided pleasant excursions. Howard described a pre-Thanksgiving ride toward the "deep blue mountains" where recent rains had restored the green of the orange trees, and even the hills were "green, green, green." The next day he joined friends for a fine New England Thanksgiving dinner with turkey, cranberries, potatoes, pickled peaches, and apple and mince pies. "If only the advantages of the east could be joined to those of the west," he wrote, "there would be little to desire."

By March 1888 the boom had quieted down. Caukin told Howard the firm's prospects were dubious. Instead of being depressed by this news, Howard was relieved. "My experience with the firm has in some ways been terrible," he wrote Aunt Nette, "deadening, soul-compressing." In Los Angeles he "led two lives, days of drudgery and evenings of study, thought, writing, sketching." At the beginning of April, in anticipation of his departure from California, Howard took a trip by train to Santa Barbara, which he had read about in Charles Dana's *Two Years before the Mast*. He wrote that the scenery he viewed from the train was fine, and the view of Santa Barbara against the mountains was enchanting. He sketched the mission and noted the dignified atmosphere of the place, while predicting that more railroad traffic would ruin it.

By the end of April he was making plans to return to the East Coast but wanted to work a month or two more to earn money, even though by this time "the idea of working in a California office is intensely distasteful." Business was very slow. "A few months ago," Howard wrote Aunt Nette, "there were six of us here in the house in the same office. Now all of us have left the office and by Saturday night only two of us will be living here."

Although the economy was weak, Howard found work with James M. Wood of Chicago, who called himself "a Theatrical Architect." Howard would have preferred to work for Ernest Coxhead, an Englishman about a year older than he, whom he described as "young and in this country only a short time, but he is beginning to do some very creditable work—thus far chiefly on paper." Among the works that Howard might have seen in Coxhead's office was All Saints' Episcopal Church in Pasadena, designed and built in 1888–89. The design showed a skillful assimilation of the aesthetic of the American Arts and Crafts movement, with Richardsonian elements that Howard would have appreciated.

Coxhead had studied at the Royal Academy of Fine Arts in London and the Royal Institute of British Architects, to which he was elected as an associate in 1886. His move to California in 1887 may have been prompted by the promise of commissions from the Episcopal diocese of California. (His father, an Anglican clergyman, may have gained his son an introduction to Bishop William Ingraham Kip, who favored high church Anglicanism.) Coxhead designed six churches in southern California for the diocese in the late 1880s and an equal number of houses for Boyle Heights and Bunker Hill in Los Angeles.

Despite this apparently busy practice, Coxhead was not hiring in the spring of 1888. In any case, Howard was interested in the opportunity Wood offered him to explore theater design. He described Wood as "middle-aged, self-confident but not offensively so, smokes unceasingly and wears a cravat of blue and salmon stripes and a diamond. Everyone wears a diamond," Howard observed. He expressed no distaste for this habit and even wondered about having one himself.

On June 3, 1888, Howard met Willis Polk, an architect three years younger than Howard who had a restless personality inclined toward flamboyancy. His father had been a "carpetect" who moved around the

Midwest, finally settling in Kansas City. Polk's own training began at the age of eight, when he worked for a contractor in St. Louis. In 1885 in Kansas City, Willis senior started the firm of W. W. Polk & Son and gave his son responsibility for the residential designs in the office. Polk was talented and ambitious. In 1887 he left the family firm and went to Boston to work for Van Brunt & Howe. Although he stayed there only six months, his ambition was whetted by this foray into the eastern professional world. He then crisscrossed the country, working for brief periods in

A drawing published in American Architect, *March 30, 1889, of All Saints' Episcopal Church, designed by Ernest Coxhead in Pasadena, California.*

various architects' offices and auditing part of a course taught by William Robert Ware, a former partner of Van Brunt who established the school of architecture at Columbia in 1881 after having founded that of MIT eighteen years earlier. Polk's professional progress was as erratic as his employment record. His few months in Coxhead's office were not spent in a congenial working relationship.

After encountering Polk on a sketching expedition, Howard wrote a sharply worded description of the man who, a little more than a decade later in San Francisco, was to become his friend and ally: "Polk is clever, brilliant, facile—but with so little depth, so little appreciation of the meaning of real art that it is more encouraging to think of another 50 years of silence in our art than to anticipate its falling into such light hands." Still, Howard recognized that Polk was a talented draftsman and not one of those "many men who reveal the disastrous infancy of architecture in this country" because their aims don't include "the development of the artistic strata—the science of the upper air in the mind."

Wood's plans for Howard changed from week to week. At first he wanted to send him to Tacoma, Washington, to assist in the construction of a large theater there, but by the end of June 1888 he spoke of sending him to San Francisco where another theater was in the works. Howard was hesitant. He felt that his year in Los Angeles had concentrated his ambition to do work that was worthwhile—meaning, one assumes, work that would further his career. His purchase of Mrs. Schuyler Van Rensselaer's biography of Henry Hobson Richardson may have strengthened his resolve to raise his sights in architecture from the low level of practice in Los Angeles. He noted, for example, that Mr. Wood and his associates were prone to commit "the fatal mistake of building their decoration instead of decorating their buildings." "The longer I stay here," he wrote his mother on July 1, "the more utterly despicable the place seems and the more hopelessly homesick I get for something true and beautiful…. The crudity of life, the ignobility of aim, the incomprehension of anything like love for and devotion to art grinds deeper into me every day and I feel literally that I hate Los Angeles, a strange sentiment to go hand in hand with the real affection I have conceived for the natural scenery, the climate and for a few—a very few—personal acquaintances and friends. Yet I cannot give up hope for the future of such a young place."

At the beginning of September Howard joined friends from his former office for a brief trip south to San Juan Capistrano, where another colonial mission was located. What with the depression, the present seemed to Howard as frozen as the past. The end of the boom had left "poor settlements stranded on the prematurely drawn-up maps…paper towns. One has to see these crude ugly settlements to perceive why in the far West every collection of a few houses is called a 'city'—far from what we in New England would call a town." Santa Barbara might be a town, he thought, but San Juan was a village, even though it had more saloons than he took the trouble to count. Mulling over his impressions of California, Howard attributed the homeliness and naturalness he liked about the place to its "Spanish" culture. Americans are "grasping, overreaching, mean and mercenary…. They have driven to the wall a simple, pastoral, peaceful and human way of living and have brought a crude, fast, undignified, vicious life to do it with."

Howard's return trip to the East Coast began on September 13, 1888, by boat up the coast to San Francisco, where he would board a ship that would take him through the Panama Canal. He described the city he viewed from the harbor as "a wretched conglomeration of shanties without dignity or beauty." After landing he proceeded to the renowned Palace Hotel. "Huge and abominably ugly, but splendidly managed" was his comment. "The central court into which you drive is imposing, admirably schemed, singularly unbeautiful." Unfortunately, no other letters from San Francisco exist to tell us if his harsh initial impressions softened; the next letters described the sea voyage to Panama on the way to New York.

Paris and New York
1889–1895

2

Back home at last, Howard prepared for his first trip to Europe, for which Aunt Nette lent him the money. On November 11, 1888, he landed in Antwerp, where he was bowled over by the paintings by Rubens in the museum. Proceeding to Paris, he stopped in Amiens and Beauvais, which surpassed his expectations. "Such a delight," he wrote, "to come across sights and buildings unexpectedly which you have studied line for line and almost stone by stone from books and photographs…like recognizing an old friend."

After a few days in Paris at a hotel at 5 rue de Beaune, Howard decided to stay a month, since drawing instruction was cheap and the opportunities for learning great. He attended the Académie Julian, directed by William Adolphe Bouguereau, in the mornings from eight to twelve, where, together with several hundred other students, many of them American and English, he sketched from casts and live models. He described the atelier's rooms as "shabby," the walls "encrusted with drawings," the participating artists "seedy, longhaired scrufs," and the atmosphere "as close to pandemonium as ever I saw, but *earnest.*" Howard's enthusiasm for Paris was boundless; he wrote that he was filled with an "indescribable feeling of inner glow." As for the built environment, he preferred the high Gothic of Amiens to the "new architecture" (by which he meant the neoclassic style) of Paris, which he found "handsome, cold, and uninspired."

A trip to Italy toward the end of January 1889 began in Rome, where Howard was overwhelmed by the Sistine Chapel but did not care for Michelangelo's architecture. Howard's reactions to the major styles and the historic centers of culture he encountered were mixed. He was repelled by the baroque and rococo styles, finding them "full of distorted motifs and vicious details." Rome struck him as tame and commonplace, though he didn't say why. Florence filled him with inexpressible joy, while Naples was unsettling. "It is an extremely interesting place," he wrote Aunt Nette, "but very full of bad smells. It is peculiarly Italian, this smell, allied closely to the flavor which one encounters in almost everything one eats. Even in some candy I ate this afternoon there was this distinctively Italian flavor. I don't really object to it—it is too delightfully Italian for

John Galen Howard at age 26.

me to be able to do that; but one records it as a novelty and for a little while refrains from forming an opinion of it. Some end by detesting it; I simply don't object."

Venice, Howard's last stop in Italy, was snowy and very cold in February; sightseeing was limited and inspired no written comments. From Venice he returned to Paris and thence to London, where he looked for work without success. On February 22 he sailed for New York. After visiting his family he found work in April in the Boston office of McKim, Mead & White. The office was on the verge of closing because of lack of work, and in August Howard transferred to the New York office. In a letter to his mother he described the city as "big and harsh and crude.

I have seen more eating houses and fat men than in all my life." But New York offered a wider field for experience and observation than Boston, and Howard thought that he would like it very much, even though it was "the noisiest place and full of robbers—even the doormats have to be chained."

In the fall of 1889 Howard moved to an apartment at 137 E. 21st Street on Gramercy Park, which gave him some proximity to nature. New Yorkers, he observed, were insensitive to the "country"; it hardly seemed to exist for them. But the cityscape was attractive, particularly the views of the two rivers at the end of long, straight streets. "One of the real and unique pleasures of New York," he wrote, "consists in a walk at twilight out over the Brooklyn Bridge," an experience he compared to being at sea.

The office atmosphere was pleasantly harum-scarum, "full of papers and books and casts and men devoted to the work." Assigned to work on a new building for Madison Square Garden under Stanford White, Howard wrote his mother that he expected White (who was then in Europe) to be "a terror to deal with as he is said to have a fiery temper and a sure knowledge of just what he does and does not want, which is exactly what Mr. McKim, for instance, never does quite arrive at knowing." McKim "is most charming, if fickle," and Mead "is the effectual bond of the firm— methodical and punctual."

By the end of September he was immersed in the Madison Square Garden theater project. He was also sketching in pastels, and planning to take a clay modeling class at the Art Students League. Such classes were not simply a dilettantish interest of Howard's. Drawings and soft clay models of classical ornament from the Grecian, Roman, or Renaissance periods were required as part of the admission examination for the École Nationale Supérieure des Beaux-Arts in Paris, as well as standard components of the course work there. Howard would have been familiar with the école's approach to design from working with Richardson, whose experience at that illustrious school influenced the office atmosphere. "It was one of Mr. Richardson's principles," Howard had written, "always to have photographs and casts of all the best old work, as a constant unconscious means of educating tastes." Proficiency in rendering classical motifs and the orders was a practical necessity; they could be integrated into the design vocabulary, modified, and recreated for real projects.

A letter dated October 13, 1889, announced that "the greatest event of the last few days has been the arrival of Mr. White from Europe. He is a great, hulking fellow with a little round head, hair a la Pompadour, and a big red moustache with no method to it at all. He is addicted to swear words, and everyone mimics him. I am prepared to love and hate him in the same breath—he's that sort of man." Two weeks later Howard wrote that "Mr. White is not half so bad as he has been painted though utterly untamed and thoroughly eccentric."

As for Howard's standing in the office, Mead, in whom Howard expressed "perfect confidence," told him that he was regarded as a fixture and should stay as long as he liked. Although the firm had been cutting expenses and staff, in January 1890 White raised Howard's salary from $20 to $25 a week and put him with two or three other men at the head of the office. Such signs of approval boosted Howard's self-esteem; nonetheless, he allowed to Aunt Nette that he felt "the cruel need of betterment."

In June Howard won *Cosmopolitan* magazine's competition for a public bath. The $200 prize, he wrote his mother, would pay some doctor's bills and buy a new coat. He also moved to 46 E. 21st Street, "a quiet house with a number of pleasant men, artists, literary men and engineers." October's news was that McKim wanted to send Howard abroad and had offered to lend him enough money for eight to ten months of study in Paris, presumably at the École des Beaux-Arts, which McKim had attended from 1867 to 1870.

The école exerted a magnetic attraction on young American architects in the latter part of the nineteenth century and into the twentieth. For Howard and others who craved instruction in the principles and methods of design, no course of study in the United States equaled that of the école. Much of its influence came from the fame of American architects such as Richard Morris Hunt and Henry Hobson Richardson, who, having attended the école, had started successful practices and attracted important commissions. (Hunt started an atelier in New York City in 1858 in an effort to bring some of the école's spirit home; among his students was William Robert Ware, who in 1865 founded the School of Architecture at MIT.) In the 1890s the circle of architects who had studied at the école worked mainly in the eastern part of the country and maintained ties to each other through professional clubs such as the Architectural League of New York, established in 1881.

Although the expense of ship passage to Europe and lodgings in Paris made it costly for Americans to attend the école, the instruction itself was virtually free. Nor were there any academic prerequisites.[1] Students set their own pace in acquiring the credits needed to pass from the second to the first class and then working toward the diploma, eligibility for which ended at the age of thirty.

In November 1890 Howard sailed on the *SS Westernland* to Antwerp. Proceeding to Paris, he stayed again in the hotel at 5 rue de Beaune and wrote that he was enjoying everything just as much as before. A most welcome bit of news from New York was that "Stanny" White had purchased a watercolor from a New York dealer to whom Howard had consigned it. According to McKim, who relayed the news, White had admired it in the window and bought it without knowing that Howard was the artist.

After some weeks of preparation in the atelier of Paul-René-Leon Ginain, a normal procedure for foreigners, Howard took the March/April entrance examination for the École des Beaux-Arts. He placed third among 230 applicants, only thirty of whom were admitted to the école. Howard's score was higher than any American had attained previously. After passing additional tests in drawing and modeling, he wrote that he had been received into the school with a rank of fourth place. Only two other Americans out of the fifteen who took the examination were admitted at that time.

The next step was to settle on an atelier, or design studio. Howard chose that of Victor-Alexandre-Frédéric Laloux, one of the largest and most prestigious ateliers then and for some years to come. Typically, the *patron*, or head, of an atelier was a recognized competition winner, often a winner of the Grand Prix de Rome. Laloux had won the Grand Prix in 1878. The amount of instruction the patron gave his students was not fixed, nor was the amount of time he spent in the atelier predictable. For this and other reasons the atelier had evolved into much more than a workshop; it was an invaluable home base with its own organizational rules. Howard described the operation of the atelier as having an element of "communism." New students served a half-year apprenticeship during which they were obliged to slave for the upperclassmen, known as the *anciens*, in a variety of ways, including the manual labor of building frames for the large drawing boards and moving them in carts, or *charrettes*. (Hence the expression "en charrette"—still in use—for being in the final stage of a design problem.) At the end of the apprenticeship the "new man" became an *ancien* and could vote for officers and participate in the management of the atelier.

Upperclassmen were entitled to help from fellow atelier members, both in the form of critiques of their work and, in the case of lengthy design problems that required huge drawings in pen, pencil, and ink washes for plans, sections, and elevations, artistic assistance. The painterly additions to the students' final boards—landscapes, cloudscapes, figures, etc.—might be executed by talented fellow studio members. Although the members of teams working on the competition problems cooperated with each other, a competitive spirit, both within and between ateliers, was encouraged, as were boisterous behavior and practical jokes.

On the scientific side of the école's curriculum were courses in descriptive geometry, stereotomy (the cutting of solids into certain figures or sections), and perspective. On June 28, 1891, Howard wrote that he was the only person to win a medal in the descriptive geometry examination. He was also the only one awarded a medal for a project in the stereotomy course, for which he made "carpentry" drawings of structural details to accompany the presentation of a building designed according to a program.

Introductory projects, or *analytiques,* required rendering of the classical orders, window and door treatments, and other minor features taken from historical buildings. These preliminary problems led to what Howard described as "competitions of plans," which were for small structures such as a loggia or courtyard or a small public building. A knowledge of historical prototypes was necessary to formulate a solution and finish the problem within the required time period. These competitions were called *concours,* and the student's achievement of first or second place gained him the points required to advance to the next stage of instruction. A medal was worth several points.

These courses were all prerequisites for construction, the most challenging course of all. Construction consisted of a series of lectures followed by an arduous oral examination and a design project that featured, on several panels, structural drawings, working drawings of details, accurate dimensions, and computations.

Since the construction course was one of the most important parts of the training, Howard very much wanted to stay another year to take it. But he needed more money to do that. McKim offered a loan, but Howard turned to his mother and Aunt Nette, who sent him monthly checks during the next year. He rewarded their confidence in him by continuing to win "mentions" in his courses. When a Paris architectural journal published one of his designs with favorable comments, he wrote his mother that he took it as a good omen.

In October he moved to 54 rue Vaugirard, where he had an attic room overlooking the Jardin du Luxembourg, his favorite Parisian garden. He wrote of having completed his half year of atelier service making frames and wheeling the carts that carried drawings submitted for judgments. Now he was entitled to serve the upperclassmen doing renderings. In November he finished his first "regular" project in architecture with help from his fellow students in the atelier. Thus far he had the highest standing among those who had entered the école with him, and he was now eligible for the course in construction. Soon he wrote that he was attending the construction course twice a week and that only one other student had more points than he, because he had done two problems that Howard had not yet done. Still, he reined in his confidence: "The chances of success," he wrote, "depend on the opinion of too many men for one to feel at all sure of his mentions, especially on esquisses [sketches]."

The year's end was hectic, what with examinations for the next phase of construction, work on a three-month problem, and preparation for a final exam in January 1892. Howard was under great pressure to finish up work for the second class in order to enter the first class in the very short time of seven months. Despite his rapid progress, Howard was circumspect about the value of continuing his training at the école. "There is coming a time," he wrote on November 8, "when no advantage which I could gain by remaining could offset the disadvantage of weighting myself with additional debts…. I feel that I must not eat too far into my life with a training which, however valuable in itself, might prove only a hypersensitising influence on my own faculties, already perhaps too exquisite in certain directions for my own happiness or that of those about me."

In addition to his work at the école, Howard was committed to assisting McKim's effort to convince Puvis de Chavannes, a renowned Parisian artist, to execute the murals for the main staircase in the Boston Public Library. In late April he had the time-consuming task of getting a large model of the library staircase sent by McKim through customs and into good repair after its sea voyage. After renting a space for the model, he had the satisfaction of showing it to some members of the atelier. At the end of May, Howard wrote McKim that he had had a "long and interesting talk with M. Puvis de Chavannes," who still would not confirm whether he would take the job—the distance from Boston was too great and he had many other commitments. Still, Puvis expressed his deep interest in the scheme, which a close examination of the model had renewed. Howard requested drawings with exact dimensions of all the surfaces of the staircase that were to be painted.

In the meantime, he finished the construction course and by the beginning of August had taken his last examination for admission to the first class. In September Howard wrote that the LeClaire Prize, the award for finishing the second class and proceeding to the first in the minimum amount of time, was divided equally between himself and another American named Storghton. Howard's goal was to complete five months of the first class and return home in February 1893. Since he would be thirty in May, he would be ineligible to pursue the diploma.

In early October Howard moved to a seventh-floor apartment—up 139 steps—at 5 rue de Médicis. The winter's major course was archaeology, for which he did a restoration of a Roman bathhouse. His two-month project won the first medal given in this subject in two years.

On January 1, 1893, Howard wrote his family that he was engaged to marry Mary Robertson Bradbury, an art student whom he had met in New York. Mary had come to Paris to study painting, which she had previously studied in Chicago and New York at the Art Students League. She paid her way by writing magazine articles about a student going to Europe on a shoestring. In Paris she was hired by an American clergyman and his wife to manage a club that the couple had started on the Left Bank as a place for Americans to meet. In return for her rent-free room she served four o'clock tea to visitors and acted as a chaperone in the evenings. When Howard came to the club with some friends, they renewed their acquaintance. But this time, as John wrote, they continued to meet and fell in love.

Although they were supportive of each other's work, correspondence indicates that John's commitment to architecture was stronger than Mary's to painting. He described her as having "a strong fine face" and a personality "as gay as a bird.... She is all that I am not," he concluded. By all accounts this statement was fairly accurate, for Mary was gregarious and extroverted. In a memoir written in 1987, their daughter Janette Howard Wallace described her mother's exuberant personality: "She loved to dress up...she would turn a coat inside out—just anything to make an

Mary Robertson Bradbury sketching on a trip to Spain in 1886 with family and friends.

outlandish costume, and then she'd act the 'Jabberwocky' with enthusiasm and much laughter."[2]

By early February, virtually working around the clock, Howard had accumulated more than half of the points required for the diploma; McKim and others urged him to stay on. The final hurdle was the thesis: the design of a building and its complete presentation in plans, sections, and elevations, with working drawings, construction details, an outline of specifications, and cost estimates.

In late March, however, fate intervened. Howard's mother became seriously ill, forcing him to depart for home; she died before his ship reached New York. The subsequent press of family affairs and his approaching marriage made a return to Paris unwarranted.

Although he failed to finish his last year, Howard had reason to be proud of his record at the École des Beaux-Arts. Of the thirty-one points required to finish the program, he had earned twenty-seven. (Although he wrote his mother that he had accumulated thirty-one, four were extra points, which raised his rank but did not count toward the diploma.) No other American had ever advanced so far toward being *diplômé*.

Although a diploma from the école certified that its holder could practice architecture in France, it was of little practical use in the United States, where the process of certification for architects had yet to be regulated (Illinois became the first state to institute licensing for architects, in 1897). Hence for most Americans the école's diploma seemed hardly worth the time and effort needed to acquire it. The prestige of having attended the école, however, was a generally sufficient entrée to the most desirable offices, particularly during the building boom that followed the Civil War. In the decades from 1870 to 1910 the country's population more than doubled; some cities increased in population more than fivefold. A nationwide labor shortage and the westward migration encouraged mechanization of industries and trades. The number of factories with assembly lines increased; corporations grew in size and number. In such prosperous (and unregulated) times, virtually anyone with some experience in construction could set himself up as an architect-builder.

Those men with academic training or who had experience as an apprentice in a recognized architect's office found the situation deplorable. Architects began to lobby state legislatures to enact licensing laws; they established professional societies and journals, founded new schools, and published their views whenever possible. Young men attended the École des Beaux-Arts in increasing numbers, with American attendance at its highest from 1890 to 1914.[3] The fraternity of école alumni was close-knit and intent on raising the standards of architectural practice in the United States. Howard, too, on his return to the country, began what was to be a lifelong involvement in this cause by cofounding the Society of Beaux-Arts Architects in New York City.

Predictably, the increasing prominence of architects with ties to the école aroused jealousy within the profession, which was by no means solidly in the Beaux-Arts camp.[4] Efforts to denigrate the school's system took various forms. For example, in an article titled "The Case against the École des Beaux-Arts," published in *American Architect* on December 26, 1896, Ralph Adams Cram—prefacing his remarks with the disclaimer that he knew nothing about the école—addressed the issue of whether it was proper to use iron, an industrial material, in the construction of buildings in the United States. Iron had been used structurally to great effect in many famous Parisian buildings, notably in the École des Beaux-Arts' own Grande Salle des Antiquités (1863), designed by Félix Duban, and in the Bibliothèque Nationale's Salle des Imprimés (1858–70), by Henri Labrouste. Considering the growing structural use of iron in office and commercial buildings in the United States in the late nineteenth century, the matter would seem to have been settled. Yet Cram, a confirmed medievalist, thought otherwise. He cited Ruskin, who said, "God never

A rendering of the Hotel Renaissance in New York City published in Architect and Engineer *in June 1937.*

meant iron for anything but decoration purposes unless perhaps for nails when you can't use wooden pins. You are flying in the face of the Almighty to turn a metal to purposes of support." Howard, however, in a letter to the editors of *American Architect* published on February 15, 1897, demurred: "Far be it from me to enter at this time into a discussion of the rights of iron to assume functions other than mediaevalists allow it. I will merely say that there is no civilized nation today which denies itself the use of iron for support…. The École des Beaux-Arts might reasonably countenance its use in obedience to the dictates of common sense." Howard then asked the editors to present a "serious and faithful outline of the actual course of study at the École" to forestall misrepresentations of the program.

Howard launched his private practice in 1893 in partnership with an engineer, Samuel M. Cauldwell. In spite of a severe economic depression that year, the firm had several commissions that enabled them to open an office at 31–33 Pine Street in New York City. Partnership between architects and engineers was not unusual, particularly when the work included large buildings such as hotels that required more knowledge of structural engineering than was addressed in architects' training. Among Howard and Cauldwell's projects were the Hotel Renaissance (1897–98), the result of a competition, and the Essex Hotel (1896–98)—both representative of the rather ornate French style of hotels being built in New York at the time—and several houses, including a townhouse for Mr. A.D. Julliard (1896). In 1897 the firm was at work on the Newark, New Jersey, High School, also the result of a competition. That same year, Howard and Cauldwell were awarded second place in the much publicized competition for the New York Public Library. The firm of Carrère & Hastings was the winner, and the principals of the other competing firms were all école men. Another important project was the Majestic Theater in Boston (1901–2), a commission that Howard received through James M. Wood, with whom he had worked in Los Angeles.

Meanwhile, the Howard family had grown to include two sons, Henry Temple, born in 1894, and Robert Boardman, 1896. In 1898 the family moved to Upper Montclair, New Jersey, where another son, Charles Houghton, was born in 1899—a fateful year for the Howards.

3

The University of California and the 1898–1899 International Competition for the Hearst Architectural Plan

For late-1890s California, which in 1900 would celebrate its fiftieth anniversary, the century ahead promised unlimited opportunity. The state's population had grown to almost one and a half million, and the economy, once based firmly in mining and agriculture, had grown to embrace large-scale commerce, transportation, and manufacturing. Although San Francisco dominated the Bay Area, other cities, such as Oakland, were taking shape. Berkeley had two foci: an industrial center on the western waterfront and a largely residential district with some commercial development to the east around the University of California, founded in 1868.

The university's location on the east side of the bay opposite San Francisco was somewhat fortuitous. The concept of a state institution of higher learning, embedded in the state constitution, had been discussed in and out of the legislature since the early days of statehood. Although various sites were promoted for the institution, none was backed by a strong commitment of money and energy. The income of state residents was not especially high, making the notion of taxation for higher education unpopular. Many citizens thought that the government was usurping new power in even considering the idea. Compulsory education even at the elementary level was not enacted until 1874; by 1879 the state had only sixteen high schools.

Publicly supported higher education had long been a missionary undertaking, espoused by Congregational and Presbyterian clergymen such as Horace Bushnell and Samuel H. Willey, chaplain to the state constitutional convention. They were joined in the cause by influential lawyers and businessmen such as Frederick Billings, John W. Dwinelle, and John B. Geary. After several unsuccessful starts, this grassroots movement finally gained momentum and financial support in May 1853, when the Reverend Henry Durant, who was to be the first president of the new university, arrived in California and professed his goal of establishing a women's seminary. Shortly thereafter, a joint meeting in Nevada City of the Congregational Association of California and the Presbytery of San Francisco resolved to open an academy called the Contra Costa College in rented space in Oakland. In 1855 this preparatory boarding school was incorporated as the College of California.

The college trustees, headed by Billings, acquired four blocks of land bounded by 12th, 14th, Franklin, and Harrison Streets in what was to become the downtown area of Oakland. Funds for the new "seminary of learning" would come from the sale of 46,000 acres of public lands granted in 1853 to the state by Congress. Buildings were constructed for residence and instruction, but the site soon proved problematic. The city was growing up around the campus, increasing the value of land beyond

View of the University of California campus from the east, ca. 1890.

the college's means to acquire it and threatening the students—as the trustees saw it—with unwholesome influences. They therefore began to explore new sites in less populated, more pastoral areas. After acquiring several tracts and a ranch about four miles northwest of Oakland, the twelve trustees stood with friends of the college on a large rock (later named Founders' Rock) that commanded a sweeping view of the area and dedicated the new grounds as a Seat of Learning. Although this event took place on April 16, 1860, financial instability postponed the college's move to the new site for over a decade.

A view of the central campus from the north showing Bacon Hall on the left and North and South Halls on the right. The ca. 1885 photograph shows a loop road defining the grassy plot for the flagpole and footpaths criss-crossing the surrounding grounds.

In 1862, the Morrill Act gave each state 30,000 acres of surveyed public land for each of its U.S. senators and representatives for the establishment of a land-grant college. Four years later, the California legislature used the proceeds from the sale of its 150,000-acre grant to found an Agricultural, Mining, and Mechanic Arts College, to be located on land near the new College of California site.

During a meeting of the trustees that took place in 1866 at the base of Founders' Rock, Frederick Billings, surveying the grand view, quoted several lines from an essay, "On the Prospect of Planting Arts and Learning in America," by the eighteenth-century Englishman George Berkeley, bishop of Cloyne: "Westward the course of empire takes its way;/the first four acts already past,/A fifth shall close the drama with the day;/Time's noblest offspring is the last." He suggested that the town in which the new college was located be named after the bishop, and at a later meeting, on May 24, 1866, the board of trustees of the college unanimously endorsed his proposal.

The next year the trustees of the impoverished College of California offered its Berkeley and Oakland properties to the state on the condition that the humanities would be added to the state college to create "a complete university." The legislature then repealed the 1866 act founding the Agricultural, Mining, and Mechanic Arts College, and in its place passed a charter act establishing the University of California, signed by Governor H.H. Haight on March 23, 1868. A board of regents was appointed to govern the university, and Henry Durant was elected its first president. The University of California graduated its first class of twelve men—called the "Twelve Apostles"—in 1873, by which time 17 faculty members served 191 students.

In the expansive post–Civil War era, the country badly needed more educational institutions to create a skilled population for the development of the sparsely settled West. A postwar migration of people to cities had taken place on an unprecedented scale, creating chaotic social conditions along with new wealth. But while social and political reformers focused on the problems associated with urban growth, a growing number of civic-minded leaders were attracted to loftier projects, including the Beaux-Arts–inspired architectural visions that took shape during the 1880s.

A much published and discussed embodiment of these visions was the Boston Public Library (1887–95). Designed by Charles Follen McKim of McKim, Mead & White, the building drew inspiration from Italian Renaissance palaces and the Parisian Bibliothèque Sainte Geneviève (1838–50), an internationally famous building designed by Henri Labrouste. As a publicly funded institution supported by Boston's wealthy and cultured citizens, the Boston library testified to the power of art and architecture to express civic pride.

Before its completion, however, a far grander expression of civic art took center stage: the World's Columbian Exposition of 1893 in Chicago. An ensemble of monumental buildings, the "White City," as it was called, gave form to the aspirations of the civic-minded whether in government, business, or the arts. The Chicago event opened the way to a succession of expositions in the first decade and a half of the twentieth century: the Pan-American Exposition in Buffalo, 1901; the Louisiana Purchase Exposition in St. Louis, 1904; the Alaska-Yukon-Pacific Exposition in Seattle, 1909; the Panama-California International Exposition in San Diego, 1915; and the Panama-Pacific International Exposition in San Francisco, 1915. Under the combined influence of the expos and various reform movements, municipal art leagues, civic improvement associations, and city art commissions were established in major cities. Such organizations provided a client base for architects associated with the École des Beaux-Arts who had been trained in the classical language of architecture.

Given the enthusiasm for civic-minded construction at the turn of the century and beyond, the idea of an international competition for a permanent architectural plan for the University of California campus was not surprising. By the end of the 1890s, the school was growing quickly, with the faculty numbering around one hundred, and student enrollment nearly two thousand. Within a few years it would rank among the nation's top ten in size. Although the university was nicknamed the "Athens of the West," the physical campus with its hodgepodge of buildings did not come close to matching its reputation. In addition, there was competition from the rival school to the south to consider: in the mid-1880s, Leland Stanford had attracted national attention by enlisting the talents of leading architects to design a master plan for the university he planned to build in Palo Alto as a memorial to his son. Stanford University opened in 1891.

In 1895 the prominent San Francisco lawyer Jacob B. Reinstein, one of the Twelve Apostles and newly appointed to the board of regents, asked his fellow regents, the faculty, and the alumni to suggest ways to improve the university. Bernard Maybeck, a mechanical drawing instructor in the engineering department and once a student at the école, proposed an architectural competition. At first Reinstein dismissed Maybeck's idea as unrealistic, even calling Maybeck "a freak," whom he and his fellow regents did not take seriously. But soon he was won over—possibly by Maybeck's infectious enthusiasm for the grand vision—and endorsed the proposal, saying that state legislators and private individuals would give more to the university if they could see an "actual picture" of the architecture that would perpetuate their names in stone. In December 1895 Reinstein publicized his views in a newspaper article, stating, "Let us build, not rapidly, not lavishly, but slowly, yet grandly, that there may greet the commerce which shall whiten the Golden Gate and the civilization which shall

A portrait of Phoebe Apperson Hearst in the Trustees Publication of the International Competition of 1899.

grace this western shore an architectural pile of stately and glorious buildings which shall rival the dreams of the builders of the Columbian Exposition, which shall do honor and justice to a superb Republic and to its most
favored State, and which, even in their ruins, shall strike the beholder
with wonder and rapture."[5]

Following the regents' approval of the competition in May 1896, a
campaign to raise funds received such enthusiastic support that within
a few months $4 million had been pledged. The major donor was Phoebe
Apperson Hearst, widow of Senator George R. Hearst, who, in a letter to
the regents dated October 22, 1896, offered to pay both for the competition and for two buildings of the accepted plan.[6] One building was to be
a memorial to her late husband, who had made his fortune in mining. "I
desire to say," wrote Mrs. Hearst, "that the success of this enterprise shall
not be hampered in any way by a money consideration." (Mrs. Hearst had
approached then President Martin Kellogg in late 1895 with the intention
of funding a building for the College of Mining in memory of her husband. News of Maybeck's proposal may have caused her to see her building project as an appropriate part of a grander scheme.)

Her magnanimous offer accepted by the regents, Mrs. Hearst then
appointed a board of trustees for the competition. J.B. Reinstein was the
chairman; the members were California governor James H. Budd and
William Carey Jones, professor of jurisprudence. As the coordinator of the
competition, Maybeck seems to have been largely responsible for the
prospectus, which outlined an unparalleled—indeed, scarcely believable—
opportunity for architects:

> The purpose is to secure a plan to which all the buildings that may
> be needed by the University in its future growth shall conform. All

the buildings that have been constructed up to the present time are to be ignored, and the grounds are to be treated as a blank space to be filled as a single beautiful and harmonious picture as a painter fills in his canvas.

The site of the University of California at Berkeley, California, comprises two hundred and forty-five acres of land, rising at first in a gentle and then in a bolder slope from a height of about two hundred feet above the sea level to one of over nine hundred.... It is thought that the advantages of the site, whose bold slope will enable the entire mass of buildings to be taken in at a single coup d'oeil, will permit that production of an effect unique in the world, and that the architect who can seize the opportunity it offers will immortalize himself.

It is seldom in any age that an artist has had a chance to express his thought so freely, on so large a scale, and with such entire exemption from the influence of discordant surroundings. Here there will be at least twenty-eight buildings, all mutually related and, at the same time, entirely cut off from anything that could mar the effect of the picture. In fact, it is a city that is to be created—a City of Learning—in which there is to be no sordid or inharmonious feature. There are to be no definite limitations of cost, materials, or style. All is to be left to the unfettered discretion of the designer. He is asked to record his conception of an ideal home for a University, assuming time and resources to be unlimited. He is to plan for centuries to come. There will doubtless be developments of science in the future that will impose new duties on the University, and require alterations in the detailed arrangement of its buildings, but it is believed to be possible to secure a comprehensive plan so in harmony with the universal principles of architectural art, that there will be no more necessity of remodelling its broad outlines a thousand years hence than there would be of remodelling the Parthenon, had it come down to us complete and uninjured.

In the great works of antiquity the designer came first, and it was the business of the financier to find the money to carry out his plans. In the new building scheme of the University of California, it is the intention to restore the artist and the art idea to their old pre-eminence. The architect will simply design; others must provide the cost.[7]

The plan was to provide buildings for administration, the library, a museum, auditoriums, gymnasia, areas for military exercises, habitations, clubhouses, an infirmary, general service buildings for such things as heat, power, and light, and the means of "approach and communication," or access roads and pathways. Fifteen departments were projected, within divisions classified as Higher Historical and Literary Instruction, Higher Scientific Instruction, and Higher Technical and Applied Instruction.

There was much to do to get the competition under way. Maybeck and Professor William Carey Jones spent several months seeking advice from presidents of large universities, leading educators, architects, painters, and sculptors. Meanwhile, Maybeck and Reinstein set out for Paris to consult eminent architects about the program for the competition.

Apparently Maybeck did not discuss the competition with the local architectural community, even though he certainly knew its leaders. The choice of Paris as the headquarters for his work on the competition reflects his devotion to the place where he had spent several memorable years studying. Having arrived in San Francisco in 1890 and settled in Berkeley, where he started an as yet very modest practice working in other architects' offices, he was aware of the region's provinciality regarding architecture. That many of those who entered the competition would have no real knowledge of the site and its geographic context was not a disadvantage, in Maybeck's judgment, for great art was universal. At the école students worked on projects for distant places they knew nothing about. Indeed, winners of the institution's highest award, the Grand Prix de Rome,[8] often created buildings for fictitious sites: a hospital in the Alps, for example, or a government center for "a capital city."

Maybeck spent most of two years working on the competition in Paris. The "programme" (the French term was used, a nod to the École des Beaux-Arts' legacy of such competitions) was written mainly by Julien Guadet, professor of theory at the école, and William Ware, head of Columbia University's School of Architecture. In 1897, after the program was completed and the jurors selected, Maybeck visited various European cities to promote the competition. Sets of photographs of the campus, maps showing boundaries and indicating some of the topography, and copies of the programme in English, French, and German were deposited with architectural societies and with city officials at home and abroad. In addition to J.B. Reinstein, who represented the university, the jury was composed of eminent architects: Jean-Louis Pascal of Paris, Paul Wallot of Berlin, Norman Shaw of London, and Walter Cook of New York. The competition had two stages, judged, respectively, in Antwerp, Belgium, from September 30 to October 4, 1898, and in San Francisco from August 31 to September 7, 1899.

The published European responses to the news of the competition often alluded to the American disposition toward materialism. The *Spectator,* a London review, commented favorably that the projected "city of learning on the slopes of the Pacific" reflected "the desire to identify California in the thought of the world with something else than mines, ranches, and newly enriched millionaires." On a more envious note a speaker at Oxford said, "To us Oxonians who bear uncomplainingly our poverty and lessened revenues there is brought a report that in California there is a university furnished with so great resources that even to the architects (a lavish kind of men) full permission has been given to spare no expense." In the United States, an 1898 issue of *Harper's Weekly* exclaimed, "There has never been anything in the history of education or of architecture quite like the competition which the University of California owes to the munificence of Mrs. Hearst." Linking the competition to Leland Stanford's creation of the eponymous university down the peninsula from Berkeley, the article went on to state that "the multimillionaires of California have attested their interest in education on a scale which has excited the wonder of mankind."[9]

By July 1, 1898, the deadline for the first round of the competition, 105 entries had been received in Antwerp, where they were displayed in the Royal Museum of Fine Arts. The jury met from September 30 to October 4 and awarded prizes to eleven plans, the authors of which were invited to compete in the second round. The finalists were also invited to make an all-expenses-paid visit to the site, of whom nine did so. Considering that three of the finalists were from France, one from Austria, one from Switzerland, and six from the eastern United States, the offer was indeed generous. Only three California firms entered the competition—B.J.S. Cahill, Alexander Oakey, and Coxhead & Coxhead—and none was among the finalists. Strangely enough, none of the architectural firms most prominently associated with the École des Beaux-Arts, such as McKim, Mead & White or Carrère & Hastings, submitted designs.

One of the finalists was the New York firm of Howard & Cauldwell, and in January 1899 John set off "to the Golden Gate," arriving in San Francisco on January 29. His mission was to study the site and assess the strengths and weaknesses of his proposed scheme. In letters to his wife he reported that he had called on Regent Reinstein and then hurried to Berkeley to see the site: "and wonderfully beautiful it is!" he wrote, "the air is full of Spring." After lunch at the Bohemian Club in San Francisco hosted by the mayor, the superintendent of the city's parks, John McClaren, drove Howard around the city. That night he dined with Regent Reinstein and friends and later wrote Mary that he had many invitations to lunch and dinner. The following days were a whirlwind of activity, his visits to Berkeley alternating with social events in San Francisco, where, for example, he viewed the sunset from the Cliff House. Given the relatively slow pace of transportation at the time, his periods of rest and reflection were few and short.

On February 6 Howard described a strenuous day on the campus talking to the heads of the Departments of Chemistry and Mechanical Engineering about their needs. The next day he wrote Mary that "the air in Berkeley is an elixir; the views are an inspiration. Tomorrow I go to Reinstein's office for a consultation with Friedlander, Stokes and May- beck." Howard was also to have lunch with Professor George H. Howison of the Department of Philosophy, an eminent scholar, who had come from the Massachusetts Institute of Technology and occupied the first endowed chair in the university.

As a competition finalist, Howard was guaranteed access to power- ful figures in the university. He also knew the architects Willis Polk and Ernest Coxhead from his year in Los Angeles in 1887, both of whom had by now made names for themselves in San Francisco. Although Polk was ambitious by nature, he did not enter the competition. Coxhead did enter with an interesting scheme that, unlike those of the finalists, did not dis- play a strong Beaux-Arts bias.

Alas, Howard's letters from San Francisco contain no reflection on his triumphant return to San Francisco in 1899 relative to his disdainful dismissal of the city eleven years earlier. After an extended stay marked by congenial meetings with university figures and new acquaintances on both sides of the bay, Howard returned to New York.

For those finalists who chose to visit the site the main revelation lay in its topography. The competition prospectus noted the 700-foot change in elevation from sea level to the range of hills to the east but did not describe how hilly the land designated for the campus buildings was. Since preliminary site visits had been out of the question for distant com- petitors, the assumption followed in the winning designs of a uniform flat or sloping site for ensembles of buildings was logical. Further, the combination of increasing elevation and an obvious westward orientation to the "Golden Gate" made tiers of buildings rising from west to east only natural. True to the prospectus, the finalists' competition boards pre- sented the "entire mass of buildings" so that they might be taken in "at a single coup d'oeil."

The programme for the second stage of the competition was substantially the same as that for the first. However, on behalf of the competition trustees J. B. Reinstein clarified certain of the competition guidelines. The first concerned student housing. Although the number of students was projected to be 1,500, he now qualified the question of how they were to be housed with the statement, "Whether or not dormitories will be neces- sary for the students will not be decided for many years," thereby dimin- ishing the importance of the dormitories to the composition as a whole. He also lowered the space requirements for military exercises and a botan- ical garden; both elements, said to have been exaggerated in the first-

phase submissions, were now to be located away from the campus.[10]

A more important issue was the treatment of the existing landscape: "Some competitors have, in their arrangement of their plans, almost entirely covered up the water courses and conducted them in subterranean conduits under different parts of their plans. We again call attention to the great importance attached to these water courses and to the more important groups of trees on the grounds." He referred specifically to the hilly nature of the site, stating the university's "wishes to reserve, for the construction of its edifices, all the resources at its disposal.... It cannot devote them to costly remodeling of the grounds, such as would necessitate extensive or deep excavations or fillings, or any considerable work in erecting embankments, which, besides the disadvantage of excessive expense, would cause preliminary delay and inconvenience." The competitors were expected to "respect the general topography of the grounds and to follow it as closely as possible ... and to permit only such remodelings and gradings as might be necessary for a general system of roads and means of communication."

The final submissions did not reveal serious consideration of these amendments to the guidelines. Dormitories still contributed importantly to the plans, although they often seem to have been used as compositional pawns. Some of the finalists made a feature of the south fork of Strawberry Creek and its wooded environs, along with other wooded areas. Most of the building groups still appeared to rest on graded land. This apparent lack of concern for the last and most emphasized of the trustees' points is not surprising, since even those who visited the site would not have had time to study the lay of the land in great detail. Nor would the surveys provided them have been adequate to the task of making the architectural forms reflect the site with any accuracy. In any case, this was the kind of issue usually addressed once the competition winner had been declared.

Then too, Mrs. Hearst's munificence doubtless raised false expectations of the university's wealth. In fact, the university was far from financially secure.[11] In 1887 the legislature had imposed a one-cent tax on every $100 of taxable property in the state; a decade later this ad valorem tax was raised to two cents. Little of this money went to the new university, however: powerful interest groups, notably in agriculture, generally opposed legislative support for development of the campus, perceiving the university as elitist. Thus, it was only with the help of such donors as Mrs. Hearst that the university president at the conclusion of the competition, Benjamin Ide Wheeler, was gradually able to build a roster of wealthy donors who would fund the campus buildings erected during his administration (1899–1919).

The second stage of the competition was judged in September 1899,

33

in San Francisco. Submissions were to be deposited at a post office or railway or steamship company office having regular mail service to New York; the parcels would then be sent by fast train to the secretary of the University of California in Berkeley. These instructions call attention to the fact that nearly half of the eleven entries came from Europe; the rest would travel from the northeastern United States: five from New York City and one from Boston. The finalists, notably, were from those areas most in the shadow of the École des Beaux-Arts.

The four jurors—Pascal, Wallot, and Cook, plus John Belcher from London, replacing Shaw, who was ill—met from September 1 to 7 to make their judgments. They visited the site twice to verify compliance with the program, the second time using photographs of the drawings to assess the adaptability of each submission to the local topography. As anticipated, the jury members found the quality of the final entries to be of "high character" and to bear evidence that their authors had expended "great thought and study" on their presentations.[12]

The jury listed several points that they considered of particular importance in their deliberations. First was whether the submission represented a university as opposed to a mere architectural composition. Second, it was critical that the grouping of buildings would allow future expansion without crowding. Third, the purpose of several departments had to be apparent from their building's design. And finally, the architectural forms were to fit the configuration of the grounds and preserve their natural beauty.

The first-place winner, Émile Bénard of Paris, had submitted one alternate to his final scheme (he had submitted two schemes in Antwerp) and had added three drawings to the plan, section, and elevation requested for the study of one of the building groups. Bénard had won second place in the 1866 competition for the Grand Prix de Rome; in 1867 he was the first-place winner. Entering competitions was a staple of his career, as indeed it was of many outstanding graduates of the école. His drawing skills were exceptional, as the plates for this competition demonstrate (of particular note are the perspective view of the gymnasium, the interior of the gymnasium vestibule, and the gratuitous detail of a sculptural group on the capital of a pilaster supporting part of a balustrade).

Bénard's scheme won unanimous praise for having successfully addressed all of the jury's concerns. The elevations were judged to be "excellent in scale, character and nicety of proportion," and the drawings "beautifully rendered." The only weakness noted was that some of the buildings in the upper part of the plan were too far from those with related departments, making some rearrangement perhaps necessary. In the end, "The jury, after an examination of the references and certificates submitted by M. Bénard, declare that this architect offers the guarantees which justify his being entrusted with the execution of the work."

The second- and third-place winners, Howells, Stokes & Hornbostel of New York and Constant Désiré Despradelle and Stephen Codman of Boston, were criticized politely, with their strong and weak points noted. The fifth-place submission by Lord, Hewlett & Hull of New York was all but dismissed for requiring an "immense expenditure for retaining walls, grades, etc." and for being more of an "interesting study than a practicable plan for a university."

Howard & Cauldwell placed fourth. Their plan had changed significantly from the one submitted for the first phase, the tightly organized, more or less equilateral composition having been drawn out along an east-west axis and embellished with landscaped terraces. Rows of nearly identical rectangular buildings flanked the central element, and two main cross axes connected to the gymnasium complex on the south as well as to the city blocks and other building groups on the north. At the west end, streets radiated from a grand plaza out into the still sparsely developed city of Berkeley. At the east end a domed auditorium building flanked by large halls (of as yet undetermined use) provided a focal point for the terraced central element. On the hillside above the auditorium were rows of dormitories and a domed, basilica-like building, serving as a coda to the composition. The use of individual buildings rather than building complexes minimized the amount of grading needed for foundations and made incremental development of the plan possible.

The jury noted that the design had a general reasonableness, but that the author (the use of the singular acknowledges Howard's responsibility for the design) had not "taken advantage of the possibilities of his scheme.

Howard's auditorium building, while modest compared to the gymnasium depicted in Bénard's entry, was still at odds with the reality of the university's prospects. The domed building recalls McKim, Mead & White's library at Columbia University as well as other versions of the Roman Pantheon. In this rendering from Howard and Cauldwell's submission to the 1899 international competition, the white building and its subsidiary structures appear to hover above an undefined landscape. The unreal effect was prophetic; the auditorium was never built.

The disposition of his buildings on a long avenue facing the Golden Gate is somewhat monotonous. He has preserved the woods and placed his athletic fields in a good position. The dormitories as placed radiating on the hillside appear better on the plan than they would in execution. The group shown in detail [the auditorium complex], though fine in many respects, is not the jury's idea of a University." The negative tone of these comments suggests the unlikelihood that Howard would ever be considered for the position of supervising architect for the Phoebe Apperson

Émile Bénard's rendering of a longitudinal section of the gymnasium.

Hearst Architectural Plan. But as events unfolded over the following year, the jury's remarks—and even the competition itself—became irrelevant to the situation at hand.

Competitions were a legacy of the École des Beaux-Arts system. The presentation requirements for a general plan, a general elevation, a general longitudinal section following the longest dimension of the grounds, and a general perspective of the scheme were familiar to those who had either attended the école themselves or worked in offices run by men who had. The dominant impression the array of presentation drawings makes on today's viewers is one of grandiosity. The plans were visionary—as in impracticable, speculative, fanciful. None of them could have been readily implemented. Their only practical value, perhaps, lay in projecting a picture that would bring gifts of money to the needy university.

The local population received the competition with enthusiasm; many architects supported it. In an approving article titled "The University Competition" in the November 7, 1896, issue of *Wave*, a journal devoted to art and architecture, for example, Willis Polk noted that "all localism in the project will tend to render the results local in effect," and he commended the international nature of the competition. But in a second article with the same title, published also in *Wave* on January 29, 1898, he denounced the procedure as absurd and too beholden to the École des Beaux-Arts. "The teachings of the Beaux-Arts and the influence of its precepts have robbed the endeavor of all individuality. Expression of character is minimized by artificial standards, arbitrarily set, and slavishly followed…. It is doubtful whether any but the Beaux-Arts students or graduates…will be in the running in this competition…. The trustees have gone forth to seek mediocrity, and have made elaborate preparations to get it. The entire programme breathes the very air of the Beaux-Arts. Ideal expression or original conception of architecture suitable to California must lose its significance when poured through the academic sieve of the Beaux-Arts."

Polk was not alone in thinking thus. Among like-minded men of some influence was the Reverend Joseph Worcester, pastor of the Swedenborgian Church in San Francisco. Although Worcester had no architectural training, he had considered becoming an architect in his youth and remained passionately interested in the field, subscribing to professional journals and keeping articles on buildings and architectural ideas he liked in large scrapbooks. His opinions on matters of taste were valued by a small but influential group of artists, architects, and intellectuals who constituted the city's avant-garde. Worcester was also a patron. The modest church built under his direction in the fashionable western part of San Francisco was designed—as was the Ferry Building—in the prestigious office of A. Page Brown. A.C. Schweinfurth in Brown's office was the main designer of the church, and others in Worcester's circle participated. Bruce Porter designed one of the stained-glass windows and probably did the garden, which was an important component of the project. William Keith painted murals, and Bernard Maybeck may have played a small part as well. The church testified to Worcester's belief, rooted in Swedenborgian mysticism, in the harmony of art and nature. The expressiveness of materials in their natural state—unfinished redwood boards on interior walls, for example—and simple detail rather than the complicated jigsawn ornament typical of late-nineteenth-century buildings were important to this harmony.[13]

In a letter to Howard (whom he apparently had met, though it is not clear how) written on October 13, 1899, the Reverend Worcester expressed his indignation at the awarding of first prize to a Frenchman. He also mentioned the local professional community's generally great disappointment with the competition. "A group of us—Polk, Coxhead, Porter, Faville, and Bliss," he wrote, wished that Howard would come and study the site with them. A letter of November 14 stated further that

Bénard not only should visit the site (something he had not yet done) but that he should also tell Mrs. Hearst and the regents that "the Americans are quite competent to do the work. He might express a preference for one or more Americans and offer to advise them, but he should retire." Worcester reported that Polk was also "politiking [*sic*] and rallying the troops for local boys"—a "politiking" that included arranging meetings between Howard and the locals. The small but influential group around Worcester opposed giving the competition winner a chance, despite the

A view of the exhibition of the international competition entries in the corridors of the Ferry Building in San Francisco in 1899.

fact that, in the jury's opinion and even based on impartial review of the entries, Bénard's plan was the most sophisticated, yet at the same time most workmanlike, of the lot. Worcester's letters suggest that among those whose opinions on issues of art and taste were most valued, Howard was not considered a "foreigner," as were the other competitors. He had at least lived and worked in California, if not in the San Francisco Bay Area, and was personally acquainted with local architects.

And what did the general public make of the competition drawings that were displayed, decorated with palm branches, in one of the long corridors of the Ferry Building's top floor for eleven days after the final judgment? The drawings were certainly eye-catchers; many were five feet long by over two feet wide, and technically they were handsome, even spectacular. Yet their meaning must have escaped most of the thousands who passed daily through what was the busiest terminal on the bay. No one was on hand to explain the graphic conventions of the site plans and section drawings of the buildings and the landscape. Except for those who had seen the Columbian exposition in Chicago six years earlier, few would have been able to bridge the gap between what was on view in the Ferry Building and what was physically on the campus grounds in Berkeley.

Postcompetition Reversals
1900–1901

Behind the scenes, the jury's award was running into difficulties in an unlikely quarter. In December 1899 Bénard came to Berkeley to collect his prize money of $10,000 and to consider altering his plans to suit comments made by the jury and the competition board of trustees. Since he had never visited the site, he had not realistically addressed the way his buildings would sit on the land. One thing was clear from the outset: the extensive grading the university officials had insisted would not be affordable would have to take place for the plan to be implemented. In meetings with the trustees Bénard revealed an inability to accept criticism gracefully. Not only did his lack of fluency in English frustrate his attempts to explain his ideas, but his volatile temperament created other problems as well. On February 13, 1900, Chairman Reinstein wrote to Theodore A. Lescher, an intermediary between the competition officials in Berkeley and their counterparts in Paris, stating that he desired to acquaint Lescher with certain facts about the "situation touching Mr. Bénard," which he also wished communicated to Mr. Pascal, the head of the competition jury:

> I do not write directly to Mr. Pascal because I do not desire to appear as complaining of Mr. Bénard's action, inasmuch as he... seems to have considered that I had not treated him in a proper manner, and he seems to have been greatly incensed at my actions in his behalf; but I think you should have quite a full knowledge of the occurrences between Mr. Bénard, Mrs. Hearst, Professor [William Carey] Jones and myself while he was here, in order that you may use your best judgment on the situation.

Bénard had arrived in Berkeley on December 1, Reinstein related. He had met with Maybeck and Reinstein and had subsequently inspected the grounds. At a second meeting, Bénard reported on alterations he could make to his plan to have it comply with the trustees' recommendations. One step was to bring the buildings that were up on the hill down to more level ground. Bénard explained that this change would not alter his scheme significantly because he had learned that only one auditorium, not two, was needed and that two dormitories could be taken out of the main area and placed on the hill. Nearly all the buildings could be reduced in size. Bénard said he had this new arrangement firmly in mind and even drew a sketch of it on a photograph of his plan during the meeting.

Bénard then requested payment for the travel expenses for himself and his wife from Paris as well as his expenses in hiring draftsmen in San Francisco and gathering information he would need for the execution of the revised plan. Reinstein agreed to these requests, but asked that Bénard consider doing his personal work gratis since it had been clear to all parties that modifications would be needed to any plan that won the first prize of $10,000 before the plan would be accepted. The changes Bénard intended to make were, by his own account, minor and could be dictated to his draftsmen. Bénard agreed to this proposition and said "he would be happy to render such service as was necessary on his part as a matter of favor." Reinstein also explained to Bénard that, following the submission of the first-, second-, and third-prize plans to the board of regents, the duties of the competition trustees would end. It would then be up to the regents to select one of the three plans and see it through to realization. After the meeting Mrs. Hearst reserved lodgings for Bénard and his wife, as well as workrooms for the draftsmen, and hired both an interpreter and an office boy who spoke French. "I supposed," Reinstein wrote, "[that] matters were arranged."

Shortly thereafter, however, Mrs. Hearst informed Reinstein that Bénard was not satisfied "and was evincing a lack of confidence in the good faith of the Trustees, of the Regents, Mrs. Hearst, and, in fact, everybody connected with the adoption and carrying out of the plan." A meeting was called at Mrs. Hearst's home in Berkeley with Bénard, Reinstein, William Carey Jones, and Professor Paget of the French department. Bénard reported that he had interviewed

> a number of representatives and influential citizens of the state of California, and he had been informed by them, and believed, that the Regents would never adopt his plan because he was a foreigner, and that there was no money to execute the plan, and that he had been basely deceived; that he had been informed by Mr. Pascal that he was to come to this country to make the contract for the execution of the buildings, and not to modify his plan at all; that he had no faith in the enterprise, or in the honesty of anybody connected with it.

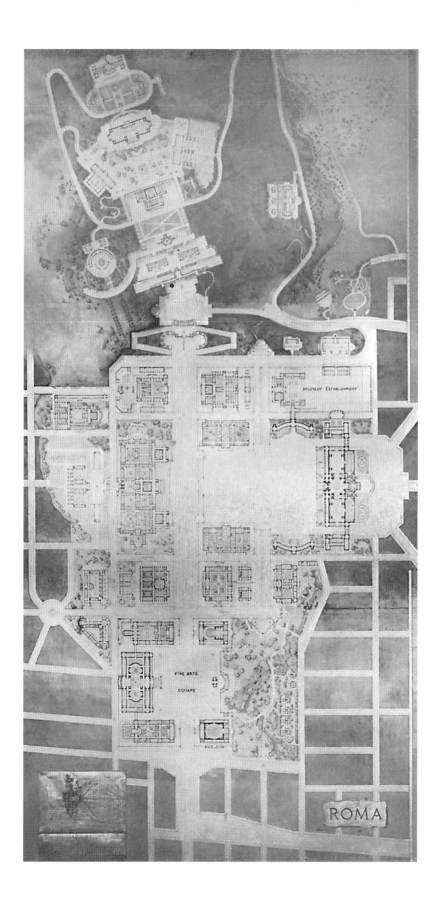

The plan of Bénard's winning scheme showed the campus's main axis joining University Avenue, a linkage that implied a more urban context than the existing orientation to the Golden Gate. The so-called Fine Arts Square at the western end of the plan (bottom) was a major campus center intended to link the university to the city. An elaborate composition was created for the hill to the east of the central campus, where non-academic buildings and dormitories were located.

Bénard, Reinstein wrote, had been foolish to talk to the enemies of the plan (who are not identified) and listen to them rather than the friends of the plan, who were Bénard's real allies:

> However, Mr. Bénard showed himself a man who was incapable of listening to reason; excitable even to the point, almost, of hysteria; and irritable to such a degree as to indicate to all of us who were there, that he was not a fit man to entrust with the execution of any work whatever, at least in this country; and he most grossly insulted everybody there present, including Mrs. Hearst, to such an extent, that only the fact of his being a guest in that house prevented him from being forcibly ejected therefrom. He shouted at the top of his voice, and raved and stamped about, said all he wished was to be permitted to go back, and that he had already been made the laughing-stock of the world. But he demanded thirty thousand francs to prepare any new plan…together with all his expenses for coming and going from Paris; and for all expenses that were to be incurred here.

A second meeting a few days later in Reinstein's office with Bénard and his interpreter, Mr. D'Aquin, and Maybeck was, according to Reinstein, nearly a repeat of the first except that Reinstein reminded Bénard of his agreement to render his personal services for the revision of the plan at no charge. After Reinstein had reiterated this point several times, Bénard admitted that he had so promised. But "he simply stated that he had been in error as to the amount of work to be done…and he adhered to his determination to obtain thirty thousand francs; and that it should be placed to his credit in the Bank of Paris before he would do anything further." Reinstein concluded:

> It is perfectly evident to me, as it was to everybody present at all these interviews, except Mr. Bénard,…that he desired to make an arrangement with the trustees, or with Mrs. Hearst, by which he was to be charged with the execution of all of the work under the new plan; and when he found that it was utterly impossible for us to make such arrangements, inasmuch as it was beyond our duty, or our power—the matter resting entirely with the Board of Regents— he made up his mind that in any event he would get thirty thousand francs out of the matter…. Under these circumstances I prepared a letter submitting the entire question of the controversy between us to Mr. Pascal, and there the matter rests; except that after Mr. Bénard received the letter and became assured that he would… receive thirty thousand francs or at least the equivalent in value for his work in modifying his plan, he became very gentle, very apologetic, claimed that he had misunderstood those on whose statements and judgment he had relied, or at least he pretended to a

greater confidence in us than ever before. But we cannot forget his acts…and if Mr. Bénard's temper as evinced to us, his suspicions, his lack of calmness and judgment, and, in fact, of good American horse sense, are to be in the future what they have been shown to be in the past, he would simply be out of the question as a man to construct the buildings he has designed…. We feel that this idea of ours should be communicated to Mr. Pascal, or at least, that he should understand this whole situation.

This was not the first word Pascal had received concerning Bénard's disastrous meetings in Berkeley. On December 26, 1899, following Bénard's departure from Berkeley for Mexico City, where he had won another competition, Pascal wrote to Mrs. Hearst excusing Bénard's tantrums. In particular, he mentioned career disappointments that had resulted in his being stuck in the provinces, where he was embittered by the lack of appreciation for his talent. Mrs. Hearst's reply reiterated Reinstein's account. She understood that Bénard was an architect of great merit and talent, but, she wrote, "between us, he is a very difficult man to understand." More important, before his departure from Paris for California Bénard had written that his numerous commitments in France prevented him from spending more than six months out of the country, a statement he repeated on his arrival in Berkeley. "This is a state institution," Mrs. Hearst observed. "Obviously the work must be done here with the architect on the site…. We wonder if we are justified in putting Bénard in a position where, because of his brusque and irresponsible temperament, he could seriously injure the future of the university."

Meanwhile, Maybeck had discussed the situation with President Wheeler. In a letter to Mrs. Hearst of January 28, 1900, Wheeler reported that Maybeck hoped that Constant Désiré Despradelle, a winner of the competition's third prize, would become an instructor and the head of the future Department of Architecture. Maybeck had also suggested that Despradelle "could do such practical architectural work as you might desire," a roundabout way of proposing him as the campus architect. "Mr. Maybeck is particularly anxious to have a Frenchman occupy the position," Wheeler wrote. "He says it would smooth matters over with the people in Paris." Still, Maybeck had agreed with Wheeler that Howard "represented the line of least resistance when all the difficulties were considered." Howard possessed all the right character traits, in addition to "first rate training." Wheeler saw no need, as he put it, "for smoothing down the French people." He considered that Mr. Bénard "had received ample remuneration and glory for all that he had done." This interchange between Wheeler and Maybeck revealed the latter's close ties with "the people in Paris," formed while he was at the école and during his two-year stint in Paris coordinating the competition.

After visiting the site in 1900 Bénard revised his winning scheme, reducing its size as well as the amount of leveling of the site needed to accommodate some of the buildings. The so-called Fine Arts Square of the original scheme was changed to Library Square, and Hearst Avenue defined the northern boundary of the campus.

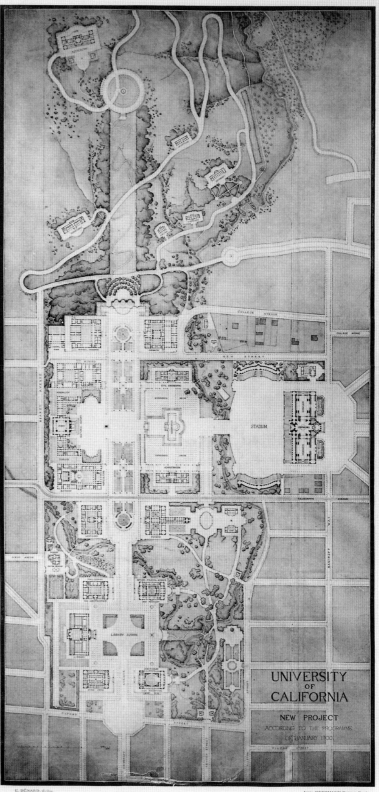

UNIVERSITY
OF
CALIFORNIA

NEW PROJECT
ACCORDING TO THE PROGRAMME
OF JANUARY 1900

Bénard chose to revise his plan in Paris. On March 16, 1900, he wrote Mrs. Hearst that he had prepared some sketches of the reworked plan and sent them off to Berkeley. In a letter of the same date to Mrs. Hearst, Pascal commented on the sketches, saying that he had advised Bénard to send only two. "The grand axes, avenues and beautiful aspects are unchanged," he wrote. "Only the dimensions of the different departments and the division of services have been modified in accord with the new program and inspection of the grounds." The reduction of built space had resulted in "a park containing University buildings rather than a University City." In closing, Pascal endorsed Bénard as an experienced and practical man, adding that he had known him for over thirty years. (They had met in 1866 in Rome when Pascal was the first-place winner of the Prix de Rome and Bénard won second place. Today their friendship would be considered a conflict of interest, but it seems not to have been a cause for concern at the time of the competition.)

Indeed, Bénard had worked assiduously on his revisions, turning out five new plans. On June 28, 1900, William Carey Jones wrote Mrs. Hearst that he had met with Bénard and Pascal in Paris and discussed the changes: grading had been minimized, the creeks preserved, and various buildings had been regrouped. But a letter dated the following day from Pascal to Mrs. Hearst lamented the siting of the president's house—a commission separate from the campus plan, being undertaken by école alumnus Albert Pissis (perhaps as a reward for Pissis's professional support for the competition)—without consideration for Bénard's plan.

Although Howard was not privy to the correspondence between Paris and Berkeley, he was aware of the drift of events in his direction. In February 1901 he went to Washington, D.C., to meet Mrs. Hearst. He wrote his wife that they had had long talks. "She has asked me to take up her building [memorializing her husband], the first of the great scheme," he enthused. "I am to go to California the middle of this month to look at the site and requirements, and later abroad to study the best buildings of this type. She intends to spend from $300,000 to $400,000, the future is assured!"

On February 18 Mrs. Hearst telegraphed Wheeler of her decision to give Howard the commission for the mining building. Wheeler replied that he looked forward to seeing Howard in Berkeley about the end of February. This news must also have reached "the people" in Paris, for a telegram soon came from Lescher on the subject. "It was to be anticipated," Wheeler wrote in reference to the telegram, "that Bénard and his friends would not wish to allow the opportunity of further emolument to escape them without a final effort and protest. So far as I know there is no obligation, legal or moral, binding us to further regard Mr. Bénard in the matter."

On March 3, in a letter to Mary from Berkeley, Howard described the summery weather and the hyacinths and buttercups he had seen on a stroll around the campus with President Wheeler. He had also attended San Francisco's Swedenborgian Church and been given a hearty welcome by Joseph Worcester. "There has been ferment here," he commented. "What the outcome will be I do not foresee. But there is time enough." Four days later he wrote Mary that he had moved to Berkeley to be nearer the site, and that he had had another meeting with Mr. Worcester, who "has espoused my interests with ardor. Bruce Porter said, when I told him about the circumstances of my coming here, that he loved fairy stories when they came true, and he believed that this was all due to that wizard on the hill, that is to say, Mr. Worcester. I told you about his tiny perch cresting Russian hill, did I not? I lunched there Monday off bread and marmalade, fruitcake, nuts and tea." Worcester's teas, which seem always to have featured the best bread and butter with fine marmalade, tea cakes, and perhaps some pecans, were described almost reverently by Howard and others.

Howard also wrote of having lunched at the Bohemian Club with Porter, Coxhead, and Maybeck and of spending that evening with the Maybecks. He had, he now wrote, just returned from dinner with President and Mrs. Wheeler and had met several professors. "I have had the most cordial welcome on all sides, apparently everyone had hoped that I would win the competition, resented Bénard's having anything to do with it, and was relieved to have me come to start the work at last. I am evidently very much wanted by those in authority, and others, as architect in chief, to take charge of the whole thing. The President is sure they can bring it about so that it will be worth my while."

The social round continued with Howard writing nearly every day about congenial lunches and dinners. "There is a charming circle of people here who have received me with open arms and whom I thoroughly like and feel in my element with." On March 9 he dined with the Coxheads, whom he described as "charming people with a lovely home." Bruce Porter's sister and her husband were there, and Worcester joined the party later. Much of the conversation was devoted to "the university work."

That Worcester was the "wizard" behind Howard's involvement in the project became clearer in the following days. The reverend seemed to be present at every social occasion. On March 10 Howard wrote that he had dined with the family of a young architect named Bliss, who lived "far out" in a house overlooking the Presidio, with a superb panoramic view over the Golden Gate, the bay, and the surrounding mountains. Worcester was the other guest. His influence was also noted by Charles Keeler, a man who wore many cultural hats in the East Bay and was an ardent publicist for the Arts and Crafts movement. In an essay titled "Friends Bearing Torches," Keeler described Worcester as always dressed in well-tailored black suits and speaking in a deep, low voice. His word was law, Keeler stated, in "a select group of connoisseurs of which he was the center."[14]

A second letter dated March 10 described spending the afternoon with Jacob Reinstein, who had been ill and unable to meet with Howard before that time. "Things are advanced," he wrote, "I feel one peg further. I begin to see an arrangement I can make without sacrificing my foothold in New York and yet taking up this work in such a way as to justify a reasonable hope of its success. Perhaps not, probably not, a full professorship in addition to the architect-generalship, but a sufficiently close relationship to the school [i.e., university], and the rest wholly in my hands. Whether they will see fit to meet me halfway I do not know, but I cannot help feeling that they will come farther." Later in this letter Howard referred to surveying work he was conducting on the grounds around the mining building site: "One of the difficulties which presents itself at the first touch is a difference of level of 68 feet!! between two corners of the Mining Building, as indicated in Bénard's drawings. That is to say, if the building is placed just where he shows it, one corner where it touches the ground is 68 feet higher than the opposite corner, five good stories difference! Absurdity number one for the buildings are supposed to be two stories high at most."

Howard's optimism about his prospects also stemmed from meetings with President Wheeler, who in turn reported their contents to Phoebe Hearst. A letter of March 8 related conversations Wheeler and Howard had had about the problems with Bénard's plan, the most immediate of which was the height discrepancy between the building's northeast and southwest corners. Howard told Wheeler that a revised plan containing Bénard's fundamental concept could be carried out, but only if the locations of other buildings were adjusted. He also said that he was reluctant to leave New York, where he had a million dollars' worth of business, and he wanted assurances of freedom of action and noninterference from the regents. Wheeler thought Howard might be persuaded to come to Berkeley if he were offered a professorship and the position of supervising architect, as well as control of the building program.

By mid-March Howard had decided to stay on another week or so. "Bénard's plans are so utterly impractical," he wrote, "that it looks as if the whole thing would have to be restudied before anything can be put on the ground. Everything has to be demonstrated by surveys." He planned to convince Reinstein that the plan was unworkable by showing him the mining building implanted on Bénard's drawing, "tip-tilted on the side of the hill 71 feet and more out of level. Were it not for this kind of absurdity Bénard's vision might preserve its enchantment.... [The drawings] possess just that factitious semblance of reality which is calculated to hoodwink the layman and even the experienced architect unless he studies the problem sufficiently to grasp its significance. Ah me!"

On March 20, Wheeler wrote Mrs. Hearst:

> The more I study the plan of Mr. Bénard and the more I become acquainted with all that it involves, the more certain I am that he dealt with his work rather as a problem for creating a picture on paper than for locating buildings on the earth. I do not think it is right that we should undertake a plan which would involve five to ten million dollars of expenditure for grading.... The most serious oversight involved in it, however, seems to me to be this: the main axis of the plan steers for University Avenue instead of for the Golden Gate, the library facing directly toward [the avenue]; a line drawn from the Golden Gate to the top of the hill which dominates the campus passes, strange to say, directly through the depression or valley extending from Oxford Street clean to the eastern limits of the campus. If this axis were used the amount of grading would be reduced to a minimum. Mr. Bénard's plan arranges the grounds according to the streets of the present Berkeley instead of according to the great features of the landscape. The disposition of the buildings in the plan...is on the whole beyond criticism. I find that Mr. Howard regards himself as in a delicate position if Mr. Bénard retains any relation to the plan. He consented to consider it only on the understanding that Mr. Bénard's connection with the work had terminated; he understood what I believe is correct, that Mr. Bénard has been fully remunerated for the work which he has done and that his work has come to a definite conclusion. It is understood by Mr. Howard and everybody that Mr. Bénard's plan is to be the basis for the work which is to be undertaken from this time on. The work involves the adjustment of the general plan to the practical necessities of the grounds and of the special constructions.

Mrs. Hearst's reply to Wheeler on April 1 reveals the level of distrust that Bénard's behavior had created: "I have felt all the time that it was Bénard's purpose to confuse the land so that he would have to be employed to work it out."

Later that spring, at Wheeler's invitation, Howard addressed the university's students and faculty as part of a regular lecture series. Curiosity about the much-discussed plan and the future of the campus brought more than one thousand people to the university gymnasium to hear Howard, and two newspapers covered the event. Howard wrote Mary that he was "extremely nervous, trembled, but got through it somehow and was complimented." His anxiety may have come from a feeling that the audience's judgment would affect his future. However, the audience—which was much larger than he could have mustered outside the university setting—may have been impressed by Howard's appearance as much as by his presentation. He was well over six feet tall and formal in his bearing. In photographs he appears severe. Although his New England background meant that formality came to him more or less naturally, his somewhat forbidding demeanor was more likely the defense of a shy person. In social situations he was quite cordial and displayed courtly manners, as those who knew him often noted. Wheeler, for one, considered him "a gentleman, an artist, and a scholar."

President Benjamin Ide Wheeler on horseback below Hilgard Hall, ca. 1917.

After Howard's midday lecture he and Wheeler toured the grounds discussing their concerns about the campus plan. "We are curiously alike in some ways," Howard wrote Mary. "I surmise in him similar weaknesses, held more or less in check by similar qualities in the upper region …he let slip one little expression which startled me about the longing he frequently had to retire to utter seclusion. Then he caught himself, but not until I had cried out, 'Why, do you have that feeling too?' and we looked at each other as if we had found each other out…. What we win, we win by brain driving character not by character using brain."

Like Howard, Wheeler was a New Englander. He too had benefited from a European education, having spent four years studying in Germany after graduating from Brown University. In 1885 he received a Ph.D. degree summa cum laude in comparative philology from Heidelberg University, and the next year he was hired by Cornell University as a professor of Greek and comparative philology. Three years later he was offered the presidency of the University of California. His acceptance was contingent on the board of regents agreeing to certain conditions, including making him the sole means of communication between the faculty and the regents; giving him the initiative in the appointment and removal of professors and in matters of salary, as well as in control of the university employees; and obligating the board of regents to support him in all his actions. These conditions being met, Wheeler accepted the offer of the presidency on July 18, 1899.

Wheeler combined the intellect of a scholar with administrative skills and the ability to speak eloquently to the needs of the university as he saw them.[15] Although his autocratic approach to administration brought him some unpopularity, his strong interest in bonding university and community affairs and his support for student government won general approval. He was a familiar sight on the campus, which he often toured on horseback, stopping to converse with people along the way like a paternal commander-in-chief. Believing in the power of architecture to mold character, Wheeler saw the architectural plan for the campus as a physical expression of the university's destiny to be "the Athens of the West." In this respect his arrival in Berkeley was a surpassing piece of good fortune for the future of the university—and for Howard as well.

The machinations over ending Bénard's involvement with the campus plan continued through the summer of 1901. In a letter dated June 6, Wheeler told Mrs. Hearst that he had consulted John Carrère (a member of the competition advisory board) about runners-up in the competition who might be considered for the position of supervising architect. Carrère agreed with Wheeler that the chosen architect should move to California, adding that "a man who is competent for the task and who has been engaged in work of the larger sort will be hard to move…and will require assurances for continual work and employment." Carrère thought Howard would be more likely than others to view the venture favorably because of his acquaintance with California. He went on to say that "all architects regard him with the highest respect" and mentioned his accomplishments, which included taking second place in the 1896 competition for the New York Public Library. Carrère judged that competition (which Carrère and his partner, Thomas Hastings, had in fact won) to be the equivalent of the university plan competition in Berkeley. He also noted that Howard had

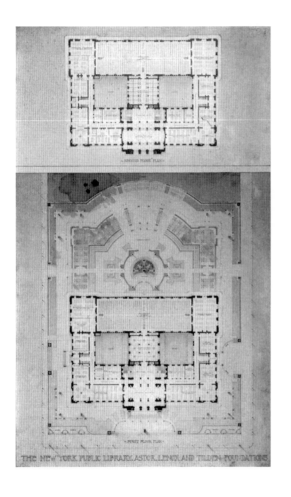

Floor plans and elevations for Howard and Cauldwell's second-prize entry in the 1896 competition for the New York Public Library, which show strong similarities to those of the winning submission by Carrère and Hastings.

charge of the design for the central tower of the 1901 Pan-American Exposition. (One of eight architects involved in the design of buildings for the expo, Howard was chosen by his fellow designers to execute this beacon for the exposition. Known as the Buffalo Electric Tower, the structure was studded with electric globes and resembled the Madison Square Garden tower that Howard had worked on for Stanford White. The American Institute of Architects awarded Howard a gold medal for the structure.)

But Bénard and his supporters had not given up. On June 9, 1901, Pascal wrote Mrs. Hearst:

> We hear repeatedly that it is Mr. Howard—of whom I appreciate the honesty and the talent—who is appointed by the regents of the University of Berkeley—and doubtless by yourself also—to start the magnificent plan destined to constitute in California one of the beautiful works of our generation. If Mr. Howard...is to be entrusted ...[with] the direction of operations and the setting to work of those studies and details furnished by the creative artist, no one will raise an objection; at the same time it seems to me that...the artist himself should have been consulted. If nothing of the execution is assigned to Bénard, no graver mistake could have been made. The plan in an architectural work is like the skeleton of a beautiful creature, like the woodwork of a noble structure, the libretto of an opera, the branch of a tree. Without the form, without the covering, it is not a work of art—without the budding there is no spring. The work in its entirety will have been crude. Thus if done by a stranger, justice will probably be denied the work and it will not be that model of which we have dreamed to show to coming generations.... If you have not the stamp of the artist's talent in elevation as well as in plan your work will be incomplete.

This impassioned protest failed to impress Wheeler, who continued to negotiate with Howard over his appointment as supervising architect. In a letter to Wheeler dated June 12, Howard asked for a salary of $10,000 for the position. In addition, he requested a fully equipped office and a budget for draftsmen, travel expenses, and so forth. He was also willing to assume the duties of professor of architecture and to establish a school provided he received adequate support and equipment as well as proper assistance in administration and instruction. For that he requested a salary of $4,000 a year.

On June 21 Wheeler wrote to Mrs. Hearst suggesting that they offer Howard $3,000 a year. As for Howard's request for complete control of the plan in order to revise it, Wheeler had consulted Charles McKim, another member of the advisory board, who said that Bénard's plan was only a suggestion and that "the jury had no other idea than that the man

Howard's design for the Electric Tower of the 1901 Pan-American Exposition in Buffalo, New York, published in American Architect and Building News, *June 1901.*

who would be selected would create the plan afterward." The fact that Howard was a protégé of McKim's may explain this offhand dismissal of the official status of Bénard's plan. In any case, as this correspondence suggests, Howard had by now been as good as offered the position of supervising architect, and his requirements for acceptance of the offer had been largely met.

On July 28, Howard was on board the RMS *Lucania* bound for England. The purpose of the trip was to gain ideas for Mrs. Hearst's commission by visiting European mining colleges and related chemistry laboratories identified by Samuel Christy, head of the mining department. (The two men had already toured several mining colleges in the United States and Canada together; this time they would be making separate tours.) After several stops in England Howard proceeded to Germany, where he stopped at Aachen, Heidelberg, Göttingen, and Berlin. Except for his stay in Berlin, where he reported seeing up-to-date chemical labs and received much helpful information, the results of the tour were disappointing. From Freiburg he wrote Mary that he was doing a lot of "scientific cramming" that he would be happy to forget when the science buildings at Berkeley were completed. After more study stops in Prague and Vienna as well as a visit to Switzerland, he reached the end of his itinerary in Paris the first week in September. In addition to stopping at his official destination, the school of mines, he took nostalgic tours of the city, looked up friends, and made new professional contacts.

Howard's personal agenda on this trip included meeting some of the competition jurors. He had gotten together with Paul Wallot, the juror from Berlin, at his home in the Vosges Mountains, and in Paris he had called on Jean-Louis Pascal. Pascal wanted Howard to meet Bénard. On September 9 Howard wrote Mary that Pascal "was discretion itself and avowedly the staunch partisan of M. Bénard whom he considers, judging from what he says, the right stuff. The meeting can certainly do neither the cause nor me (whom I consider as part of the cause) any harm, and it may serve to simplify things for the future to have a thorough-going understanding all round at the start. But I don't see how the meeting, if it occurs, can be anything but painful to both M. Bénard and me."

The meeting with Bénard was arranged for September 11. Howard took along a young friend, Peter Willingale, who was then at the école. "I think it well," he wrote,

> to have a witness to the doings and sayings of that interview besides the support that a strong and friendly presence will be to me in what must be a more or less trying experience. Think of Bénard, a veteran, and an old man feeling himself wronged, and the youthful... whipper-snapper who like David is come with his sling to slay

Goliath. I am not so conceited as that metaphor would seem to make me out; nor is the result of the coming encounter likely to be similar to the biblical one; but something is likely to happen. I hope I am not blinded by my own personal interest in the outcome. What I want to see…is [that] the best for the university prevail, and if justice's doing brings success to me and advancement, I look to enjoy that apart from the greater good which is to accrue to the cause…. I fully believe that I am better fitted than M. Bénard to bring order out of the present chaos of affairs.

As it turned out, both Bénard and Despradelle were at the meeting. Afterward Howard wrote Mary that the interview, though not pleasurable, had been friendly and productive. He thought that Bénard saw himself as "definitely out of it," alluding to the position of supervising architect, but that his friend Pascal was still trying to see him reinstalled. It seems that Bénard proposed himself—or was proposed by his friends—as Howard's collaborator, an arrangement that Howard considered impossible both for himself and for the university.

Following Howard's visit to Bénard, Pascal wrote to Wheeler on September 26, calling his attention "to the disastrous error" that the Berkeley administration would commit if Bénard's participation was limited to design alone. "We would have neither the Louvre, nor Versailles, if any such procedure had been followed," he stated. Howard's arrival in Paris, he wrote, prompted his letter: "The very courteous visit of a highly esteemed architect, whose conduct is absolutely correct, shows how great a mistake is made in putting, as we say, the wagon before the oxen. Mr. Howard is a man of talent and of honor who might, nevertheless, deceive himself, and this impression was so clearly borne in upon me that I took the responsibility of proposing to him an interview with M. Bénard, despite the embarrassment I must so cause the latter."

The point of Howard's visiting the members of the jury, Pascal observed, was certainly to gain approval for his shifting the axis of Bénard's plan toward the Golden Gate instead of University Avenue. According to Howard, this would not change the essence of the plan because the disposition of the buildings would be preserved. "On paper," Pascal noted, "this interpretation is specious; confronted with the reality of things it is not correct," and he said as much to Howard: "If you do this pivoting, you cannot construct a single separate building, without having re-studied the whole plan." The new axis would, he said, disrupt the unity of the avenues and the vistas. "All the ingenious effort of the general combination would be compromised; the value of the park, of the fine trees, of the streams, whose happy conservation we had admired." In Pascal's judgment, a final, most grave effect would be that the university would be placed in "disaccord" with the town—as if that accord had been a mandate of the competition program.

If Howard presented his argument about minimizing the grading of the site by following the natural drainage in the valley that corresponded to the Golden Gate axis, he did not report it in his letter about the meeting with Bénard. Nor is it likely that he told Bénard and Pascal about his talks with Wheeler about adjusting the plan to meet other practical needs. On his return to Berkeley he continued his study of the grounds, even as he began the design process for the mining college building, for which the drawings were prepared in the New York office. On November 6, 1901, he wrote Mary that after two more weeks studying the overall site he planned "to put the Regents in possession of the facts on which to judge the situation."

Supervising Architect for the
Hearst Architectural Plan

1901–1903

5

On December 21, 1901, Reinstein submitted a resolution to the University
of California board of regents that Howard be appointed supervising
architect, subject to approval by the jury in charge of the competition. In a
letter to Mary, Howard relates that he had been out with Mrs. Hearst and
the other regents reviewing Bénard's plan, which had been staked out on
the grounds along with Howard's suggested revisions. "Everyone appears
delighted with the change of axis as shown on the site," Howard wrote.
"The advantages of my adjustments sing out well, and my calculations are
significant as well." By this time Howard had brought two men out from
New York, Charles Peter Weeks and Frank Jackson, to assist him in drawing up further proposals.

Christmas was approaching. Howard wrote that he would miss
being at home for it. However, he would be well taken care of what with
celebrations both at the Hacienda, Mrs. Hearst's Pleasanton estate, and
at the Pacific Heights home of Charles Wheeler, Mrs. Hearst's attorney
(no relation to President Wheeler). After the holiday, Howard provided a
detailed account of the Wheelers' party, at which both men and ladies
wore "old English" costumes.

> The whole room was hung with crimson sown with golden fleur-
> de-lis and caught at intervals by great brass sconces with clusters of
> red candles. The cornice was massed with greens and from the ceil-
> ing hung enormous baskets of strange design, Indian and Oriental,
> filled with green branches and red berries. The table instead of being
> spread with white was covered with a rich green cloth like moss;
> and in the center of the great circle was an enormous mound of

A map of the campus dated 1897, the year the competition prospectus was published, shows the sparsely developed state of the grounds. However, the growth of the university during the decades after its creation resulted in heavy use of existing buildings, which were inadequate for future needs.

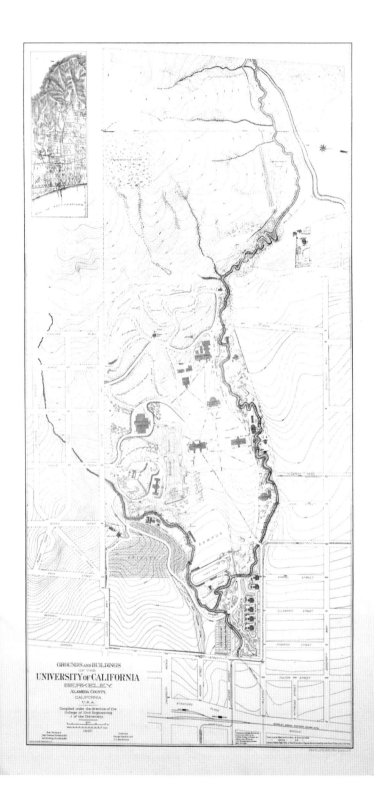

all the fruits of the earth—pumpkins, cabbages, oranges, grapes, artichokes, bananas, all the green and yellow and purple things that grow and please the palate or the eye. This luscious pyramid was surrounded by rivers of roasted turkey, haunches of venison, sides of beef, etc., whose brown crispness set off the mossy green of their field. Beyond them, just within the cover, was a garland of greenery interwoven with tiny scarlet and yellow apples. A boar's head was brought in and children came singing old English songs, then innumerable toasts and more good things to eat. Then old fashioned dances like the Virginia reel and tableaus. Mrs. Hearst was gorgeous in white crepe brocaded in delicate pink, and she wore an enormous white wig of innumerable ringlets.

Howard's dinner partner was the sister of Orrin Peck, a fashionable portrait painter. Mrs. Hearst herself was seated at Howard's left—confirming his inclusion in the university's innermost circle—and she sat at Mrs. Wheeler's right. After the festivities ended Howard returned to his hotel in San Francisco, where, he wrote, "I rendered up all that I had taken in."

After spending February and March in New York, Howard returned to Berkeley the first week of April. The mining building site in the densely wooded, upper part of the campus grounds was being cleared of trees so that excavation for the building could proceed. Wheeler reported that good stone had been found in the White Rock Quarry in Oregon.

With support from President Wheeler and Regents Hearst and Reinstein, Howard was now free to consider alterations to Bénard's plan. The questions that required his consideration were which new buildings would be needed immediately and whether any existing buildings could be demolished to accommodate new ones important in the plan.

Howard was also overseeing construction of the Greek Theater, located in the hillside east of the main campus. The site, a natural bowl known popularly as Ben Weed's amphitheater, had already been used for several years in its natural state for music and drama events.[16] Although the competition program did not mention a theater, President Wheeler, an ardent Grecophile, promoted the idea as a way to further the dramatic arts within the university curriculum and to provide a proper setting for ceremonial events. William Randolph Hearst, Phoebe's son, was the donor for the project. In October 1902, Wheeler wrote Hearst that he would have no regrets over his contribution when he saw Howard's plan for the theater: "The slope of the ground is almost exactly that of the Dionysiac Theater at Athens, and the seats can be anchored to the ground with a minimum of excavation." However, the funds Hearst gave were not adequate to pay for Howard's design in its entirety, as can be seen by comparing the final state of the theater with Howard's original drawing.

The cost of constructing the concrete stage proscenium and tiers

of seating for ten thousand people was $447,000. Howard had intended to have all the exterior surfaces—walls, seats, and the fluted columns of a colonnade—clad in marble, but when the estimate came to $384,000, the proposed design was abandoned. The amphitheatre tiers were left in rough concrete, and the colonnade intended to crown the top was omitted.

The Hearst Greek Theater was used for the first time on May 16, 1903, when Theodore Roosevelt delivered the commencement address there. It received its formal dedication on September 24, at which William

Randolph Hearst remarked matter-of-factly, "I am interested in this university and want to help it. This is no great thing, but it seemed to be a need, and I am happy to supply it." Howard also spoke at the dedication, citing the "monumental and festive character" of the theater and the brilliant contrast "afforded by the wide, long sweep of the line of the semi-circular auditorium and the crisp rectangular form of the stage…. The pure, simple, big classic forms harmonize exquisitely with the forms of hill and canyon."

On the main part of the university grounds, the situation hardly matched the picture painted by the 1897 competition prospectus, which had announced that all existing buildings were to be ignored and the campus grounds treated as empty space. Although the regents had approved Bénard's plan, no endowment existed to implement the building program. Consequently, most of the buildings constructed during Howard's tenure were named for donors whom Wheeler solicited to supplement appropriations from the state legislature.

The campus was still very open, preserving the pastoral quality the

OPPOSITE

Bird's-eye view drawing of the proposed design for the Greek Theater, ca. 1901–2. Howard's design embodied the traditional form of the Greek theater, with a 135-foot-long raised stage backed by a stage building with five entrances that overlooked a semicircular orchestra. A section of tiers wide enough to accommodate movable chairs rose from the orchestra to the level of a wide aisle at the height of the stage. Marble "seats of honor" to be provided by donors were to line a wall at the back of the aisle. Behind this a second section of concrete seating divided into ten wedges rose to the height of the stage building. Atop the stage building a colonnade with caryatids supported a richly ornamented covered cornice. The rim of the hillside seating was to be a covered colonnade or peristyle.

LEFT

Although the basic elements of Howard's scheme for the theater were constructed, those that would have completed the grand setting were not, as this photograph from the 1960s reveals. The truncated stage building with its engaged Doric colonnade was not clad in marble; the row of marble "seats of honor," designed by Melvin Earl Cummings, is incomplete, although many seats have been added to it during the theater's history. The upper tiers of seating blend into the hillside without the interruption of the peristyle.

College of California trustees had envisioned for it. Five buildings of brick or brick and stone occupied a central open space bordered by stands of trees planted on the recommendation of Frederick Law Olmsted, who, together with Calvert Vaux, had prepared the first plan for the College of California. A major axis began at Bacon Hall, built in 1891 to house the library and an art gallery, and continued westward toward the Golden Gate. South and North Halls flanked that axis on a cross-axis running north and south. South Hall, one of the first two buildings constructed in 1873, was a fireproof structure of brick and stone that housed laboratories for the physical and natural sciences. Designed in the so-called Second Empire style by David Farquharson, a Scottish architect who came to California in 1850 and prepared the first plan for the university,[17] it is the only original campus building that has survived to the present day. North Hall, a wooden building demolished in 1931, housed mainly classrooms for the humanities. The brick Mechanics and Mining building to the northeast of Bacon Hall conformed to the 1870 Farquharson & Kenitzer plan, but the wooden engineering and chemistry buildings, which stood to the east of Bacon Hall, did not. With the exception of Hearst Hall, designed by Bernard Maybeck and built in 1898 with a gift from Mrs. Hearst, a group of other wooden buildings—East Hall and the four buildings for botany, agriculture, philosophy, and civil engineering—were architecturally undistinguished, as was the Harmon Gymnasium (1879), also of wood. The gym was near the southwest corner of the campus, as were five wooden cottages for students. The wooden Leuschner Observatory of 1886 stood near the north entrance to the campus. A smattering of provisional wooden buildings and sheds completed the inventory of structures.[18] Around all these, enough open land existed to permit construction of those new buildings stipulated in the campus plan for which funding was foreseeable.

As for Pascal's protest that shifting the axis would break the connections between town and gown, no urban fabric of any density really existed to be fractured. Shattuck Avenue, west of the campus, where streetcars ran and where the Southern Pacific railroad had a terminal, was the main commercial artery. South of the campus was Telegraph Avenue, which extended from Oakland to Berkeley; it had a horsecar line started in the 1860s that was later converted to electric streetcars, which provided the main transportation for students, many of whom lived in Oakland. The main residential area for faculty and administration was also south of the campus, in the College Homestead Association district, and meanwhile the north-of-campus blocks were fast being developed. The north-south streets of the College Homestead Association district did not match those to the north, though some were close enough to provide a basis for important cross-axes. Even though cross-axes were considered part of the campus circulation plan, they were not really drawn on maps; nor did they demarcate the campus like city streets. The campus was a discrete site and has remained so to this day.

The design of the mining building and the Greek Theater took up most of Howard's time in 1902. Designating sites for California Hall (the administration building) and the new library also required his attention, as did additions to existing buildings. The details of his contract as both supervising architect and professor in the fledgling architecture department were matters of constant concern. Meanwhile, at his New York office, which he shared with his new partner, Dan Everett Waid, attention was being given to several large houses and a library in Montclair, New Jersey, that were under construction and to working drawings for the Long Island City Hospital.[19]

On October 22, 1902, Howard and Waid went to Boston to inspect the nearly finished Majestic Theater. Howard was immensely pleased, and following the theater's opening early in 1903 he relished the reviews that appeared in several newspapers. "When all is said and done," he wrote Mary from Boston on February 15, "and every criticism made, it must be acknowledged a superb success, this building, and I am proud of it as I have never been proud of anything before. It is a genuine contribution to theater design and to art in general...but less perfect than the Mining Building is going to be.... All this sounds mighty conceited, doesn't it? But one must bank on something, and why not on self esteem?"

Despite these other jobs, work on the Berkeley campus was never far from his mind. In January 1903, in a lengthy article titled "The Architectural Plans for the Greater University of California" written for the *University Chronicle*, Howard stressed the university's extraordinary growth, in response to which "rapid headway is now being made upon the plans." He then argued his case for changing the competition-winning design:

> It may not be generally understood that the plans secured two years ago through the munificence of Mrs. Hearst and prepared by M. Bénard were not, and made no pretense of being, other than preliminary sketches. They were on the very small scale of fifty feet to the inch and showed little more than the outline of a scheme.... Later on, after a visit to Berkeley, M. Bénard prepared a revised scheme, making many important modifications and improvements. It is these drawings which form the basis for the further studies that are now in hand.
>
> As all who have had to do with building operations well know, there is a long step between the preliminary indications of a scheme and the execution of working drawings....
>
> Starting from the basis of the plan as presented by M. Bénard, the task seems to be...to evolve a scheme for the university which shall

preserve the fundamental idea of his plans without being so overly punctilious in that preservation as to allow the plans to impose themselves dogmatically upon actually existing conditions with which they may prove to be out of harmony and with which the original designer may fairly be supposed to have been unfamiliar.

Howard described the "fundamental characteristics" of Bénard's scheme as being the east-west–running esplanade that divided the grounds in half, and the two north-south axes, each of which crossed the esplanade, though at some distance from each other. The more westerly cross-axis established the center of the great court—variously called the Fine Arts Square or the Library Square, depending on whether the museum or the library was given the place of honor on the square. The easterly cross-axis terminated in the athletic field at the gymnasium, located on the campus's southern boundary. The academic buildings were grouped around these axes "in accordance with well recognized principles of formal architectural competition" and were diverse in respect to their size and form; yet even with this diversity, Howard noted, "the architectural treatment is nevertheless consistent in its generally classic character."

Howard emphasized following the spirit rather than the letter of the plans and acting according to principles "based on the necessity of economizing [on] materials…and of not violating the grounds but of interpreting them":

> It signifies little, architecturally speaking, that in a great plan one building is called Library, another Museum, another Auditorium. It is not the names to which these buildings answer but the mass and the general disposition of parts which count in the effect of the whole…. It should not be considered in itself, then, a general change of parti if the Library, for example, be moved from the western to the eastern side of the square, or the Mining Building from the southwest corner to the northeast corner of the plan. The present studies are being made on this assumption, that a mere shuffle of the buildings among themselves cannot justly be considered a material change.

Howard then questioned the idea of fixing the plan in all its details for all time: "Future generations will consider themselves bound by our preparations to the extent, and only to the extent, that we have foreseen their needs and have planned wisely for them."

Having prepared his readers for a pragmatic approach to the planning process, Howard spoke of the first challenge to the implementation of Bénard's plan: establishing the main axis. The backbone of Bénard's winning scheme had been an axis obtained by continuing University Avenue to the eastern boundary of the campus. However, because this axis did not follow the rise and fall of the land in a natural way, extensive grading would have been required to create building sites. Bénard had recognized this problem and had solved it in his revised plan "by a bold device": he had lowered the crown of the hill above Oxford Street by an average depth of twelve feet and crossed the succeeding valley with a broad causeway that followed the length of the botanical garden, thus raising the axis by ten feet. "By this means," Howard wrote, "virtually a single magnificent slope, at a very easy inclination, held from the entrance at

The west elevation of South Hall, ca. 1880. The main entrance of South Hall was originally on the west side, like those of most of the campus buildings. With the completion of Wheeler Hall in 1917 the west entrance was less accessible, and the east entrance became the main one. The west entry porch and staircase were transferred to the east side in 1968–70.

Oxford Street to a point...east of the Mining Building.... Only a man of lofty power of imagination could have conceived so thorough-going a transformation of the grounds, only a designer with supreme architectural courage could have envisaged such a task as that contemplated in this project. It is a pleasure to acknowledge the advantage of having a great idea constantly before one as inspiration in a task like the present."

Although we do not know what level of irony, if any, Howard intended with these statements, his next comments signify that he meant to honor Bénard's grand concept more in the breach than in the observance: "The University is bound to be an immense gainer by reason of the largeness of conception which has marked the initial steps in this undertaking. Nevertheless it is necessary now to look upon the practical side of things, and to weigh all the arguments...before committing the University to its course of architectural development."

To retain the effect of Bénard's plan, Howard proposed a new axis that called for a much smaller expenditure of money and less risk to the natural beauties of the site. The new line, which corresponded to the natural drainage and emphasized the view to the Golden Gate, extended from Center Street past the northern edge of the eucalyptus grove and up through the gully that divided North and South Halls and eastward to the great hill above Ben Weed's amphitheater. This line, Howard noted, had "the advantage of preserving the entire middle portion of the grounds at approximately their present grade." Howard then devoted several pages to describing the views and vistas that would greet the campus visitor who followed this path. In a burst of purple-tinted prose he ended this section by saying, "What a field here for a flight of symbolic poetry! The boundless waste of the Pacific cloven by the axis of the University and brought into the system of its actual architectural composition! What vast horizons open to the mind's eye beyond that wondrous passage to the sea! What far oriental realms lie ready there for Alma Mater's peaceful and beneficent conquest!"

In the rest of the article Howard addressed the division of the grounds according to their topography. The hilly northern half of the campus, he noted, presented problems for the construction of monumental building groups; its western quadrant in particular suggested a park or arboretum—a "vestibule" between town and gown. "This section," Howard observed, "is remote from what must always be the center of the University group. It is admirable for agricultural purposes throughout." Yet in Bénard's plan, the northwest corner of the grounds was occupied by the Library Square, one of the plan's most monumental building groups— the better to tie the campus to the town through University Avenue, according to his vision—while east of Library Square the grounds were nearly covered with buildings. The park in Bénard's plan occupied the southwest corner of the campus, where a eucalyptus grove, a meander of Strawberry Creek, and stands of oaks were to be left untouched. To the east and extending south above the Hillegass tract Bénard placed the grand gymnasium complex. As Howard observed, however, the Hillegass tract, which extended from Telegraph Avenue to College Avenue, was well suited for athletic fields, being more level and uniform than any other portion of the grounds.

Summing up, Howard found the grounds naturally divided into four parts. The central portion, already the location of the main buildings, would continue to be developed with monumental buildings. The area to the west, rather than being linked to the town as in Bénard's plan, would be left in a largely natural state to give the central grounds "seclusion and distinction." The high hills to the east would form "a majestic natural background and climax to the composition." As for "human habitation," Howard wrote, "we see in the four portions of the grounds, as above defined, the House with its Forecourt or Garden to the west, its secluded Retreat and Promenade to the east, and its Playground and Field for

Sports to the south." In his closing paragraphs, Howard defended his aesthetic goals for the university plan:

> Above and beyond any of the considerations which have been enumerated, is the principle that it is owed to the people to establish on these grounds a standard of artistic excellence. It is the University's bounden duty to cultivate artistic ideals just as distinctly and indisputedly as it is its duty to teach the beauties of literature and the wonders of science. The University fulfills only a part of its mission when it teaches the theory of beauty without its practice. Its duty is to inspire, to cultivate, to edify. And to do that completely it must have fine buildings. By fine is not meant elaborate or even costly, but buildings… so beautiful that the student coming into their presence is uplifted.… Men and women come here at the most impressionable period of their lives, and lost is the most important of opportunities for raising the standard of their taste and cultivating their higher instincts, if they do not find themselves at once in an atmosphere of fine artistic surroundings.

6 The Move to California in 1902

With his commitment to the university deepening, Howard decided to move his family to California. Mary Howard and their four sons, Henry, Robert, Charles, and John Langley, came to Berkeley in the summer of 1902. They rented a house on Arch Street where they had as neighbors the family of Warren and Sadie Gregory. The Gregorys lived in San Francisco but came to Berkeley in the summers to escape the fog. The close friendship that developed between the two families lasted through two generations. Other Berkeley friendships, mainly with faculty and university personnel, followed, along with a strengthening of ties to the San Franciscans Howard had met before his family arrived. The Reverend Worcester continued to be a mainstay in Howard's life.

Although Howard's attachment to California was growing, his trips to New York raised doubts about a long-term commitment. In a letter to Mary of March 3, 1903, he wrote of the excitement of being in New York, where some of his projects, notably the Hotel Renaissance, that had been stalled for years were now proceeding.

It is astonishing how much money is flying around these parts now…. One hears of three, five, ten million dollar buildings on every hand, and even vaster undertakings. And the flattering thing is that we seem to be in the swim of it, and if only I were here continuously it is certain some of it would come my way. My California campaign is building up my reputation and standing without a doubt, but it hurts my immediate practice here woefully, of course. All the same I know where my heart is for the next few years. The work before me there [in California] is unique, no fortune in it, but an opportunity to do a great work such as the children will like to look back on one of these days.

On April 28, 1903, Howard's doubts were resolved, at least for the time being, by official notification of his appointment as supervising architect and professor. "So we are for it!" he wrote Mary, suggesting that she get "a proper gown" for receptions.

After moving to another rented house on Euclid Avenue, Howard acquired property north of the campus on a hill whose crown was intersected by Ridge Road and Le Conte and Scenic Avenues. Phoebe Hearst had purchased most of the hilltop from Frank Wilson, developer of the north Berkeley tract adjacent to the campus called Daley's Scenic Park. Wilson had built his own house on the hilltop near the intersection of Ridge Road and Scenic Avenue in 1894. Howard now bought half a parcel of Wilson's land that stretched between Le Conte Avenue and Ridge Road east of the hilltop. The house he designed for the property in 1903 had the address 2421 Ridge Road.

The Howard and Gregory families on a Thanksgiving Day picnic in the Berkeley Hills in 1902.

According to William C. Hays, who wrote an article about the house in the February 1907 issue of *Indoors and Out,* Howard did not draw detailed plans for the house in advance of its construction. Instead, he made a foundation plan for his workmen, and at the beginning of each day he visited the site and specified the work for that day. Presumably, he provided detailed drawings when necessary.

Designed in the Arts and Crafts tradition, the house had an L-shaped plan with the ell on the east side filled in by a terrace. A flight of steps descended from the terrace to a garden. The main entrance on the west

The Howard family's first home in Berkeley, at 2421 Ridge Road, reflected the current Craftsman style with a bow to California's missions in the square tower. The orientation of the house to the south and the terrace and porches to the east took full advantage of the climate and also allowed Howard to survey the progress of his work on the campus below the hill.

RIGHT
The first-floor plan of the house shows the prominence of the main living spaces and the circulation from the entrance on the west side to the ground floor rooms and the outdoor terrace.

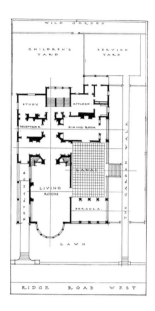

side of the house was at the end of a gravel-surfaced walkway that proceeded from the street past the living room to the door, which Hays described as an "immense, solid plank of redwood." A broad, low-pitched gable roof with a wide, plain bargeboard covered the south wing, which faced the street. This wing featured a wide, polygonal bay window. The walls up to the first-story window heads were finished in "dashed cement" (heavily textured stucco). The two-story east-west section on the back of the house was clad in long redwood shingles laid in overlapping rows in which the bottom row extended about two inches below the row above, producing a deep shadow line. (This technique was used to create the more plastic effect of a masonry wall rather than a thin-skinned wooden wall.) Retaining walls of round river boulders contributed to a rustic look. The dominant element of the house was a large, central tower, also stuccoed, with a tiled roof that suggested the colonial missions Howard had admired during his year in Los Angeles.

Inside the entrance door one had the choice of entering a small

This view of the terrace, called a lanai, on the southeast corner of the house shows it furnished as an outdoor living room.

The path on the east side of the house bordered the garden and provided access to the terrace.

reception room that preceded the study at the north end of the house or turning right into an octagonal central hall that preceded the living room. A smaller octagonal room led to the dining room. The main south-north axis had three cross-axes that afforded views through either windows or doors to the outside. The pergola on the southeast corner provided the perfect vantage point for viewing the eastern hills and, more important for Howard, the campus to the south.

The living room was a grandly proportioned space with an exposed, heavy-timber ceiling that peaked above a mezzanine. The decorative panels on either side of the living room doorway were made from old wooden doors from Mexico. In her "Reminiscence" Janette Howard Wallace, who was born in Berkeley in 1906, recalls this spacious living room with its massive, copper-hooded brick fireplace and the mezzanine balcony from which she and her brothers peered down at guests who came to the many social gatherings in the house. Among these were subscription concert

Two views of the main living room showing the mezzanine balcony over the passageway to the reception hall and the massive brick fireplace with a copper hood.

series with string quartets whose musicians were paid with money from friends, theatrical performances, and dances. John, who enjoyed writing poetry, organized a poetry club with twenty or so members that continued to meet for many years in one location or another.

The neighbors, a close-knit group associated with the university, met for frequent social and cultural activities and were regular attendees at the concerts. Howard designed houses for Lucy Sprague, dean of women from 1906 to 1909, and for her sister, Mary, and her husband, Adolph C. Miller, the first chairman of the university's Department of Economics, established in 1902. These two houses stood, respectively, to the east of the Howard house and across Ridge Road from it.[20] From 1900 to 1911 the

Wheelers lived around the corner at 1820 Scenic Avenue in a house designed by Edgar A. Matthews next to Mrs. Hearst's property. A mansion that Howard planned for Mrs. Hearst on the hilltop was never built, though a house and a reception hall designed by Ernest Coxhead were constructed, respectively, in 1900 at 2368 Le Conte Avenue and in 1902 at 1816 Scenic Avenue. Presumably Hearst moved here from her south Berkeley home to be near the Wheelers. The palm trees that still stand along Ridge Road and Scenic Avenue signal the importance of the original development.

The hilly topography of the area north of campus encouraged such small enclaves of development. East of the Howard houses Ridge Road sloped downhill to Euclid Avenue and then rose again to end at Highland Place, where another cluster of houses stood, designed by Bernard Maybeck in the 1890s and mainly owned by faculty. On the way up the eastern hill, at 2800 Ridge Road, was Cloyne Court, the first faculty apartment building, designed by Howard and built in 1904. Cloyne Court was a project of the University Land and Improvement Company, a development group whose membership included Phoebe Hearst, Jane K. Sather, James K. Moffitt, and John Galen Howard. A sales brochure described the complex as a "high class modern apartment house" catering to faculty and graduate students of means. Part of the building was a residence hotel and had its own chef; a large living room accommodated music recitals and lectures. Many prominent faculty members, including Howard, lived there over the years.

Although the Howards' main residence was in Berkeley, their close friends the Gregorys prompted them to explore the artists' colony of Carmel-by-the-Sea. The people and the landscape of the Carmel area appealed to them so strongly that in 1903 they purchased half a block of property at 13th and Monte Verde Streets, which John named Copsey Court. Eventually they built a modest house in the pine trees and manzanita, but for some years, Janette recounts, "we would sleep on the ground and use an outdoor privy—it was really camping." Charles Sumner Green, already a well-known architect in Pasadena, and his family were among their closest friends in Carmel.

Like many easterners transplanted to California, the Howards had boundless enthusiasm for the landscape of the Sierra and the redwood forests of the coast. Camping trips to the mountains were regular events, and Janette Howard also recalled frequent overnight stays at the lodge on Mount Tamalpais and hiking in the wooded areas around the bay. Moreover, unless he was away on business, John Galen never missed the annual celebration called "the Jinks" at the Bohemian Club's redwood grove near the Russian River.

7

The President's House, California Hall, and the Hearst Memorial Mining Building

1901–1907

The first building constructed after the Hearst Architectural Plan was adopted was the president's house, the groundbreaking ceremony for which had taken place on May 16, 1901, with Mrs. Hearst presiding. Albert Pissis had designed the residence in a classical Mediterranean style, and the state legislature had appropriated $215,000 to pay for it. This sum, however, was inadequate to complete the interior in a manner appropriate to the president's use. Work on the building stopped after September 1902. Until Howard remodeled the interior for President Wheeler and his family, who occupied the house in 1911, the building was used for classrooms.

Indeed, classrooms were in such short supply that Howard designed California Hall, the main administration building, with classrooms and a variety of department offices in addition to administrative services. A 500-seat auditorium, intended mainly for the large classes in history, English, and botany that could not be accommodated in other campus buildings, would occupy the north end of the ground floor along with smaller classrooms. The central part of the second floor, a square room lit by a skylight and defined by columns, was compared to a Roman house atrium and to a bank lobby because it provided easy access to university services such as registration and the recorder's office. The south end of this floor had rooms for faculty meetings, administrative offices, and the offices of the president in the southeast corner. The top floor would house the university herbarium and the university press.

A state appropriation of $250,000 and an additional $19,000 from university funds paid for California Hall, which opened for partial use (the interior remained unfinished) in August 1905. The building was

The president's house has generous semicircular bays projecting from the east and west sides and an entrance portico with triple arched openings. The red tiled roof and classical detail complete the image of an Italian villa. This view, taken ca. 1915 from the southwest, also shows the Miller house that Howard designed on the hill to the left.

The first- and second-floor plans reveal that California Hall was not designed as a simple container for offices. The large lecture hall occupied more than a quarter of the first floor. The second floor featured a wide hallway illuminated by a skylight and lined with Tuscan columns to recall a Roman atrium.

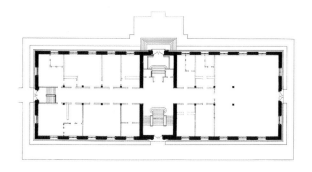

praised for having been constructed with the most advanced methods and materials. A key consideration, on a campus that already had many wooden buildings, was the threat of the destruction of valuable records by fire. The *University Chronicle* stated in September 1905 that "if there is a building in the State that is perfectly fireproof, in which a fire cannot start, or could find nothing to make headway on if possibly started, it is California Hall."

Interior flexibility was a priority. Because the interior partitions were made of metal studs, wire lath, and fireproof plaster, they could be replaced with relative ease. Numerous windows gave the exterior a modular appearance and at the same time revealed the spatial division of the interior. The steel frame covered with reinforced concrete was clad in Raymond granite (a stone of exceptional quality because of its uniform light gray color and hardness) and lined with brick. The copper finials and other ornament that enriched the rooftop skylight were the crowning embellishments for a structure that was otherwise quite austere. Except for the ornament below the projecting window heads on the ground floor and around the doors, the building had little classical detail. Howard wrote that "in style the building is a free study of modified classic forms without recourse to the much over-used, and in fact much abused, columnar orders. An attempt has been made to realize in this building a type of architecture characteristic to Central California."[21]

In a long article in April 1908 titled "The New University of California," Herbert Croly, a critic for the *Architectural Record*, noted "the admirable effect" of California Hall, which "has not been imposed upon its frame, and does not disguise its function, but is the direct expression of the substance and the life of the building." He praised Howard's adaptation of the prevailing classical style in American architecture to California's distinctive landscape and ambitions for the future.

Croly's article begins with a discussion of the unusual combination of private and public support enjoyed by the University of California. Thus, he observed, the university was able to combine the authority of its tie to the state with the freedom gained from its affiliation with Californians of wealth and intelligence, who recognized the importance of the "intellectual sphere" in their state's future. These advantages, he said, were evident in the campus architecture. (He did not mention President Wheeler's successful pursuit of donors for campus buildings, without which implementation of the campus plan would have proceeded at a much slower pace.)

The campus buildings that predated the new architectural plan were not, in Croly's opinion, "worthy of perpetuation." Since the university had no strong architectural tradition, unlike Princeton or Harvard, a local one could take root on the campus. "Californians," he stated in a

OPPOSITE, BOTTOM
An aerial view of California Hall taken in 1945 from the west shows part of Doe Memorial Library and Sather Tower in the background. The uniform treatment of the elevations with molded, bracketed hoods over the tall casement windows on the first floor, smaller unadorned windows on the second floor, and hooded entrance doors on all sides emphasizes the functional nature of the building. The ornament is confined to friezes of bound reeds under the window hoods, a running frieze of rose pateras beneath the roof cornice, and acroteria studding the ridge of the copper-framed skylight.

boosterish way, "are united, much more than the inhabitants of any Eastern State, by the future they are building; and the really formative [architectural] influence in that future is not a tradition so much as an adequate and fruitful idea."

After reviewing the history of the international competition and the winning plan by Émile Bénard, Croly proceeded to repeat almost word for word the justifications for altering Bénard's scheme that Howard gave in his 1903 article "The Architectural Plans for the Greater University of California." In Croly's opinion, "Mr. Howard has proved his ability to devote himself with disinterested enthusiasm to the fulfilment of an idea." Croly noted that Howard's approach to style was fundamentally classic. "No doubt the adoption of such a style was practically implied," he observed, "when a French architect was awarded the prize in the original competition." Howard's departure from the conventional classic style, as exemplified by California Hall, succeeded in satisfying what Croly perceived as a demand that local art, architecture, and literature be Californian rather than national.

Previously, the search for a regional style had turned to the colonial missions for inspiration. "This experiment," Croly stated, "has been responsible for a truly appalling number of flimsy and fantastic plaster copies of the sober conventual buildings of the early Franciscan friars." Stanford University was one of the better examples "of the experimental use of the style for a group of collegiate buildings." Designed by the prominent American firm Shepley, Rutan & Coolidge, the Stanford buildings offered an antidote to the "frivolous and exasperating popular version" of the Mission Revival style. Still, he judged the result a failure. "The attempt to adapt an ecclesiastical style to the needs of modern museums, libraries, laboratories, and lecture rooms must necessarily be a forced attempt...as a matter of fact, we understand that certain of the buildings [at Stanford]...are very inconvenient places in which to work.... The rude but charming archaism of the old Mission is wholly out of keeping with the needs of modern American building."[22]

Howard had gone a different route, looking to classical forms for inspiration, but engaging them with a fresh vision. The University of California buildings, Croly noted, had been "emancipated from an embarrassing allegiance to a narrow or a rigid architectural tradition" and stripped "of the merely French accessories, with which it was originally entangled." Cleansed of extraneous trappings, "the classical architectural ideal and forms...are peculiarly well adapted to the California landscape."

Credit for the architectural flowering of the "Athens of the West" belonged, in Croly's view, to the genius loci:

California is more closely allied to Latin civilization than is any other part of the American republic. It was settled by people of

Spanish descent and while the tie which connects California with the missions and the friars is merely literary and sentimental, there exists a much more significant connection with the social tradition represented by the early Mexican inhabitants…. [Californians] have tended to exhibit some characteristics which are more Latin than they are Anglo-Saxon. Under the influence of the open-air life and really temperate climate, they are gayer socially, more expansive and much more willing to spend more time giving pleasure to

themselves and to other people…. In the course of time Californians should be able to give a more genuine and a more idiomatic expression to the Latin or the classic tradition in art and architecture than will their fellow countrymen further east…. It should be added also that the Californian landscape…is peculiarly adapted to a classic type of building. The whole country lying between the Sierras and the sea, except that nearest the highest ridges of the coastal range, is composed of extremely simple elements…. A landscape of this kind demands a type of building which has been simplified in the classic spirit.

Howard's proposed design for the buildings flanking the Golden Gate axis of the campus, ca. 1911. To the left is California Hall; to the right, Boalt Hall and Philosophy Hall (the latter never built; see page 108).

As for the campus plan as revised by Howard, Croly felt that it would enhance the natural beauties of the site. Moreover, "the scale of the buildings is fitted to the scale of the countryside and of the trees. Their white walls and tiled roofs will look particularly well in the California sunshine and atmosphere. Their lay-out will take advantage of the actual shape of ground, and will lead naturally to the most interesting points of view."

The Hearst Memorial Mining Building, dedicated on August 23, 1907, was perhaps the most urgently needed of the new campus buildings. When construction began in 1903, the University of California's mining college was the largest in the world, and its 247 students made up about

20 percent of the university's total enrollment. The first major building designed under the aegis of the Phoebe A. Hearst Architectural Plan, it was funded entirely by Mrs. Hearst, who paid $1,065,000 for it. It was also Howard's first commission for the campus and in many ways the biggest challenge of his tenure as the plan's supervising architect. Not only did the building's program call for considerable technical innovation, but its prominence on the campus also demanded an appropriate aesthetic expression of that technology.

In his speech at the dedication ceremony Howard recalled that during his first interview with Mrs. Hearst she had impressed upon him her wish that the building be "as perfect for its specific purpose as it could be made, but also as beautiful a structure and as noble a part of the great plan as possible." It was to this end that she had sent him and Professor Samuel B. Christy to visit the important mining schools in the United States and abroad. "In fact," Howard stated, "no school of mines was found which had been built under anything approaching conditions which were fundamental here." Most of the mining schools abroad were in buildings constructed for other purposes, while in this country they were in undistinguished workshop structures that recalled the mines themselves. Howard feared that the absence of reliable prototypes meant that mistakes would likely be made. The same kind of standardizing that hospitals and libraries, for example, had undergone over the past several decades would be necessary before mining schools would be error free. Howard's tactic for guarding against mistakes was to make the plan as elastic as possible.

The main structure that housed the technical part of the school was therefore designed as a shell; this would allow the interior to be replaced without compromising the strength of the whole and with minimum cost. The numerous chimneys and ventilating flues for the furnaces—the elements most vulnerable to wear and tear—were made independent of the larger structure and could be torn down without affecting the building or its equipment.

The plan of the building was innovative. The administrative and more public parts were located in the south portion on either side of the great memorial vestibule, which would house the museum. Windows in the three two-story arches of the facade and three low glazed domes beneath the roof skylight furnished daylight for the vestibule. An administrative wing with the offices of the dean flanked the vestibule on the west; lecture rooms and an office for the curator of the museum occupied the east wing. Extending north behind the vestibule and its adjacent blocks were the central court, which housed the mining laboratory, and, along the east and west sides, metallurgical and research laboratories.[23] A series of drafting and lecture rooms occupied the upper floor above the labs, along with a private study and drafting room for the dean. The three-story,

Second- and third-floor plans of the Hearst Memorial Mining Building.

BELOW
View of the Hearst Memorial Mining Building from the southeast.

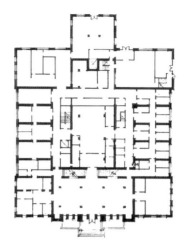
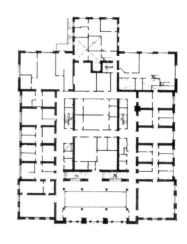

fifty-foot-square tower for crushing dry ore projected thirty-six feet beyond the north wall of the building. The tower was flanked on the east by the copper and lead smelting laboratory and on the west by the gold and silver mill.

"Within," Howard continued,

> everything is work-a-day, substantial and, I hope, convenient, but totally devoid of ornament, as a building of this character should be…. Yet the building is intended to take on a progressively more civilized aspect, and a more monumental beauty as one goes from the work shops of the rear toward the public portions of the front, and sounds the highest note of dignity and impressiveness in the great museum-vestibule. The [memorial] motive reaches on the exterior its first full development and orchestration…and [is] further enriched by the recall of the classic type of architecture, which the great ground of the University as a whole will approximate. We have sought to secure beauty not by easy masquerade and putting

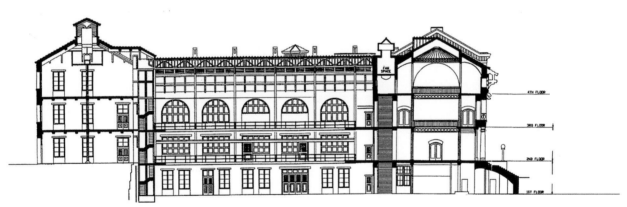

LONGITUDINAL SECTION · HISTORIC CONDITION

> on of architectural stuff, but by organic composition, working from within out, and letting the heart of the thing speak.

The longitudinal section of the mining building.

Five years earlier, in an article about the Hearst Memorial Mining Building written for the *University of California Magazine,* Howard had stated his goal for the mining building with even more passion:

> The aim has been to give expression to the character of a College of Mining Engineering as distinguished from one of Art, Letters, or of Natural Science. The expression of belles-lettres in architecture demands a more purely classic character than that of scientific studies. Such a building as a library, for instance, may without inconsistency rejoice in all the sumptuous glories of Roman architecture or

the Renaissance; the tradition of the world leads one naturally enough in this direction. But…such delicate and highly organized motives find little place in a Mining Building, which demands a treatment, while no less beautiful, much more primitive, less elaborately developed in the matter of detail, less influenced by the extreme classic tradition either as a canon of proportion or as an architectonic schema. The profession of mining has to do with the very body and bone of the earth; its process is a ruthless assault upon the bowels of the world, a contest with the crudest and most rudimentary forces. There is about it something essentially elementary, something primordial; and its expression in architecture must, to be true, have something of the rude, the Cyclopean. The emotion roused must be a sense of power, rather than that of grace…. To produce a design for a Mining Building which shall in all sincerity express its purpose and at the same time harmonize with future buildings quite as sincere in the expression of their purposes— purposes in almost every case of greater amenity—this has been the aim of the architect in approaching his task in its artistic phase.

Herbert Croly closed his article "The New University of California" with praise for the mining building, echoing many of Howard's statements. He declared the building to be organically conceived and carefully and elaborately wrought. It embodied "such a transfigured version of the classic ideal that many ministers of that faith would not recognize the allegiance." Still, the building could not, he judged, be "wholly justified or appreciated until…it is properly approached, properly planted and properly surrounded with its neighboring buildings. In the meantime its novel appearance will make many architectural observers doubtful."

Observers approaching the mining building today are not likely to describe its appearance as novel; *idiosyncratic* seems a more valid term. Croly had expressed doubts about the "propriety" of placing a tiled roof with bold timber brackets upon a facade pierced with three arched openings enriched with classical ornament. For Croly, this combination of vernacular and classical elements impaired the beauty of the building "without contributing anything essential to its character." But the rules that governed Croly's judgment of impropriety have long since been dismissed. Today, the very combination of elements that Croly criticizes is what gives the facade its impression of power.

The scale of the largely glazed, two-story arched openings in deep reveals is complemented by that of the architraves, set on free-standing Tuscan columns, that project slightly beyond the plane of the wall. The pattern of the voussoirs on the walls echoes that of the radiating windows in the lunettes of the arches and serves to extend their upward thrust toward the attic section below the roof. Two wreathed medallions, typically used as a secondary ornamental motif, are here enlarged and so placed that they appear as giant nail heads anchoring the wall. The descent of the heavy tiled roof with its generous overhang supported on heavy wood brackets effectively counters the lift of the arches, while the blocks that tack down the bead-and-reel stringcourse are upheld by sculptures. If one were judging by the norms of the time for classical facades, Howard's composition would be termed outlandish. This was not an adjective Croly would have thought it proper to use, but it may have been what he meant.

In Howard's view, the exterior had "an extremely simple, dignified character, based upon the classic tradition, but strongly influenced by the naif and charming work of the Spanish Fathers in the land." To compare the mining building to the colonial missions seems farfetched. Even the tile roofs could be attributed to ancient Mediterranean classicism generally, rather than to California missions specifically. But Howard's words were directed to an ideological goal that was important at the time, which was to tie the mining building to a period that had receded sufficiently into the past to become a way of validating what was genuinely Californian.[24]

The sensuous male and female sculptures by Robert Aitken on the granite corbels supporting the wooden roof brackets conveyed the building's symbolic intent. Howard spoke of the sculptures with characteristic verve in his dedication speech: "The two male sculptures to the west symbolized "the primal elements" and the two to the east "the eternal forces." The female sculptures in the center of the facade represented "the ideal arts, the final flower of life—fresh, mysterious, pure—emerging from the void of chaos."

The very form of the memorial vestibule block conveys its importance to the overall structure. Not only does the facade project in front of the walls of the wings, but the skylit roof rises well above the adjacent roofs. The cross-walls of the vestibule, which rise still higher, delimit the width of the block and give it integrity as a form complete in itself. Although the composition of the facade relies on the classical means of symmetry and hierarchy to achieve its unity, Howard has rescued it from predictability by deftly interweaving the voids and solids with an unconventional use of ornamental detail.

The real revelation of Howard's innovative approach to the design of the mining building comes when the visitor swings open the golden oak entrance doors and enters the vestibule. Instead of the anticipated classical interior there is a high rectangular hall in an industrial aesthetic that sparks a breathtaking moment of surprise. The shallow, glazed domes fifty feet above the floor are set on pendentives clad in Guastavino tiles. The interlocking tilework creates a delicate woven pattern that contrasts in a lively way with the brick walls. The pendentives in turn taper to columns composed of steel beams, with rivets and other structural detail exposed; the columns extend through two floors of balconies with cast-iron railings supported on steel lattice trusses. The blue-green metalwork complements the buff-colored walls and beige tones of the Guastavino tilework. Refinement and grace are the dominant impressions.

The success of the vestibule is due in no small measure to the use of the structural system developed and owned by the Guastavino family

This partial view of the memorial vestibule interior shows the herringbone pattern of the Guastavino tile in the pendentives supporting the shallow glazed domes. The industrial character of the metal railings and the beams supporting the second and third floor galleries is a fitting expression for the mining profession.

company.[25] Rafael Guastavino and his son had come to the United States in 1881 from the Spanish province of Catalonia, where they had developed a vaulting system based on local tradition. The company they established in 1889 was very successful and brought them work from major architectural offices such as McKim, Mead & White, for whom the Guastavinos constructed vaults in the Boston Public Library in the early 1890s. The company installed vaulting systems and shell domes in many well-publicized buildings in New York that Howard would have known about. While Howard's familiarity with Henri Labrouste's Bibliothèque Nationale reading room from the 1860s, with its vaulting and domes, may have had some influence on his thinking, his awareness of the Guastavino Company's work in the United States was probably more important in informing the industrial aesthetic of his vestibule design.[26]

Howard sent the Guastavino Company three schematic drawings for the structure of the vestibule ceiling: a quarter plan of the framing for the tile in the pendentives, a detail showing the location of the tile in section, and a plan showing rods, floor beams, and angles. Company employees made working drawings from these schemas and provided trained work-men and materials for the construction of the domes and pendentives.[27] As photographs taken at the time show, the domes were fabricated within the shell of the vestibule before the roof was constructed. They were then

This 1905 photograph of the memorial vestibule of the mining building under construction shows the metal frame-work being put in place for the glazed domes and tiled pendentives.

set like crowning jewels in the frame that Howard had designed for them.[28]

The building's main interior axis extended across the vestibule from the main entrance doors and through a matching archway to follow the center line of the atrium, traced by the roof skylight. The axis terminated in the crushing tower at the north end. Three-story wings flanking the tower housed the copper and lead smelter and the gold and silver mill. The flues rising above the roofline that punctuate the north and south elevations vented the draft forges and high-temperature assay furnaces that occupied the laboratories in the atrium. The south elevation, also symmetrically composed, had entrance doors in the central bay that accommodated the transport of materials into the atrium for use in the labs.

Within the rectangular form of the building, the Beaux-Artsian norms of symmetry, axiality, and hierarchy were strictly observed. Loren Partridge's comparison of the mining building's plan to that of a "great church," with its narthex, nave, transepts, and apse, is well taken.[29] If not a cathedral, the edifice was certainly "a new temple of science and industrial arts," as Martin Kellogg put it in his invocation at the ceremonial laying of the cornerstone on November 9, 1902.

Croly's closing remarks regarding the mining building were prescient: "The building emphatically constitutes both beauty and character, and the writer does not doubt that fifty years from now it will constitute one of the buildings erected by the present generation of American architects which will have worn best, and which, in the opinion of that day, will best deserve indefinite perpetuation." The passing of nearly a century has confirmed this judgment. The mining building stands today as one of the state's, and even the country's, most distinguished architectural monuments.

University Work, Private Practice, and the Alaska-Yukon-Pacific Exposition

8

1904–1907

Howard's tenure as supervising architect was never trouble free. Having secured authority over all aspects of the physical development of the campus, he had to cope with the petty details of alterations and repairs to existing buildings, which, as he observed in letters to the Committee on Buildings and Grounds, prevented him from attending to the more important task of implementing the architectural plan. Roads and pathways between buildings, connections to the campus from city streets, and infrastructure such as pipelines were important issues, as was the campus landscaping. Howard was also concerned with making "resting places" on the campus, to be furnished with heavy wooden benches of his design. Even repairs to the creek banks came under his review.

In the fall of 1904, Howard submitted plans for South Drive. This paved road, which was nearly finished by March 1905, began at the Center Street entrance to the campus, curved south past Harmon Gymnasium and then north to pass Bacon Hall, and completed its eastward course at College Avenue.

The operating budget of the supervising architect's office was increased from $2,000 to $4,000 in 1904. Howard used half of this amount to commission a model of the campus that revealed the topography of the grounds and the character of new buildings: the Hearst Memorial Mining Building, California Hall, the Greek Theater, the president's house, and the power plant. The model was particularly useful in showing the logic of Howard's shift to the south of Bénard's axis to University Avenue. The new axis followed the natural vale that traversed the campus from the hills to the east, focusing visually on the Golden Gate. Under the new scheme, the main western gateway to the campus was at Center and Oxford Streets, where a monumental entrance gate was planned. A crescent-shaped road was plotted to tie University Avenue to Center Street. Although this roadway was created at that time, the Center Street gate was not built until later.[30]

As the work in the supervising architect's office increased in volume, the space Howard was leasing in the Eastman Building on the southwest corner of Center and Oxford Streets began to feel cramped. He therefore petitioned the regents in April 1904 for authorization to open an office in San Francisco, where, he argued, qualified assistants, contractors, and materials were more available and less costly. The regents granted his request, but Howard did not move to San Francisco right away. Instead he leased space on the sixth floor of the National Bank Building a block away at Center Street and Shattuck Avenue. At that time Howard had ten or more employees. Arthur Markwart, who along with William C. Hays became a junior partner after 1906, came from New York in September 1904. He and Ira Wilson Hoover, another member of the firm, had known each other from student days at the University of Pennsylvania. Other employees were George T. Plowman; John Hudson Thomas, son of a Berkeley mining engineer; Walter Ratcliff, who had just graduated from the University of California; Harvey Harris; Max Lempke, who had come from Germany to work for Howard; and Harriet Young, the only woman in the office after Julia Morgan left to start her own practice in 1904. W. F. Scott was the office engineer. Most of these young architects went on to establish their own offices and contributed in significant ways to Bay Area architecture.

The tenor of Howard's office in these early years was described by William Gray Purcell, who had come to California at age twenty-three— as had Howard—in search of work and adventure. (Purcell later formed a partnership with George Grant Elmslie that produced many notable buildings in the Prairie School tradition in Minnesota and other parts of the Midwest.) Purcell, again like Howard, had started his California sojourn in Los Angeles, where his aunt lived, but his real destination was Seattle, Washington. In Los Angeles he applied for work in the office of Myron Hunt. Although Hunt did not hire him, he did suggest that Purcell stop in San Francisco and see John Galen Howard, who hired him after a fifteen-minute interview. Purcell worked for Howard from early January to the middle of August 1904, mainly on California Hall. In an oral history from 1950, he recounted the office routine:

> Each morning about 10:30 Mr. Howard, accompanied by his office superintendent, and sometimes by his engineer, would make the

The architecture building, known as the "Ark," photographed from the west ca. 1910.

rounds of the tables, observing the progress of the work, discussing details or making comments, but orders as to what to do always came through his executives.

Now as to the impression which Mr. Howard made upon me and his personality. He seemed taller than I, and as I am 6 feet tall, he must have been quite a tall man. He had a reddish, sandy beard... and hair somewhat darker than his beard. He carried himself very well indeed, but his manner was genial rather than proud. He was exceedingly pleasant spoken and gave you the impression of being very sincere and wholly interested in you as a person and in whatever you happened to be talking about. He gave you his absolute, undivided attention as long as the interview lasted. I never saw him exasperated or disturbed in any relations in the office. He spoke in a vigorous way..., seemed at all times to have complete mastery of any situation, knew exactly what he wanted to accomplish, and was quite ready to accept the views of others. No one had any hesitation in offering their opinion, and he received it and considered it for what it could be worth. I have attended office parties at his home, meeting his wife and children. This atmosphere was most pleasant and hospitable.[31]

In 1905, the supervising architect's office moved to the Italian American Bank building at 456 Montgomery Street in San Francisco. Although the catastrophic earthquake and fire of 1906 damaged the building and destroyed drawings and records, the drawings for the Phoebe A. Hearst Architectural Plan, the surveys of the university grounds, and the incomplete drawings for Doe Library were rescued from the building by an employee, Henry A. Boese, the only draftsman who lived in San Francisco. Boese went to the office, pushed his way past the police, and climbed to the sixth-floor office to save whatever he could carry. By the end of the year the firm, now Howard & Galloway,[32] had reopened in the Atlas Building at 604 Mission Street. Howard was later hired to design the replacement building for the Italian American Bank.

In Berkeley, although chimneys toppled and cracks appeared in walls, in comparison with San Francisco, damage from the earthquake was minor. On the campus, the modern construction technique of reinforced steel frames with masonry cladding was credited with protecting the newer buildings, which came through unscathed. Janette Howard Wallace recalls the earthquake's effects in her 1987 memoir:

There were people in Berkeley, some religious sect, who thought the end of the world had come; they all went up on the hills, in white robes, and stayed up there for two or three days singing hymns....
Since Pop and Mom had this great big house [on Ridge Road], they

took in a lot of refugees from San Francisco; people poured over from across the bay after the fire started…. Pop and Mom had people who stayed for several months…. Among them was William Keith, the painter, from whom Pop bought a lot of pictures…. One of Keith's good friends was John Muir. Mom said she could remember John Muir coming and visiting him after the earthquake at the Ridge Road house, these two old men sitting out in the sun and chatting.

Two buildings designed by Howard that were not part of the permanent architectural plan were constructed in 1906. A two-story wooden building clad in redwood shingles for the new Department of Architecture, begun in December of 1905, was occupied on January 23, 1906. The 1,800-square-foot structure, thirty feet wide and seventy-five feet long, cost $4,393.59; it contained Howard's office, an instruction room, and the library, which was started with a collection of books on architecture donated by Phoebe A. Hearst. Howard's curriculum for the

The Ark photographed from the northwest, showing the recently completed 1908 addition, which housed the drafting rooms.

department, approved in 1905, included courses in architectural history, theory, and engineering. Having spent their first two years fulfilling requirements in the university's College of Letters and Science, architecture students devoted their last two years to these specialized courses. The new building provided enough space that classes in watercoloring, pen-and-ink drawing, and modeling might be added to the curriculum.

The department's small size did not diminish the high hopes President Wheeler had for its future influence on California architecture. In his biennial report of 1904–6 Wheeler wrote, "I am convinced that the work of no department of the university more honestly meets an existing need than does the work for this; for, though the number of students who may go forth from it annually may not exceed a dozen, they will be well trained and will bring a much needed forward impulse to the standards of building and art in California."

From the beginning, the department's atmosphere was intimate and informal. Because these juniors and seniors were not required to take courses in other departments, they spent most of their time working together in the architecture building. The eight students in Howard's first class called their self-contained world "the Ark." Howard was "Father Noah."

The demanding nature of the architecture program bonded the students. Howard described the course of study as demanding "a cruel lot of time, for which twenty-four hours a day are not enough." Under such pressure, he said, the department became "a little community of good will, off by itself on the edge of the campus."

Howard grew so fond of his building that in June 1908, when Mary's family considered renting the Ridge Road house for two years, he wrote her a letter in which he suggested, probably not seriously, "Perhaps we could build a bungalow in the back lot, on the basis of the Architecture Building, but a grade better." Whatever Howard meant by this offhand comment is not known, nor did he ever write about the design of the building. His statements about its nurturing quality, however, indicate that he thought it a success.

In December 1907, less than two years after the architecture building was occupied, Howard requested funds to expand it. Already in August he had written President Wheeler that the increase in the number of students enrolled "has been so rapid that our building has overflowed…. The number of students in design alone has increased from fifteen to twenty-seven, and the Drafting room should be at least doubled in size." The regents granted Howard's request for $6,000, and in 1908 a 3,400-square-foot structure with two drafting rooms was added to the east side of the original building. The entrance to the addition that Howard designed with his first Bay Area partner, engineer John Debbo Galloway, was on the south side, where the courtyard was later built. The drafting rooms were lit by a bank of windows on the north side. Inside the drafting rooms, industrial lamps with green shades hung from wires that crisscrossed below the ceiling's exposed framework. The lamps could be moved along the wires to wherever they were needed. Former students recalled that the first occupants of the drafting rooms would cluster the lamps over their desks, causing a genial fracas when others arrived and tried to rearrange the lamps to get their share of light.

Although the Ark was enlarged several times over the years, it maintained its informal quality and domestic scale. Since the monumental, granite-clad building dedicated to the arts that Howard envisioned for the north side of the campus was never built, the simple structure that he designed as a temporary home for the school of architecture remained in use until 1964, when Wurster Hall was constructed to house the new College of Environmental Design.

Several other buildings not part of the Hearst Architectural Plan were constructed around this time as well. The Senior Men's Hall, paid

A photograph of the Senior Men's Hall from a pictorial album of campus buildings published by the Students' Co-operative Society around 1907. The Order of the Golden Bear, a secret honor society for senior men founded in 1900, proposed the building in 1903 and began raising money to build it. Howard waived his fee for the plans he prepared in 1904. As completed in 1906, the outsized log cabin had two spaces: a large front room available to senior men, alumni, and faculty for meetings and social gatherings and a smaller back room on the east end for the exclusive use of the order. The two rooms were separated by a wall of logs with a two-sided fireplace of clinker brick. Some 2,940 redwood logs from the Russian River area were used without removing their bark. Furnishings for the rooms also used the logs in their natural state. King post trusses set on log pilasters between the sections of windows supported the roof. The Order of the Golden Bear continues to use the building.

for with a donation of $4,500 by the Order of the Golden Bear, a senior men's secret society, was built in 1906 of 2,940 redwood logs. Howard studied log cabins in the California mountains to guide its design and hired as contractor for the 60-by-30-foot structure a man who had built log cabins in Alaska. Other incidental buildings designed by Howard were of brick. One such was the power plant, built in 1904 but not put into operation for lighting and heating until 1906.[33]

Howard was on leave from January to June 1907 to work on the 1909 Alaska-Yukon-Pacific Exposition in Seattle.[34] On February 4, he and John Galloway met with the exposition design team, which included the Olmsted Brothers and Edward Frere Champney, a Seattle architect whom Howard had known in the East and had himself employed in San Francisco. As supervising architects for the fair, Howard & Galloway had prepared a scheme for the grounds. Three of the expo buildings were to be permanent additions to the University of Washington campus and thus had to be designed for the dual purpose of exhibition and learning. "This is rather a hard task," Howard wrote to Mary, "especially in the case of the chemistry building, which is to be used by the show as a fine arts museum! Such transmogrification requires some species of magic I doubt I possess." By May 15, Howard and Galloway had signed a contract with the regents of the University of Washington to undertake the project. "Our star is certainly in the ascendent," he wrote Mary. "Everyone seems delighted

A drawing of the plan for the 1909 Alaska-Yukon-Pacific Exposition, for which Howard and Galloway were the supervising architects.

with all we have done, and affairs are moving as smoothly as possible."

The regents of the University of California, meanwhile, continued to take a proprietary interest in the operation of the office of the supervising architect. In 1907 the board suggested an on-campus office for all university work because it would require a smaller organization. Howard defended the operation of the San Francisco office for both on- and off-campus work, expressing doubts that he would be able to hire a good staff for a campus office at the university's low rates of pay. He was required to submit a monthly record of the office expenses, a continual source of aggravation because of lack of agreement on the division of expenses between his private work and that for the campus.

On January 16, 1908, V.H. Henderson, the board of regents' secretary, wrote to Howard reviewing a conversation the two men had held that day. In the letter Henderson stated his understanding that Howard was prepared to carry on university work—which included new construction, alterations, additions, repairs, temporary structures, monuments, fountains, roads, bridges, and engineering construction—after April 1 for a fee of 4 percent of costs, in addition to Howard's salary of $4,000 as professor of architecture.[35] (Until March 1908, Mrs. Hearst contributed Howard's salary of $6,000 as supervising architect. After that date Mrs. Hearst no longer contributed to the architectural expenses of the permanent plan.) Advice on landscape gardening would be given free of charge except when such work was executed under contract. The university proposed the 4 percent fee, rather than the 6 percent recommended by the American Institute of Architects, because of payment for work already carried out. The fee would cover all architectural service and all necessary engineering service as well as the expenses of supervising construction. Howard would forgo payment if the university employed a collaborating expert.

In the case of the Doe Library project, the first part of which was already under way, Howard proposed that he complete the plans, specifications, and working drawings for this portion of the building so that bids could be solicited. Plans, specifications, and working drawings for the second phase, estimated at $1 million, would also be completed so that bids could be obtained at a future time, after the first phase was finished. The two sets of plans would be furnished for a fee that represented Howard's costs, calculated on the basis of employee time cards and a proportion of office expenses. There would be no charge for Howard's personal service. Supervision of the construction of the library after April 1 would be recompensed at a rate of 1½ percent of costs.

On January 20, 1908, Howard replied to Henderson's letter stating that he agreed to the arrangement for the library of a fixed amount for partial and completed work of $5,000 and $4,000, which represented his actual expenses for the preparation of plans. He believed that would eliminate "to a great degree the constant bickering over monthly accounts, which," as he wrote Mary, "has worn me so thin."

9

Doe Memorial Library, Boalt Hall, and Sather Gate

1907–1917

From the time of the international competition, the library had been considered the most important building on the university campus. The library should, Howard wrote in 1903, be "almost equally accessible from each and every department." As a result, the library site "has been more seriously considered, perhaps, than any other single question relating to the plan, unless it be the main axis."[36] Bénard's scheme placed the library immediately east of Oxford Street and south of Hearst Avenue, in the northwestern corner of the campus—a location that, though immediately visible beyond the entrance to the grounds, permanently removed it from the center of the campus, since the university could not grow beyond its western and northern boundaries. The "artistic" advantage of this siting, Howard noted, was clearly outweighed by its inconvenience.

A site in front of the existing library in Bacon Hall, though central, was too restricted to allow for future expansion. "On the whole," Howard wrote, "everything seems to point to the ground immediately west of North Hall and south of the Botanical Garden as the most advantageous position for the Library. This is the geographical center of the portion of the property readily adaptable to building operations. It lies midway between the two cross[-campus] axes...[and] is a prominent, sightly spot facing the central avenue or esplanade,...a building placed here would give an exceedingly fine architectural effect."

The revised version of the Hearst Architectural Plan that Howard submitted to the regents in 1908 showed the library building in the central location Howard had described five years earlier. The northern edge of the site was aligned with the proposed grand "avenue" or esplanade that was to encircle the enlarged botanical garden (a garden with specimen trees and other vegetation already existed in the swale that marked the main axis but did not extend as far west as the revised plan indicated). The library block that housed the main reading room would overlook the esplanade; it also projected beyond the north ends of North Hall and California Hall to emphasize its importance. The library's south wall lined up with the buildings east and west of it that defined what would later be called Campanile Way.

A gift of $779,000 from the estate of Charles Franklin Doe, a lumber baron and bibliophile, initiated construction of the library. (The final cost of the building was $1,439,000; most of the balance came from a state bond issue of $525,000.) During the first construction phase from 1907 to 1911, the east-west block was completed, as was the adjacent five-story block that would house the books. This phase was dedicated in March 1912. The lower level of the rectangular east-west block housed the library of Hubert Howe Bancroft—an unmatched collection of published and

This rendering of the north elevation of Doe Memorial Library was made ca. 1907, perhaps as a final presentation drawing to show the reading room block with landscaping and a sequence of terraces and stairways descending to the esplanade.

unpublished materials on the western part of North America, with emphasis on California, Mexico, and Central America, acquired by the university in 1905[37]—and the reserve book room (now called the Morrison Room). The main reading room and the catalogue/delivery room were on the upper level.

Excavation for the library basement took several months. This involved both creating an earthen platform to level the site (which resulted in the library's west side being significantly higher than California Hall) and removal of much of the excavated earth to the west side of California Hall to reduce the slope of the land there. In 1911 construction stopped at the height of the first story on the east, south, and west sides of the building for lack of funds. The final phase of construction, from 1914 to 1917, completed the upper stories of the building. The library's steel frame was clad in Raymond granite backed by reinforced concrete that was poured in wooden forms behind the stone.

President Wheeler appointed a faculty committee to plan the program for the library. The members were Charles Mills Gayley, who had organized the English department in accord with the growth of the university; Henry Morse Stephens, professor of history from 1902 to 1919; William Cary Jones, head of the Department of Jurisprudence from its creation in 1894 and a member of the advisory board of the Hearst architectural competition; and Andrew Lawson, professor of mineralogy and geology from 1890 to 1928. The acute shortage of teaching space on the campus prompted Lawson to press for seminar rooms for every field of study. As finally planned, the seminar rooms wrapped around a fifteen-foot-wide corridor on the first floor that encircled the central core of stacks on the east, south, and west sides. The block of stacks, with capacity for some 300,000 volumes, was capped by a pyramidal copper-framed skylight from which natural light filtered down through glass floors. The close relationship between the study rooms and the stacks was not typical of the large public libraries of the times, where readers and books tended to be completely separate. Howard considered his plan to be more appropriate for a university community.

As built, the reading room block is symmetrical, with the entrance doors in the central bay of the north facade. The entrance portal conveys its importance by breaking through the lintel that caps the basement story. Syntactically, the entrance bay is a hyphen in the longitudinal thrust of the facade. Two slender Ionic columns rise above the portal's pediment and divide the large window into three sections, a division that also distinguishes the central window from those on either side. A stone plaque inscribed with the words "The University Library" set into the frieze of the entablature above the central bay marks this as the entrance. (The plaque, thirty feet long, four feet nine inches high, and eighteen inches thick and weighing about fourteen tons, was said at the time to be the largest stone mounted on a Western building.) If the sequence of terraces and stairways descending from the library entrance down to the formal botanical garden and across the esplanade to the proposed museum on the opposite hilltop had been constructed, the central bay would have been imposing indeed. This grand scheme, however, was never carried out.[38]

OPPOSITE, TOP
Floor plans for the first, second, and fourth floors of Doe Memorial Library reveal how efficiently Howard packed the rectangular building with functional spaces while designing the reading room block as an imposing frontispiece.

BOTTOM
A photograph of Doe Memorial Library from the northeast taken ca. 1917 shows the building rising above the botanical garden. The raised masonry base of the demolished North Hall, visible to the left of the library, remained in use until 1931.

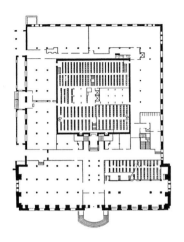 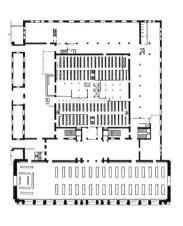 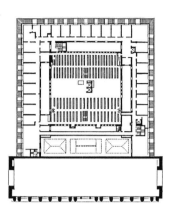

(The present configuration of the raised terrace and stairway opposite the main entrance is the result of constructing new stacks underground to meet seismic code requirements.)

Initially, Howard appears to have had two building types in mind for the reading room block: a Greek temple and a Roman basilica, both signaling wisdom and authority. The final design in a sense combines the two. The rhythmic progression of engaged Corinthian columns standing on the raised basement and separated by tall windows—voids that create the

PLANTING SCHEME
WEST ELEVATION OF THE UNIVERSITY LIBRARY
JOHN GALEN HOWARD
ARCHITECT

This rendering of the west elevation of Doe Memorial Library, made ca. 1917, emphasizes the proposed land-scaping, which creates a smooth transition from the building to the ground. The planting was executed more or less as shown.

illusion of a freestanding colonnade—evokes the Greek temple, while the gabled end walls, with their monumental arched windows that break through the entablature, hint at the Roman basilica.

For President Wheeler, an ardent Grecophile, however, the library was to be the Parthenon of this Athens of the West, a shrine of knowledge presided over by Athena, the Greek goddess of wisdom: the idea that it should be polluted by Roman influence was blasphemous. Heated conversations occurred whenever Wheeler came to the office to discuss the library program. As William Hays, who worked on the library in Howard's office, observed, "Somehow he and Howard were magnetically opposed—one was a pure artist; the other a classic scholar." Howard was on the point of giving up the arch when, one day, he asked Hays to talk to Wheeler about it. Hays met with the president and stated the case for the arched windows as follows: "This great [reading] room…needs these great arch windows at the ends. To have columns, which would allow only very small windows, would give a feeble accent at the ends." Wheeler was unresponsive. "To me," Hays continued, "Roman architecture is classic. Compared with the finest of the Greek I think it is inferior, excepting in majesty of size. But this [library] is big. This isn't the scale of even the Acropolis. This is bigger.... If we take the point of view that arches are inappropriate, then do we not have to take the point of view that the Greeks had almost no windows? There isn't a window in the Parthenon, but in the very nature of a library we're going to be full of windows."

Daylight from the windows on the north side and on the east and west ends, along with the skylights, provides the reading room interior with the even illumination appropriate to a great hall of learning.

Finally Wheeler replied, "Well, you might try the arches."[39]

With space for 400 readers, the 210-by-50-foot reading room was at that time exceeded in size only by the reading room of the New York Public Library. The lofty interior—forty-five feet from the floor to the top of the barrel-vaulted, coffered ceiling—received light from three skylights set beneath corresponding skylights on the roof. The north-facing windows and the arched windows on the east and west also admitted a generous

UNIVERSITY OF CALIFORNIA

THE LIBRARY FROM THE GAR

The image of an acropolis bearing a
temple of learning is strongly conveyed
in this ca. 1917 rendering. The view
from the northwest shows not only Doe
Library but also a corner of California
Hall and a distant glimpse of the new
North Hall, which was never built.

amount of daylight. Solid granite panels below the windows provided ample space for bookshelves.

The reading room echoed the symmetrical composition of the north facade. The entrance, centered in the south wall, was marked by a high arch infilled with decorative motifs above the door lintel. The catalogue/delivery room opened into the reading room on the south side. A branching stairway rising at the end of the wide hall leading from the building's entrance gave access to these rooms. The functional subordination of

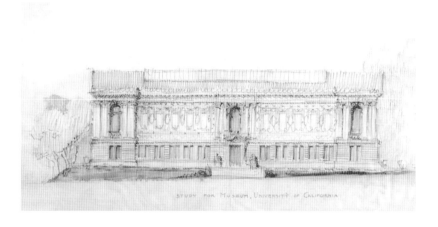

STUDY FOR MUSEUM, UNIVERSITY OF CALIFORNIA

As shown in this drawing, Howard's concept for the proposed museum of art, natural history, and ethnology, which was to stand on Observatory Hill facing Doe Library, reflects the library's north elevation. With its entrance dividing the building into symmetrical halves terminating in Greek temple forms on the east and west ends, the museum would have been a proper counterpart for the library. Perhaps to signal a building housing the fine arts, the unfenestrated wall was given an ornamented surface suggestive, at least in the drawing, of a rich brocade.

circulation space to study space was a notable departure from conventional design of libraries in the Beaux-Arts era, most of which featured space-consuming grand stairways ascending directly to their reading rooms.

The other grand interior space of Doe Library, the periodical reading room that opened in 1917, was also accessible from the catalogue/delivery room. A Renaissance decor was chosen for the room, which boasted a richly ornamented, cast-plaster ceiling. Tapestries were to hang on the end walls. Although the decoration of the completed room was not as elaborate as originally envisioned, the effect is still grand.

On the exterior, Athena (or her Roman counterpart, Minerva) was honored as the library patroness through use of her symbols. A bronze bust of the goddess overlooks the entrance doors. The Corinthian order, considered like the Ionic order to have a feminine character, was used for the colonnade. Howard even devised a special capital for the columns, which he described as having "half-opened acanthus fronds, from among which serpents [symbols of Athena] rise and coil to uphold an open book." The Ionic columns above the portico symbolize "Athena's leadership of the Ionic states," an allusion perhaps to this Athens of the West as the future intellectual leader of the United States.[40]

The gable ends of the reading room block testify to Howard's sure sense of scale and composition. The robust detail of the cornice with its courses of large and small dentils surmounted by splendid copper acroteria catches the light of different times of day to create an ever-changing pattern of light and shadow. Fluted pilasters, with another variation on the Corinthian order for the capitals, enliven the wall plane while still respecting it.

It was Howard's intention to give each building on the campus a special character through its composition and detail, an approach he had pursued with great success in the Hearst Memorial Mining Building. As regards the library, he believed that "the expression of belles-lettres in architecture demands a more purely classic character than scientific studies. Such a building as a Library, for instance, may... rejoice in all the sumptuous glories of Roman architecture or the Renaissance."

In considering the effect of the library on the campus as a whole, Howard had written in 1903: "The Library is too important a building to be placed on one side of the esplanade without a balancing mass opposite. The Museum seems to be its natural pendant, and the site immediately opposite the Library, the knoll now occupied by the Observatory, seemed in every respect an ideal site for such a building." In fact, the museum was not built on this site; the observatory hilltop remains undeveloped to this day. In 1992, the university undertook a seismic improvements project that entailed an underground addition to the north side of Doe Library and the Bancroft Library. New book stacks for the libraries were required to replace the original stacks of Doe Library, whose glass floors were judged seismically unsafe. The placement of a generous terrace above the underground stacks has given the reading room block a more appropriate setting than it previously had in the unfinished state of Howard's scheme.[41]

The building most affected by the library was North Hall, one of the two original university buildings. A wooden building set on a concrete base that had served a variety of purposes since its construction in 1873, North Hall was painted red to suggest that it was made of brick like its neighbor, South Hall. Howard suggested the demolition of North Hall at the time of the library's construction because of the threat of fire. In fact, North Hall was so close to the east end of the library that its west entrance stairs had to be removed and set on the east side. The building was finally razed in 1931.[42]

Groundbreaking for the Boalt Memorial Hall of Law, for which Elizabeth Boalt gave $100,000 in 1907, took place on July 19, 1908; the building was dedicated April 28, 1911. Because the gift was not sufficient to meet the cost of the building, President Wheeler and members of the Department of Jurisprudence attended the May 1908 meeting of the Bench and Bar Association of San Francisco to ask the lawyers of the state to contribute

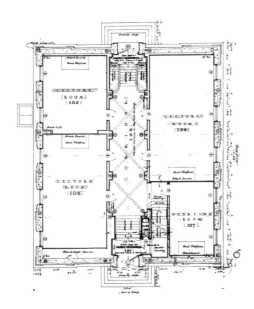

to the building fund. An executive committee composed of the chief justice of the state supreme court, eminent judges, and practicing attorneys was charged with carrying the project forward. With characteristic pride in the university, this committee stated in the circular distributed among the state's lawyers: "California must create a great School of Law and Leadership...not merely a law department of good standing, but a center of legal education of the highest rank—a Harvard and Columbia of the West; and more—drawing a student body from the western half

The section drawing of Boalt Hall reveals a complex plan with the most important space given to the Lawyers' Memorial Hall, the law library reading room, on the upper floor.

of the continent, training future leaders in the community, giving special consideration to the special development of the law of the states this side of the Rockies."

Boalt Hall was initially intended to be one of a pair of small, cubic structures; however, the other building, Philosophy Hall, was never built. Its small size—only eighty feet wide compared to two hundred feet for California Hall—meant that Boalt had the highest unit cost of any campus building. Although lawyers' subscriptions increased the original donation by $50,000, the general fund had to be tapped to meet the final cost of $163,500.

Now called Durant Hall, the old Boalt Hall is an architectural gem, a compact cube that asserts itself with surprising strength. The bold treatment of the fenestration, the molded cornice with large metopes, and the copper-framed skylight once more reveals Howard's command of scale and his ability to make all the details count. Whether intentional or not, the treatment of the building's corners—in which the granite blocks are so laid between the capitals and their bases that the shafts of the piers, though not actually there, in fact seem to exist—is an architectural pun. The phantom shafts are also present on either side of the central window bays.

As the center for the daily life of the jurisprudence department, the ground floor had club rooms and service spaces. The second floor contained lecture and debating rooms; the third floor, called Lawyers' Memorial Hall, housed the library and its stacks and a central, two-story reading room. This room, still intact, is one of Howard's more notable interiors. Fluted doric columns support a skylit coved ceiling from which are

The rooftop skylight illuminates the central part of the reading room, for which Howard designed bowl-shaped metal and glass fixtures. Tuscan columns of Sienna marble support an entablature with a molded cornice below the skylight. The San Francisco firm of Vickery, Atkins & Torrey designed the original mahogany tables.

suspended bowl-like lighting fixtures. Elsewhere in the room and on the main floor are other suspended fixtures in the shape of Greco-Roman lamps cast in bronze. The reading room conveys the dignity and gravity appropriate to the study of law.

In 1908, construction began on the Telegraph Avenue gateway to the campus. Mrs. Jane K. Sather had donated $40,000 for the gate, a memorial to her husband, Peder Sather, a trustee of the University of California from 1860 to 1863. (At that time Telegraph Avenue, an important artery, was lined with privately owned buildings from Bancroft Way to Strawberry Creek. The university acquired the property in the 1950s, extending the campus boundary to Bancroft Way.)

Although gates to the campus had been on Howard's mind since the early years of his supervision of the campus architectural plan, funding had not materialized for them: understandably, buildings had a higher priority. Of his several drawings of Sather Gate that survive, the earliest one, from 1905 and labeled simply "the Telegraph Avenue entrance to the campus," is closest to the final version of 1908; the difference is mainly in the omission of operable metal gates. The ornate metal grills that frame the openings give the gate a transparency appropriate to the entrance of a public institution of learning; the masonry piers provide solidity; and the glass globes that supplied electric light hint at the illumination that knowledge brings.

Low, balustraded walls extend from the outer piers on the north side of the gate to line the bridge that crosses Strawberry Creek. On the south side the wing walls end in round newels that support large urns. Marble plaques carved in low relief with nude female and male figures were commissioned for the piers of the gate; however, they so shocked Mrs. Sather that they were put in storage, finally to be installed only in 1979. The gate provides a graceful invitation to enter the campus.

The treatment of roadways, paths, and bridges over Strawberry Creek was addressed in the supervising architect's office as well. Because of dust produced during the long dry summer and mud in the winter, roads were resurfaced in macadam. In 1909 the block of Telegraph Avenue between Bancroft Way and Sather Gate, including the roadway over the bridge, was paved with asphalt. A new road from Sather Gate into the campus that ended north of California Hall was macadamized and laid out with an oval in front of California Hall. The road defining the oval was several feet higher on the side of Doe Library. Although it was assumed that the two levels were intended to emphasize the diversified topography of the University site and its treatment in a series of terraces, this arrangement was more likely a simple matter of expediency.

After the university acquired the block of Telegraph Avenue that became the site for Sproul Hall and the student union complex, Sather Gate no longer served as an entrance to the campus proper. Nonetheless, it is worth noting that from the beginning the gateway was a focus of political activities, religious proselytizing, and performances of various kinds, things that still go on nearby today.

10

Expositions in Seattle, San Francisco, and San Diego
1909–1915

Howard's work outside the university expanded in the years following the 1906 earthquake and fire. In San Francisco, architects competed eagerly for the many projects the rebuilding process provided. The state even created an office of architecture to allow competition for state-funded work. As a prominent professional, Howard served on various committees, such as the one charged with proposing what to do with San Francisco's old city hall, which had collapsed in the earthquake and was revealed to have been shoddily built. (Howard was joined on this architectural committee by John Reid, Albert Pissis, and Newton J. Tharp, the city architect.) In 1909 the Alaska-Yukon-Pacific Exposition opened in Seattle. Howard received high praise for his design work, and in return for their services in supervising the exposition Howard and Galloway received a fee of $60,000.

Howard also served as an advisor to Oakland's Board of Public Works and was appointed the professional advisor-coordinator of the competition for that city's new city hall, which took place in June 1910. By this time competitions routinely drew well-known professional firms from around the country. The eastern firm of Palmer & Hornbostel won the Oakland competition with what Howard described as "an exceedingly brilliant design of vast possibilities." Cass Gilbert, Delano & Aldrich, and Bakewell & Brown were among the competitors.

Although Howard's private practice appears to have taken as much of his time as his university commitments, much of this activity was a matter of professional duty and did not produce income, a source of some concern, since the Howards seem to have been in the habit of living beyond their means. Not that Howard had ever been known as a cautious spender, particularly where art and literature were concerned. In his oral history, William Hays reported that rather than repay the loan Frank Wilson had advanced for the purchase of the Ridge Road property in a timely manner, Howard bought books from the dealer John Howell and paintings from the Vickery, Atkins & Torrey Gallery in San Francisco.

Adding to this worry was his relationship with the university, which had become increasingly strained. When informed that Washington

A photograph of John Galen Howard taken about 1910.

University in St. Louis intended to offer him the position of head of the Department of Architecture, Howard was tempted. This offer may have prompted him to review his career at the university and to draft a proposal on May 7, 1910, titled, "An Arrangement for Carrying on Work as Supervising Architect of the University of California":

> In view of the special and complex conditions surrounding this matter...permit me briefly to outline the circumstances under which such work was originally undertaken.... When I was offered the appointment as Supervising Architect I looked upon the office as a permanent one, especially as the conditions showed a permanent need. Permanency of the office was a determining factor in accepting the offer.... I felt that I was at the parting of the ways, betwixt east and west, and I chose the west solely for the sake of the great

plan at Berkeley, merely safeguarding my position by an agreement covering five years, but based on financial arrangements which, while fair in prospect, proved to be enormously in favor of the University and very burdensome to me. The details of the arrangements too, while originally made as a happy modus vivendi, and recognized by all concerned in the beginning as most favorable to the University, were complicated and not always clearly understood by incoming Regents, and were in the long run a source of growing friction between the University and me. The system was briefly this: I received a salary of $4000 from the Regents as Professor of Architecture and a salary of $6000 from Mrs. Hearst as Supervising Architect. The University architectural work was done for net cost, made up of directly chargeable expenses plus a share of general office expenses.... I was free to do outside work, and the more outside work I did the more the University profited, as the proportion of general office expense (a fairly stationary sum) became less [for the university] the more work there was in the office.... The above arrangement...has been most satisfactory in quick exposition work where one administration carries the undertaking through from beginning to end, but it has been shown by experience in the University to be inapplicable to long-continuing relationships in which ...misconceptions or uncertainties creep in. In our case the University did not take the trouble to keep in intimate touch with my work. I repeatedly asked to have a representative of the University call at least monthly at my office and audit affairs, but with no result. Everything went well and my charges were accepted and paid without questions but also without knowledge or record. In time new Regents and committee members came in until the whole membership of the committees I started with had changed. Questions were asked concerning which no record existed. The questions could not be satisfactorily answered so more questions were asked. Doubt, distrust and friction came.... Toward the end of my five year contract with Mrs. Hearst in January 1908 (my contract ending April 1) feeling began to be so heated that it became evident that some change must be made; all the more because Mrs. Hearst did not care longer to subsidize the undertaking, and the Regents could not raise the salary...even had they wished. On my side the old arrangement had been most unsatisfactory too: great responsibilities, immense labors,... total lack of appreciation—rather large lumps of criticism—and profits wholly incommensurate with the tasks as judged fairly by professional standards.

Howard next referred to a "crisis" that came "at a most trying moment," in 1908 when the library was "in media res." At that time he had made an arrangement by which he would carry on the "ensemble plan" at his own expense to the end of a definite stage, thereby making sure that the preliminary studies were at least not at loose ends. The library drawings were completed at what was estimated to be net cost, but this cost was so low that the work was in fact done at a heavy loss. Between 1908 and 1910 he carried out his campus responsibilities for a 4 percent fee on the assumption that preliminary work would be completed on most of the buildings scheduled for that period. But new programs were proposed for these buildings, such that considerable restudy was required. "These two years have been lean ones for me," he commented, "all the more so because my professorship militates against my getting good financial results from outside work."

At this point in his narrative Howard broached the subject of his "retiring from the undertaking," feeling he could do so at that juncture with honor and increased prestige. "The ensemble plan is now in such a state that some other architect could carry out my vision," he wrote—though, he confessed, he foresaw difficulty in finding an architect willing to work under the conditions the university offered. In closing, Howard revealed what was probably the real point of this rambling proposal: restoration of the position of supervising architect to its former level of remuneration. He observed that since the supervising architect's responsibilities were now greater than they had been when his salary was $6,000, they should not now be worth less. However, the terms for this salary might be different. A yearly honorarium of $6,000 for consultation on the architectural plan, he judged, would cover adjustment of the plan to new conditions and its development into a consistent whole, as well as preliminary studies for individual buildings and landscape features. Howard would also give advice on the selection of architects for various separate projects, conduct the negotiations with these architects, and advise them on their designs. For campus works executed by the supervising architect that had not been previously negotiated, he further requested a fee in accordance with the American Institute of Architects' schedule of 6 percent, while a fee of 12 percent would be paid for dwellings, alterations, monuments, furniture, decorative and cabinet work, and landscape design.

Since no evidence exists that Howard formalized this draft proposal and submitted it to the regents, it is not possible to gauge the success of his efforts to recover his former salary. In any case, his mind was occupied with preparations for a sabbatical in Europe, to commence that July. His family remained in Berkeley.

Not long after Howard's departure, preparations began for an international exposition to celebrate the opening of the Panama Canal. Construction of a waterway across the Isthmus of Panama had been projected early in the twentieth century. The commercial advantages for the West

The Phoebe Apperson Hearst Plan for the University of California adopted by the Board of Regents in January 1914. Although his career was beset with difficulties in this period, Howard had achieved a major goal of his work as supervising architect: a definitive plan for the campus. Howard's 1914 revision of his 1908 campus plan (itself a revision of Bénard's 1900 plan), while never fully implemented, strongly influenced the campus's subsequent development, particularly in respect to the grouping of disciplines. The five small buildings proposed for the life sciences became one large building located opposite the College of Agriculture; an Alumni House was built south of the life sciences group in the general area of Howard's building; and the area south of the Mining Circle was devoted to the physical sciences as it is today. A number of buildings shown on the plan—Hearst Memorial Mining Building, Sather Tower, Doe Library, California Hall, Boalt Hall, and Agriculture Hall—were either constructed or underway. Roads such as Sather Road, leading from Sather Gate and South Drive, defined the circulation. However, significant elements of the plan—the domed auditorium building at the head of the central axis, the grand esplanade with fountains and gardens that began near the west entrance to the campus and continued east along much of the central axis, and the stadium and athletic fields proposed for the Hillegass tract—were never carried out.

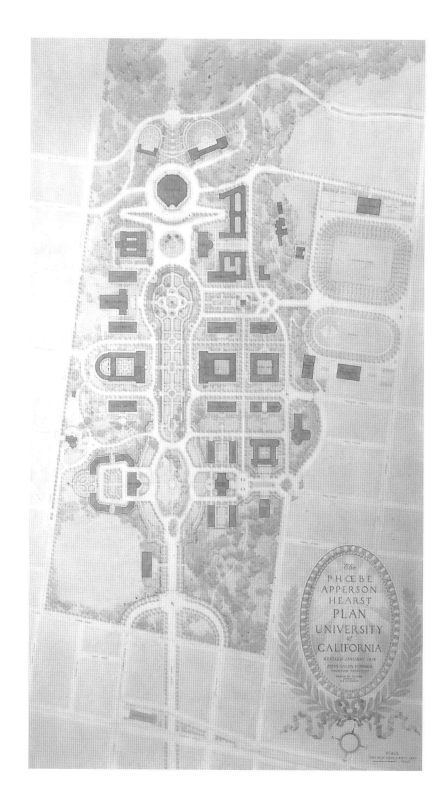

Coast of such a water route—particularly for San Francisco, with its fine harbor—were such that in January 1904 Ruben Hale, a prominent San Francisco merchant, was inspired to write to the Merchants' Association proposing that the city host a world exposition to celebrate the opening of the Panama Canal in 1915.

At about the same time that Hale wrote his letter, a movement to enhance the attractiveness of the city was launched when James Duval Phelan, a reform-minded former mayor, joined with other civic leaders to create the Association for the Improvement and Adornment of San Francisco, which was active from 1904 to 1909. As its 1904 membership brochure stated, "The main objects of the Association are to promote in every practical way the beautifying of the streets, public buildings, parks, squares, and places of San Francisco...in short, to make San Francisco a more agreeable city in which to live." By April, the organization had raised enough money to invite Daniel Burnham, a prominent Chicago-based architect, to draft a plan.

Two years later, shortly before the bound copies of the Burnham plan were to be distributed, the earthquake struck, devastating the city by shaking and fire. Yet in some quarters, the destruction was cause for optimism. Phelan saw it as "a magnificent opportunity for beautifying San Francisco," reasoning that property owners would gladly cooperate since their own efforts at improvement had been swept away. Benjamin Ide Wheeler also hailed the possibilities for change offered by a nearly clean slate. In an article published in the *San Francisco Chronicle* on April 29, 1906, he envisioned the city's famous hills "offering themselves to contour gradients," adding that "I should like to see Nob Hill [where the mansions of the wealthy had been destroyed] made into a park and that glorious view preserved for the people."

Although it might have seemed that fate had sided with the city beautifiers, conflict over the reconstruction process militated against Burnham's plan. At the first full meeting of the Committee for Reconstruction, also called the Committee of Forty, Mayor Eugene Schmitz warned against extravagance. He considered that the Burnham plan may have been affordable before the earthquake, but that was no longer the case; the cost of new public buildings alone, he pointed out, which were now a priority, might well exceed $100 million. In the face of such attacks, Phelan continued to vigorously defend the plan. As an advisor to the Committee of Forty, Howard, too, argued in its favor, emphasizing its more convenient street pattern, which allowed for better control of traffic and made all parts of the city accessible.

Much of Burnham's plan was devoted to implanting a new street system to replace the existing grid, which had been laid out in defiance of the hilly terrain. Although the advantages of the proposed changes—

widening some streets and creating diagonal ones to cut across the flat land and circumvent the hills—were clear on paper, they were problematic on the ground. Funds for acquiring property that would be affected by street widening and clearing were not readily available. Even worse, new buildings in the downtown area might have to be delayed while the new streets were being constructed. Mindful that time was swiftly passing, downtown property owners began rebuilding almost immediately, ignoring the political storms that raged around the future configuration of the city.

New storms blew up when federal agents arrived to investigate charges of corruption leveled at Mayor Schmitz and Abe Ruef, the man widely perceived as the real power behind Schmitz. By late fall Schmitz and Ruef had been indicted for corruption, and other city officials and corporate executives were under investigation. With these distractions, the Burnham plan foundered.

Meanwhile, plans for an exposition celebrating the opening of the Panama Canal were rapidly taking shape. Both San Diego and San Francisco had lobbied Congress to have their fair officially designated as the world exposition. Although San Francisco won the honor of hosting the official event, San Diego proceeded with its plans for a fair called "The Panama-California International Exposition." George Marsten, a prominent San Diego civic leader, commissioned the Olmsted Brothers to plan the exposition grounds, and he chaired the building committee. Howard's experience with both the Buffalo exposition of 1901 and the Alaska-Yukon exposition of 1909 ensured that he would be considered for a prominent role in the San Diego fair's design. His principal competitor for the position of supervising architect of the fair was Irving Gill, a talented San Diego architect who, among other works, had designed a house for Marsten in 1904.

With Howard out of the country, his office manager, William Raiguel, pursued the contract for the exposition work. Howard's old friend Warren Gregory, a prominent San Francisco lawyer who knew George Marsten, also championed his cause. On September 24, 1910, Raiguel wrote Howard in London that he had received a letter from Marsten that "seems to be a definite engagement of you as architect of the work." Marsten had sent a copy of the Panama-California Exposition plans and had stated that financing for the fair was secure, with $2 million available. Although the city had subscribed $1 million, that money was earmarked for the improvement of the park on which the fair would be located. "We need a general designer and organizing head for an architectural grouping of buildings and landscape work," Marsten wrote, "plus a general supervisor for the whole scheme."

In October, Raiguel went to San Diego to meet with Marsten and other members of the building committee. He reported to Howard that Daniel Burnham had become the chief competitor. Raiguel told the committee that, as a Californian, Howard would be able to give much more of his time and talent to the commission than would Burnham. Both Raiguel and Warren Gregory now urged Howard to come back to California and pursue the exposition work himself. But Howard was not so inclined. In any case, whether a personal appearance would have persuaded Marsten and the committee soon became moot. According to a letter from Raiguel of November 27, the Olmsted Brothers got busily to work on a plan for the grounds. The committee wanted a competition for the fine arts building. By the end of the selection process, the "offensive/defensive alliance" that Raiguel perceived between the Olmsteds and Irving Gill had dissolved. In a letter to Howard of February 9, 1911, Marsten announced that Bertram Grosvenor Goodhue had been appointed consulting and advisory architect in charge of both the plan and the major buildings for the fair.

Raiguel now focused his efforts on getting work for the San Francisco exposition. He wrote Howard that although Willis Polk had been working hard to gain the directorship, Mrs. Hearst had said that she wanted Howard to have a major role in the exposition. Raiguel wished that Howard would come home to pursue his interests, but it appeared that after having already traveled through Egypt, Greece, and Sicily, Howard now planned to join Warren Gregory for a tour around Spain.

Howard's reasons for ignoring Raiguel's pleas to return to California were expressed in bitter tones in a letter to Mary dated February 23, 1911:

> The truth is that the very thought of returning to California now fills me with an unspeakable loathing. I hate the whole kit and boodle of them except that little group of friends that mean more than all the work…and you at the head of all. And I hate expositions that eat up all a man's vitality and then go up in dust…. I didn't want the San Diego [show] and I don't want the San Francisco show…all that either of them would be is pot-boilers.[43]

He wired Raiguel that he would return for assured important work, but not otherwise. "I've had enough," he wrote, "and too much of waiting and dangling and holding my hat, and angling. Now I am going to do what my soul calls me to do for a while." Howard was referring to a project he had long planned: an epic poem that would celebrate the role of the architect as the major figure of the Renaissance. His hero was Brunelleschi, whose life he was tracking in Florence, where he had been reading Dante over the preceding three weeks. He finished the poem, titled "Brunelleschi," in April 1912, and before returning to California spent some time in New York reading portions of it to friends and looking for a publisher.

Efforts to publish his poem were not all that occupied Howard's attention in New York. On December 18, 1911, he wrote Mary that he had been asked to consider heading Columbia University's school of architecture. Coming at a time when he felt undervalued on the West Coast, the offer boosted his spirits. "I feel that my real career is all ahead of me," he wrote. "The past is past and we are going to begin again and on a higher plane." Having put his name in the running for the position at Columbia University, he returned home to await further developments.

On January 17, 1912, Howard wrote to Nicholas Murray Butler, president of Columbia University, acknowledging the honor of being offered the position of head of the school of architecture but stating that he was now involved in San Francisco's new civic center plan and hesitated to commit himself to a position in New York. The next day he wrote a letter to Mr. Cook, national president of the American Institute of Architects, to ask his advice on whether to accept Columbia's offer. Howard affirmed his deep interest in the Hearst Architectural Plan for the Berkeley campus, but complained of the lack of support for its development. More letters seeking advice from knowledgeable friends such as Grosvenor Atterbury followed near the end of January. By then Howard had come to believe that his income would be greater at the University of California than at Columbia. In a letter to Nicholas Murray Butler dated February 15, 1912, Howard proposed that he direct the school of architecture, but not teach. He further proposed a salary of $12,000 and the freedom to practice outside the university. No further negotiations were reported, and Howard remained in his position at the University of California.

1

1. *A rendering executed in 1917 of John Galen Howard's proposal for the Phoebe Apperson Hearst Plan for the University of California.*

2

3

4

5

2. *View of the south facade of Boalt Hall. The building, completed in 1911 for the School of Jurisprudence, was renamed in 1951 for Henry Durant, first president of the university.*

3. *North elevation of California Hall, completed in 1905 to provide offices for the administration as well as classrooms and faculty offices.*

4. *View of the south facade of the Hearst Memorial Mining Building. Completed in 1907 to house the College of Mining, the building underwent extensive restoration from 1998 through 2002.*

5. *Detail of the south facade of the mining building showing the sculptures of male torsos by Robert Aitken.*

6. *View of the mining building from the southeast.*

6

7. *Bronze relief panel with a bust of Minerva by Melvin Earl Cummings above the main entrance doors to Doe Memorial Library.*

8. *View of the main facade of Doe Memorial Library from the northeast. The building was completed in 1917 and named for its principal donor, Charles Franklin Doe.*

7

8

9. *The west end of the reading room block.*

10. *One of a pair of vertical panels that embellish both the east and west elevations of the reading room block. The carved granite reliefs are of staffs entwined with foliate and floral motifs.*

9

10

11

11. *View from the southwest of Agriculture Hall, completed in 1912 and renamed Wellman Hall in 1966. The first of the complex of three buildings proposed by Howard to house the College of Agriculture, Agriculture Hall was followed in 1917 by Hilgard Hall. The third building, Giannini Hall, was designed by William C. Hays and completed in 1930.*

12. Sather Tower, completed in 1914 to honor Peder Sather, a San Francisco banker and trustee of the College of California. Jane K. Sather, his widow, donated the funds for the tower and for Sather Gate.

13

13. *Detail from the frieze of the entabla-*
ture of Hilgard Hall's west facade show-
ing one of a series of bucranes, or ox
skulls, festooned with a garland and
flanked by decorative motifs in sgraffito.
Bucranes belonged to the classical
vocabulary of ornament used on tem-
ples and intended to celebrate the rites
of the harvest.

14

15

14. *View of Hilgard Hall from the*
southwest. The building was completed
in 1917 and named for Eugene W.
Hilgard, first dean of the College of
Agriculture.

15. *Detail showing a monumental*
urn laden with fruits and vegetables set
above two cornucopias. The sculpture
caps the main entrance on the west side
of Hilgard Hall.

16. *Detail from the series of monumental free-standing urns set above the cornice of the south facade of Wheeler Hall.*

17. *Wheeler Hall, completed in 1917 and named for Benjamin Ide Wheeler, then president of the university.*

16

17

18. *Head of Apollo carved in high relief and set in festoons of laurel leaves above the keystones of arched windows in the end bays of Wheeler Hall.*

18

The San Francisco Civic
Center and a Trial

1911–1913

By 1911 the issue of a new civic center was firmly tied to the upcoming Panama-Pacific International Exposition. In April 1909, in answer to a request for advice by the board of supervisors, Daniel Burnham had returned to San Francisco, met with city officials, and advocated locating the new civic center near the intersection of Market Street and Van Ness Avenue, several blocks from the old city hall site. Soon after the meeting Willis Polk, who had worked on the 1905 general plan and now headed Burnham's San Francisco office, made a drawing locating the city hall, courthouse, and library in the triangle bounded by Franklin, Fell, and Market Streets. The buildings framed a semicircular plaza on Market Street that faced a site for a new railroad depot. Five days after the appearance of the bird's-eye view in the newspapers, the board of supervisors voted to submit a bond issue of $8,480,000 for the land and for a city hall. When the bond issue failed to gain a two-thirds majority of the vote, the supervisors succumbed to inertia: it seemed that the city hall would be rebuilt on the old site at McAllister and Larkin Streets after all, though the timing was vague. Three years later, with the exposition looming, civic leaders realized that it would be unthinkable to welcome the world to their city without an appropriate municipal setting for the many public events associated with the fair.

Early in 1912 the supervisors appointed a committee of distinguished architects to determine the civic center site. The members included Howard, Polk, and Edward Bennett, Burnham's chief assistant for the 1905 plan. Predictably, Polk and Bennett argued for the Van Ness Avenue and Market Street site. Howard, William Faville, Clarence Ward,

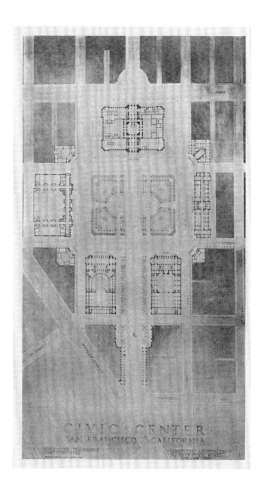

and many other architects favored a site near that of the old city hall. Not only did this choice avoid a reconfiguration of streets, but it afforded both views of the city hall from Eighth and Fulton Streets and the best route for a possible extension of the Golden Gate Park panhandle to the new civic center. An $8,800,000 bond issue was approved on March 28, 1912, and a competition to select architects for the city hall was announced in April. On June 20 a jury composed of Mayor James Rolph Jr., one member each from the board of public works and the board of supervisors' public buildings committee, the three architects on the advisory board, and an architect selected by the competitors announced that the firm of Bakewell & Brown had won first prize. While the competition was in progress, a new advisory board of architects, composed of Howard, who was elected chairman, Frederick H. Meyer, and John Reid Jr., prepared two schemes for the competing sites. A number of civic groups and architects commented on specific aspects of the two schemes. Ultimately the supervisors voted fourteen to four to approve "Scheme B," which located the city hall on Van Ness Avenue near the old city hall site.

Although the actions taken by the advisory board were widely approved, a climate of suspicion and innuendo enveloped the proceedings. In April 1912 William Hays reported to Mary Howard that the local chapter of the American Institute of Architects, which Howard had presided over the year before, was in a desperate condition. Hays communicated his views in cryptic phrases such as "The Mucker crowd have got the ascendent but will be ignored." Reflecting on the situation near the end of his life, Hays recalled a "Tammany Hall situation" in the chapter in which "anti-Howard and -Polk people got their friends elected to offices." In Hays's view, the architects who had established practices in the Bay Area before Howard's arrival had never really welcomed him. He remained an intruder and an object of envy because of his monopoly on the university work. As for Polk, Hays observed simply that "he had a knack for making enemies."

In the wake of the earthquake and with a major exposition in the future, fierce competition may have encouraged questionable practices to gain professional notice. According to Hays, "unethical people were put up for membership" in the local AIA chapter. Whether or not this was indeed the case, misunderstandings and miscommunications were sufficient to bring on a crisis of unprecedented proportions in the local chapter. At a chapter meeting on February 2, 1913, the committee on civic center buildings, composed of William Mooser, Edgar A. Matthews, William H. Toepke, and William B. Faville, submitted a report that soon became a major news item in the local papers.

On March 27 a headline in the *San Francisco Examiner* announced, "Architects at War over Civic Center." The article began: "Charging John Galen Howard, Frederick H. Meyer and John Reid Jr., members of the

Civic Center Advisory Board, with 'evasion, duplicity and discourtesy,' the San Francisco Chapter of the American Institute of Architects has launched a bitter attack against the Board, containing accusations ranging from unethical and unprofessional conduct to connivance by the Board with city officials to perpetuate itself in office as the supervising body of the Civic Center Plans."

The committee on civic center buildings, according to the article, charged irregularities in the conduct of the city hall competition in respect to the winning architects' fee and their right to supervise the project. An equally contentious charge was that the board had taken the commission for the Civic Auditorium against the chapter's wishes that the auditorium commission be open to competition. The accused stated in response that the chapter "exceeded the bounds of professional propriety in seeking to throw the Auditorium into competition, when it had already been offered to the Advisory Board." Furthermore, the accused charged that the chapter had treated the board with a "total lack of courtesy from first to last" and that its executive officer had permitted the members of the board to be insulted on the floor of the chapter's meetings.

On March 28 the *San Francisco Chronicle* published a brief article titled "An Architectural Uproar." The editors declined to discuss the charges, stating that the *Chronicle* "was not well informed as to the merits of these contentions or as to the ethical rules of the Chapter," though they did conclude that "it certainly does not comport with the dignity of the city that the designing and construction of the buildings for our Civic Center should become the subject of a local squabble among local architects."

An article in the *Call* on the same day, under the headline "Architects' Row Angers the Mayor," began: "Mayor Rolph delivered a broadside yesterday in reply to the San Francisco Chapter of the American Institute of Architects for criticizing the City's Board of Consulting Architects. He characterized the Chapter as one of the worst kind of trusts he had ever encountered, and declared he would not submit to dictation on its part as to the City's manner of conducting its business." The next day the *Call* further reported the mayor as saying that the local chapter's "attitude is harassing, unethical and undignified. Their principal object seems to be to prevent the completion of the Civic Center before 1915, and their tactics are those of obstructionists."

According to newspaper accounts, Mayor Rolph had repeatedly asked the local chapter members to visit his office and explain their charges. But in the end the chapter's board of directors declined to discuss what was termed an internal affair. On March 29 the *Chronicle* reported that the officers of the chapter admitted that they had asked that the job of planning all civic center buildings be awarded in open competitions, even though, as the mayor pointed out, the national organization was opposed to open competitions. The chapter had given in to the wishes of many members, mainly the younger ones, who wanted to participate in a public competition. Although the chapter conceded that Howard, Meyer, and Reid had taken on the work of designing the auditorium without direct profit to themselves, they had still deprived "some worthy architect of his 6% fee on a $1,000,000 contract." Moreover, by being able to claim the building as their work, the three architects benefited unduly.

In their rebuttal the advisory board members stated that they depended on the building committee of the board of supervisors, which on August 19, 1912, had passed a resolution recommending that plans for the main civic center buildings to be erected by the city be secured through competitions. Since the auditorium was paid for by the exposition company, not the city, that commission was excluded by this resolution.

The chapter contended that the resolution either had not been conveyed to it or was so close in wording to a previous resolution that the members assumed that all the civic center buildings would be open to competition. When informed by Howard, Meyer, and Reid that the Civic Auditorium, the first building to be constructed on the civic center site, would be their commission, members of the chapter accused the three architects of securing the commission by "clever wording" and connivance. This charge was countered by testimony of the board of the Panama-Pacific International Exposition Company to the effect that on June 26, 1912, the company had pledged $1 million to build a civic auditorium on land supplied by the City of San Francisco. The resolution called on the city to designate its advisory board of architects—namely, John Galen Howard, Frederick H. Meyer, and John Reid Jr.—to prepare plans for the auditorium exterior and, following the specifications of the exposition company, on the spatial arrangements of the interior.

As for the charge that the advisory board architects were responsible for the firm of Bakewell & Brown getting a fee of 4½ percent for the city hall work instead of the standard fee of 6 percent, the consulting architects contended that they had made every effort to secure the higher fee for Bakewell & Brown, but that because the city itself supervised the construction on its contracts, 1½ percent of the fee for supervision had been withheld. A letter from John Bakewell Jr. and Arthur Brown Jr. confirmed that the advisory board had requested and fought for full architectural services for the city hall on their behalf, but that the effort had not been successful. (Later that year negotiations with the city resulted in Bakewell & Brown assuming part of the supervision of the city hall construction and receiving compensation approaching if not equal to 6 percent.) Chapter members also implied that the advisory board architects had taken the 1½ percent as their fee, but this was dismissed by the citation of a resolution passed on March 29, 1912, stating that each of the advisory board architects would receive a retaining fee for his work of $2,500 plus $25 per day for every day of service.

Thus a highly unusual trial was held on April 25, 1913, in the Phelan Building on Market Street, at which it was to be decided whether the three architects should be suspended from chapter membership owing to unprofessional conduct. William Mooser and Edgar A. Matthews represented the chapter; George Kelham, the defendants. Although George B. McDougall, the chairman of the proceedings and the chapter president,

Rendering of the Civic Auditorium, 1915, designed by John Galen Howard in association with Meyer and Reid.

stated that chapter members would not be permitted to participate in the trial, Willis Polk spoke up shortly after the roll call: "The matter," he said,

> concerns ... not only the chapter itself and the gentlemen under these charges, but the Institute itself as well, and ... the profession as a whole.... It is the profession of architecture that is going to be reviewed and passed on by you [the members], and personally I regret very much that ... you feel you have to proceed with the trial now.... It is something that ought to be tried by an unprejudiced body.... You are either for or against and you will be [so] regardless of any evidence that might be offered.... Any action you may take, either favorable or unfavorable, either in approval or disapproval of the charges ... cannot be limited to members of the Chapter. It will have to be borne by the profession at large and shared in by the public at large.

Polk closed by stating that the AIA would be justified in withdrawing the charter of the local chapter if it proceeded without proper recognition from the national organization, because in fact the issue was a national one. Edgar Matthews objected to Polk's argument, stating that at present the matter concerned the local chapter only, not the national institute. Whereupon Polk announced his resignation from the chapter and left the room.

The trial then proceeded with a request by Matthews that George Kelham explain why the defendants denied that the chapter had the right to try them. Kelham replied that the chapter had not given the accused men a precise statement of the charges against them, to which they could make a proper response. There followed a restatement by Matthews of the charges that the advisory architects had usurped authority over the design of the two civic center buildings in question. The charges were once again refuted, but another round of charges and countercharges took place, prompting Kelham to propose that the chapter request a ruling from the national board of the AIA about the charges. The charges had not been borne out by the testimony, he said, and should not be sustained.

After more rancorous discussion, the trial concluded; the accused left the room, and those who remained debated a verdict. One member observed that throughout the trial there had been a tendency merely to object, without coming to conclusions. Another member, Henry A. Schultze, made a lengthy plea that the issues be judged from an ethical perspective. The accused, he said, had never spoken frankly about the civic center situation and, moreover, had been privy to special knowledge that they had not passed on to the chapter membership. He could not find a trace of any lofty ideal in their reply to the charges, nor "a single gleam that would indicate that these gentlemen were guided by anything but a grovelling commercialism, which is all too prevalent in the profession." A vote on the charges followed this statement: thirty-seven members voted to sustain the charges, while twenty-four stood opposed.

Although the charges against Howard, Meyer, and Reid implied serious consequences, none were forthcoming. Behind the scenes Howard had been informed by high-placed sources that the national AIA was not in sympathy with the local chapter's conduct.[44] Indeed, the national chapter had warned the local membership not to proceed with the trial if they wanted to keep their charter. In the meantime, Howard and others formed a new organization called the San Francisco Society of Architects, with Howard as the first president.[45] The membership was composed of an elite group of principally école men, who of course were resented by the rest of the local chapter. By July 1913, as Howard wrote Mary, who was traveling in the East, that chapter, having completed its cycle, had "censured us and restored us to the privileges of membership." Presumably the alternative organization had disbanded. However, Howard had still not collected his fee for services on the advisory board and for the design of the Civic Auditorium. He had to hire Warren Gregory to pursue the matter, and the account was not settled until mid-August.

Howard had responded to the questions asked by Matthews and Mooser during the trial with as few words as possible. He did not engage with his interrogators and seemed to be holding himself above the fray. Understandably, he was pained and exasperated by the situation. He had been accused of discourtesy, a charge that, for a man known for unfailing courtesy, must have been a gross insult. However, he had been indiscreet. He had commented to a member of the board of supervisors that one of the chapter meetings convened to discuss the issues swirling around the competition and the advisory board's work was attended by a group of "sore heads." This breach of good conduct was not only widely reported among the membership but mentioned at the trial as well. Although the chapter's accusations were false, it appears that Howard, Meyer, and Reid had taken a cavalier attitude toward the membership's right to know the details of the negotiations over the advisory board's commission for the Civic Auditorium. Their condescending attitude epitomized the schism between the architects trained at the École des Beaux-Arts and those whose training came from direct experience.

The exposition opened in January 1915 with the Civic Auditorium in use and the city hall completed on the exterior but unfinished inside. The building would not be in operation until 1916, after the exposition had closed. Both the city hall and the Civic Auditorium were much admired, and the bizarre events that preceded their design largely forgotten.

A Move and the Publication of *Brunelleschi*

1912–1915

12

In 1912 the Howard family moved from their Ridge Road home. The financial burden of the large house was resolved in an unusual way. Their close friends Warren and Sadie Gregory owned a large property a mile or so north of the campus, at the place where Leroy Avenue, then a dirt lane, ended at Rose Street. Around 1904 Howard had remodeled a small summer house on the property, making it into a year-round home that the Gregorys nevertheless continued to occupy seasonally until the 1906 earthquake caused them to take up permanent residence in Berkeley. Some years later, Warren Gregory suggested to Howard that he design a house for the northwestern corner of the property that the Howards might lease—a magnanimous gesture that testified to the families' close friendship. The new house was built in 1912, and the Howards named it "Rose Leroy."

To the north of Rose Street were rolling hills covered with grass and studded with oak trees. In her 1987 memoir, Janette Howard Wallace recalls that although the Ridge Road house had been much more spacious and suitable for a family of seven, Rose Leroy had a spectacular view of the bay and was on the edge of open fields. Just below the house was an uncovered reservoir that looked like a large blue lake. At night they slept on open decks and often heard the howls of coyotes in the hills. They took picnics out to the hillside meadows, as innocent of structures as they had been in centuries past and affording sweeping views. The Gregory and Howard houses were outposts of the north Berkeley hillside community, largely composed of university faculty. Though sparsely developed compared to the neighborhoods south of the campus, the area was populated enough to have a streetcar line that ran on Euclid Avenue to within a block of the Howards' house.

The families were independent-minded. Although the sons went to public schools in Berkeley, when Janette Howard and Jean Gregory reached school age Sadie Gregory and Mary Howard started a school that met on the Howards' deck until the rainy season began, whereupon classes moved into a shed on the Gregory property. Sadie Gregory had a master's degree from the University of Chicago, where she had studied with Thorstein Veblen; she later taught at Wellesley College. She had grown up in Oakland and graduated from the University of California, where she had met Warren Gregory. After marriage she gave up her academic career but remained interested in progressive ideas (she edited some of Veblen's papers when he taught at Stanford from 1906 to 1909), and the private school gave her an opportunity to explore education in a practical way. Janette remembered perhaps ten or twelve students at the school, which

Rose Leroy, the Howard family's second Berkeley home, viewed from the northwest. The house followed the curve formed by the meeting of Leroy Avenue and Rose Street. From the front, sweeping views extended to the southwest and north, encompassing the Golden Gate and San Francisco.

OPPOSITE, TOP
First-floor plan (left) and second-floor plan (right) of Rose Leroy.

BOTTOM
The Howards' living room photographed for publication in the January 1915 issue of Architect and Engineer. *Mary Howard's piano occupied an important place in the room, where musical performances often took place.*

met for several years. French was taught along with standard subjects, and an elocutionist trained the pupils to speak correctly and to recite. The last subject was useful in the production of plays, which were among Mary Howard's favorite activities. Music, drama, and poetry were, after all, staples of the community life that the Howards and their neighbors enjoyed. Howard always read his poetry to Sadie Gregory and so relied on her advice that, according to Janette, her mother was a bit jealous of their intellectual companionship. Howard responded by saying, "My dear, I married you. I didn't marry Sadie!"

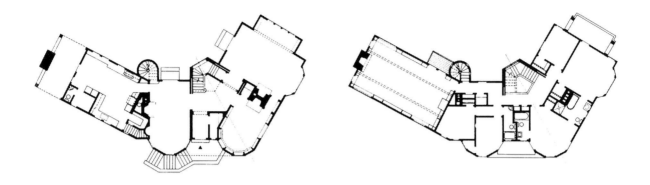

Howard designed Rose Leroy with great sensitivity to its site. Set against the hillside, the house is an open U skirting the edge of the site, with the entrance and stair halls hinging the two wings. Views to each end of the house and to the garden terrace and hillside in back extend from this circulation hub. On both floors views through doors and windows tie the hillside to the distant bay. The library and dining room, which flank the entrance hall, end in polygonal bays that barely break the line of the facade and do not rise above the roof. Like two compressed towers held

Mary Howard and her daughter Janette photographed in 1913.

together by a shingled skin, they are locked into the plan as part of a contrapuntal spatial sequence. The large living room accommodated evenings of music and poetry as well as the Thursday afternoon "tea course" that Howard conducted for his students.

The house was well planned for privacy. The parents' bedroom at the south end was separated from the children's quarters by the stair hall. The boys usually slept on an open deck at the north end of the house; there was another sleeping porch at the south end. Typical of the ideal of California living even then, the out-of-doors was readily available. Although Howard's demeanor was generally formal—he was always well attired, wore a hat and yellow doeskin gloves, and carried a Malacca cane—home life was reasonably informal. Mary was much more extroverted than her husband and inclined to plunge into life. She always tried to dissuade Howard from "dithering" over decisions and brooding over the consequences. On the whole they complemented each other well.

After rejections from Scribner's and other publishers, Howard decided to bear the expense of having John Howell, a prestigious fine arts book dealer in San Francisco, publish *Brunelleschi* in 1915.[46] Although Howard relished the enthusiasm that greeted his reading of the epic poem to friends and colleagues, the reaction of the literary world was less favorable. His friend the writer John G. Neihardt, whom he had visited in Bancroft, Nebraska, in 1914, wrote him criticizing the "bombast" and the "stilted language," though he still found much to praise. He commented that Howard's emotion, "always genuine, is sometimes slightly beyond your control."[47]

Eunice Tietjens, a critic in Pasadena whom John Howell asked to review the manuscript in May 1915, wrote:

> Mr. Howard has been so bewitched by the shimmering opalescent quality of certain essentially artificial and "poetic" words that he has completely swamped his narrative with them. His ideas are buried under a mass of verbiage.... If he were working in his own medium Mr. Howard himself would understand that it is not good art to cover every available inch of space with elaborate fret-work. This poetic monologue is an attempt by a thoughtful, studious man to transfer his creative power to a medium which is not his own.

Yet in the end Tietjens also found much to value in *Brunelleschi*, including Howard's "human understanding" and his "sympathetic grasp of the character of the great Florentine.... Somehow through the fog of words," she wrote, "the character of this man emerges, whole and compelling."

Six years later, in a letter of February 14, 1921, to Cass Gilbert, a prominent architect and friend, Howard reflected on *Brunelleschi* as a labor of love: "It is first of all an attempt to present the psychology of the typical architect, plus an interpretation of the life of one of the greatest of his kind. But I am forced to the conclusion that architects in general don't care for poetry, or at any rate don't care for mine."

13

The College of Agriculture, Sather Tower, Hilgard, Wheeler, and Gilman Halls, and Campus Landscaping
1910–1917

During the months Howard was on sabbatical and then occupied with the unfortunate civic center trial, the work on new campus buildings proceeded. Agriculture Hall (now called Wellman Hall)[48] began construction in 1910 with funds from a state bond issue and the university's Permanent Improvement Fund. The final cost was $267,000 for a 43,300-square-foot, steel-frame building clad in Raymond granite. That this was not one of the first buildings erected under the Phoebe A. Hearst Architectural Plan requires some explanation, since the College of Agriculture was one of the colleges for which the university was founded and should have had a building of its own long before.[49]

An attempt to separate the College of Agriculture from the rest of the university and locate it elsewhere in the state had caused a political fracas that for years militated against appropriation of funds by the legislature for a proper building for the college. The first agriculture building, a one-story brick structure designed by Clinton Day in 1888, was funded in part through the influence of viticulturists, who wanted experimental work done for their industry. Another year passed before an appropriation enabled the completion of two more stories and an attic of wood. In 1897, however, the building burned down to the brick story. Although reconstructed and enlarged that same year, Budd Hall, as it was called, scarcely conveyed the importance of the college to the state.

The new Agriculture Hall, dedicated on November 20, 1912, enjoyed a prominent location near the northwest corner of the campus adjacent to a large open field and across from the proposed location of the life

Rendering of the College of Agriculture buildings, December 1914. Viewed from above, the three buildings for the college defined a central courtyard with a garden and a greenhouse on the north side. The complex is shown embedded in mature landscaping, which the campus plantations nurtured by the college could have provided. The complex faced the central esplanade, to which it was connected by a formal system of roads and paths. Although the scheme duly reflected the importance of the college, it was carried out in a piecemeal manner and never attained the picturesque appearance of the rendering.

REVISED SKETCH FOR THE AGRICULTURE GROUP
UNIVERSITY OF CALIFORNIA
JOHN GALEN HOWARD, ARCHITECT.

First- and second-floor plans of Agriculture Hall.

BELOW
The south facade of Agriculture Hall, now Wellman Hall.

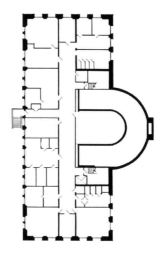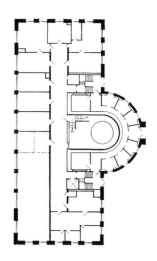

sciences buildings. It was thus the first building seen by those approaching the campus from the city. Designed along the lines of a Tuscan farm, this was the first of three buildings designed to frame a courtyard opening on the north side to a semicircular, formal garden. The courtyard was planted with olive trees, and Italian stone pines (seeds of which Howard had brought from his 1910–11 sabbatical) had been planted earlier in the area around Agriculture Hall and the president's house. The two flanking buildings, Hilgard and Giannini, were not built until some years later, and the landscaping for the formal garden was never executed.

Agriculture Hall, with its geometric forms, did not reflect the popular image of picturesque rusticity but seemed more kin to nineteenth-century French neoclassicism. An imposing semicircular bay dominates the main facade, its conical roof capped by a copper-framed skylight that joins the skylit roof of the main building block. Tiled roofs echo the Mediterranean theme of Howard's other campus buildings. Decorative detail is minimal to the point of severity, confined to fluted pilasters

between the second-story windows of the entrance bay and pseudo-quoins marking the corners of the building and bracketing the fenestrated sections. An arch with deeply scored false voussoirs projects somewhat perfunctorily from the bay wall; more delicate, double-arched windows on either side of the bay point to the Italian Renaissance. Allusions to classicism on the north facade are limited to the Tuscan columns that divide the first-story windows. The window heads on the upper story are embossed metal panels, but the window frames are wood painted dark green to mimic metal. This facade has a strikingly modern, almost industrial character.

If the oval esplanade that traced the main campus axis had been

The north elevation photographed ca. 1915. The unfinished state of the landscaping around the building is apparent.

Howard's proposed landscaping for the agriculture complex, with particular attention given to the treatment of Agriculture Hall and the descent into the esplanade.

landscaped as planned and complemented by the flights of steps descending into the esplanade, Agriculture Hall would not seem as abruptly cut off as it does today. A 1936 photograph taken from below the hilltop shows foundation planting around the building that resembles Howard's design of around 1910. Since almost none of Howard's landscape schemes were executed, their impact cannot be assessed except to say that in renderings, the buildings in their landscaped setting appear more rooted and less like geometric volumes set on earthen trays.

Although Sather Tower began construction in 1913 and was completed in 1914, Howard started designing it as early as 1903.[50] Most of the drawings were done in 1911. Jane K. Sather donated $200,000 toward its construction; an additional $50,000 was provided by the Permanent Improvement Fund. The tower was intended to dominate and unify the varied fabric of the main architectural group. Although two of the designs show the tower as a habitable structure, it is doubtful that this utilitarian format was seriously proposed. The final design bears a strong resemblance to the campanile of Piazza San Marco in Venice, a favored prototype for towers. Rising 307 feet from a balustraded esplanade with flights of steps on three sides, the tower's slightly tapering shaft ascends uninterrupted to the observation loggia with its balustrade and triple arched openings. Above the open loggia a second balustrade features obelisks at the corners capped with bronze flames. The culminating spire, set in from the balustrade, terminates in a flared lantern with four outcurving spikes and topped with a bronze spike. The campanile chimes, manufactured in England, were installed in 1917. As the university's most famous landmark, indeed one of the Bay Area's best-known landmarks, Sather Tower, once stirringly described as "a lighthouse of learning," is literally and symbolically Howard's most outstanding work.

Howard drafted several schemes for landscaping the esplanade, some of which are close to its present appearance. An undated watercolor rendering labeled "Scheme A" shows a rectangular reflecting pool continuing the line of the tower north toward a wide flight of steps flanked by pedestals with large urns. The corners of the esplanade are cut out to provide for circular pools with fountains. Another drawing of 1914 shows the formal plan for the oval end of the botanical garden. Its center, marked by a sculpture, is on an axis with the tower. But like other landscaping plans for the campus, the oval remained a tabula rasa that has devolved into a greensward lined with trees. This outcome may be more appreciated by its users and is certainly more economical to maintain than Howard's grand plan would have been.

Campanile Way, though lined with pollarded plane trees, was never envisioned as a grand allée. Ultimately, the transformation of the five life

THE JANE K SATHER TOWER
UNIVERSITY OF CALIFORNIA
JOHN GALEN HOWARD · ARCHITECT ·

sciences buildings into one very large structure and the informal nature of the oak grove around Strawberry Creek left the western end of Campanile Way undefined.

The year 1914 also saw the completion and approval of the final revision of the Phoebe A. Hearst Architectural Plan, which, though more detailed, did not depart significantly from the 1908 plan.

Although campus landscaping was the responsibility of the supervising

JANE K. SATHER TOWER ESPLANADE
UNIVERSITY OF CALIFORNIA
JOHN GALEN HOWARD - ARCHITECT -
SCHEME "A"

OPPOSITE
A presentation rendering of Sather Tower executed by Stafford Jory, a talented member of Howard's staff, who did a number of the watercolor renderings of university buildings.

LEFT
The most elaborate design for the Sather Tower Esplanade, shown in an undated watercolor rendering by Stafford Jory. A much simpler scheme was executed, but the rows of pollarded London plane trees still stand; they contribute importantly to the esplanade's formal character, as do the tall pine trees that were planted instead of the cypresses around the tower's base.

architect's office, Howard had little success in getting his planting schemes carried out. From the early days, the grounds had been planted more or less as the agriculture department's faculty saw fit, with little concern for design. Beginning in 1872, experimental plantings of many different varieties of trees, shrubs, grasses, and vines were carried out, with varying success. Increasing pressure to beautify the grounds and thus enhance the university's general reputation focused on a botanical garden, a mainstay of many European universities. In 1891 the regents reserved several acres along the swale below Observatory Hill for this purpose. Within a year hundreds of plants from near and far had been planted and a seed collection was organized. Eventually the botanical garden comprised seven acres. Still, landscape planning for the grounds seemed never to find a permanent place in the budget.

Moreover, the general public regarded the campus as a public park,

SATHER TOWER, UNIVERSITY OF CALIFORNIA
JOHN GALEN HOWARD ARCHITECT

SATHER TOWER   NORTH HALL   UNIVERSITY LIBRARY

PHOEBE APPERSON HEARST
PLAN
UNIVERSITY of CALIFORNIA

JOHN GALEN HOWARD
ARCHITECT

making fires for Sunday picnics and even building tree houses. The students were no better. A letter from the head gardener, A.L. Bolton, to V.H. Henderson, secretary to the regents, dated April 13, 1905, stated that "the bear from the Fraternity house on the northeast corner of Euclid and Hearst Avenues has been allowed to climb several fine trees west of the Botany Garden, and has damaged their bark badly."

In 1913 John W. Gregg joined the university faculty as professor of landscape gardening and floriculture. Howard and Gregg soon developed a casual working relationship, which involved decisions about plantings. According to Gregg, the pollarded London plane trees and Canary Island pines on the campanile esplanade were chosen in this informal way, as were many other trees and shrubs around the campus. In a 1915 report published by the Agricultural Experiment Station Gregg stated: "Planting plans for the Hearst Mining building have also been prepared by this division [of landscape gardening and floriculture] and the practical work in carrying them out is nearly completed... As a result of this service... the division has been instructed to prepare planting plans for the Doe library, California Hall, Boalt Hall, and Agriculture Hall."[51]

The landscaping design for the Hearst mining college circle, paid for by Phoebe Hearst, involved a circular pool in the center. The pool may have been "the practical work" that Gregg referred to in his report, though there is no evidence that the planting around it was carried out. A photograph taken from Sather Tower in 1915 shows the circle with groundcover vegetation but no shrubs or trees. As for the other planting plans Gregg mentioned, sketches from Howard's office exist for some of them but, again, it is difficult to ascertain if they were implemented.

Howard's belief that landscape architecture belonged to the discipline of architecture was shared by architects in general and particularly by those influenced by the École des Beaux-Arts. André Le Nôtre's great gardens for Versailles and Vaux-le-Vicomte, to name but two prominent examples, could not have been created by gardeners, no matter how extensive their knowledge of plants. This conviction, mingled perhaps with fear of threats to his authority, is seen in a letter from Howard to Gregg of March 21, 1914. In it he acknowledges receipt of a letter of March 10 outlining the following year's proposed course program in Gregg's division of landscape gardening and floriculture. He then goes on to say that although he wished to help Gregg develop his work, certain changes to the proposed announcement might be in order:

> It has long been the plan of this department, fully approved by the President of the University, to develop courses in landscape architecture; I am at the present time, with the authority of the President, in correspondence with various parties on the subject and looking to

View of the walk through the botanical garden as it appeared in 1917.

OPPOSITE, TOP
View of Hilgard Hall from the west, 1917. The richly ornamented exterior of this second building for the agriculture college contrasts strongly with the stark simplicity of Agriculture Hall adjacent to it. An engaged Tuscan colonnade eleven bays wide occupies the main part of the facade. The frieze of the entablature is studded with bucranes (ox skulls probably hung on ancient temples to celebrate the harvest). Above the entablature a pediment extending the length of the facade bears the inscription, "To Rescue for Human Society the Native Values of Rural Life." The array of decorative detail that appears in the window spandrels, between the bucranes, and on the walls includes garlands of fruit and flowers, representations of farm animals and native plants, and baskets and cornucopias laden with fruits of the field—all executed in two-toned sgraffito. The official state flower, the poppy, appears on architraves framing windows and doors. Above the main entrance on the west side a basketlike urn piled high with fruits and vegetables has two cornucopias at its base overflowing with the state's agricultural bounty.

BOTTOM
Ornament on the courtyard elevation is concentrated around the three entrances, where balconies overhanging the doorways feature relief panels with bound sheaves of grain flanked by winnowing baskets with crossed beaters.

the organization in this department of what I hope may eventually grow into a fully developed School of Landscape Architecture....

Of course the School of Landscape Architecture should and would count on having such subjects as floriculture, gardening, planting materials, etc., given by the College of Agriculture, just as the School of Architecture now relies upon the College of Civil Engineering or the College of Natural Sciences to give the necessary instruction in branches which are their specialties.... We should feel keen regret to

see fine arts courses offered in the College of Agriculture, not alone because of our long loyalty to the ideal development of our school but even more for what we feel should be the large, permanent policy of the University.... I am therefore more than a little surprised to note certain of your proposed courses, such as 103: Theory and Aesthetics of Landscape Architecture; Modern Civic Art, etc.

Howard did not believe that aesthetics should be taught in the College of Agriculture. He also noted that some of the courses conflicted with those offered in the School of Architecture. The term "landscape architecture" met with Howard's disapproval as well; he suggested that it be eliminated wherever it occurred in the announcement of courses. He was confident, he said, that Gregg would agree with him once he had thought about it.

Gregg's plans to infuse the study of agriculture with aesthetics had not originated with him. In 1912 Thomas Forsyth Hunt, newly arrived from Pennsylvania State College, had become dean of the College of Agriculture. A "ruralist," Hunt sought to improve the rural home and community by instilling a sense of aesthetics in the minds of students, who would then go out into the world to work in this community and with the expanding urban populations. In 1913 Hunt established the Division of Landscape Gardening and Floriculture, a department in many land grant universities around the country. John Gregg had been assistant professor in charge of landscape gardening and floriculture at Penn State from 1910 to 1913, when he came to the University of California to head the new division and formulate a program of study. Gregg had earned two bachelor of science degrees in landscape gardening/architecture in 1904, one from Boston University. Hunt had doubtless encouraged Gregg to introduce the courses that Howard found objectionable in the 1915–16 announcement.

On October 13, 1917, Dean Hunt spoke at the dedication of the second building of the agriculture group to be completed, named for Eugene W. Hilgard, the first dean of the college. Across the facade ran an inscription that expressed Hunt's ideal for agriculture: "To Rescue for Human Society the Native Values of Rural Life."

By the time Hilgard Hall was designed, granite was so costly that, according to William Hays, Howard was told to use reinforced concrete. (A state bond issue for $375,000 funded the 70,800-square-foot building.) That Howard considered concrete an inferior material may explain the lavish use of ornament on the building, which contrasts sharply with the starkness of Agriculture Hall.

Hilgard is U-shaped in plan and forms one side of the trapezoidal court that would not be completed until the construction of Giannini Hall in 1930. The facade has an engaged colonnade in an embellished version of the Tuscan order that stands on a raised base. The floor levels are indicated by decorative panels between the column shafts. The main entrance interrupts the colonnade's longitudinal rhythm with a flight of steps. Above the entrance portal a large urn overflows with fruits of the field. Symbols of agricultural bounty—cornucopias overflowing with fruits, flowers, and grains; bucranes (wreathed ox skulls used to adorn Greek and Roman temples), festoons, and rondels with animals and plants typical of California—are literally plastered over much of the building.

The ornamental detail is executed in sgraffito, an Italian technique for producing a design in more than one tone by scratching through a plastered surface to reveal a ground of another color. Paul E. Denneville, supervisor of texture and modeling for the 1915 Panama-Pacific International Exposition, supervised the sgraffito work on Hilgard Hall. Although the elevation of the building facing the court is relatively utilitarian, the entrance doors have balconies above them enriched with reliefs and sgraffitoed friezes along with other ornamental detail.

Wheeler Hall was also completed in 1917, construction having started two years earlier. The building, which resulted from a bond issue of

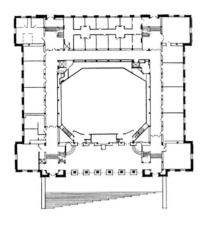
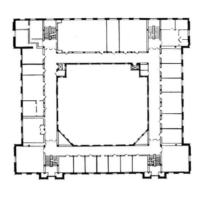

This undated rendering of Wheeler Hall exaggerates both the distance from Sather Gate and the slope of the ground. Depicting buildings poised between the earth and the sky was a much-used pictorial device for increasing their importance.

NEW CLASS ROOM BUILDING
UNIVERSITY OF CALIFORNIA

$1.8 million passed in 1914, met an urgent need for additional classrooms. As the campaign for the bond initiative revealed, between 1899 and 1914 the number of classrooms on the campus had increased by eight, from fifty-two to sixty-four, while the student enrollment had more than tripled, growing from 1,565 to 5,265. Furthermore, aside from the first two buildings, North and South Halls, built with state funds in 1872–73, the state had only contributed funds in the amount of about $500,000 for California Hall and Agriculture Hall, while gifts from individuals totaling two and a half times that amount had been responsible for the completion of Hearst Memorial Mining Building, Doe Library, and Boalt Hall. For Wheeler Hall, the bond issue generated $700,000 of the $715,994 that was the final cost of the building.

In the cornerstone-laying ceremony, the speaker for the faculty, Armin O. Leuschner, celebrated the naming of the building in honor of Benjamin Ide Wheeler, "the man with whose coming the University entered upon an era of permanence in the service of American civilization." It was the first building on the campus to be named for a living person.

Within its nearly 60,000 square feet Wheeler Hall housed sixty-two classrooms for the humanities and social sciences and forty-seven faculty offices. The classrooms and offices were located around the building periphery on the east, west, and north sides; the offices occupied the top floor. A central court opened up above an auditorium with seating for over nine hundred. On the main, south, elevation, arched entrance doors set in deep reveals on the ground floor gave access to the auditorium lobby. This important public space was announced by the special treatment given the central section of this main facade. An Ionic colonnade framed by two end bays with arched openings bracketed by pilasters runs for seven bays of this central, projecting section. The colonnaded section rises for two stories; a recessed attic story caps the central section. The six monumental urns that rest on the entablature mark the columns like exclamation points. Granite—a lighter kind than the Raymond granite used for the earlier buildings—was deemed a justifiable expense for Wheeler Hall, and finely carved ornamental detail contributes to a composition that is one of Howard's finest. In an article in the July 1917 issue of *Architect and Engineer of California*, Irving F. Morrow, a local architect and architectural commentator, wrote: "Wheeler Hall voices the best message of one of the best periods of French thought—unity, clarity, restraint, poise, centrality of intent pursued with a calculated economy of means. Our community possesses no edifice, the City Hall in San Francisco alone excepted, which delivers a message of comparable importance with equal force and address."

Still, Morrow had some reservations about Howard's other campus work. "An evident striving toward a high degree of perfection has not served to preclude a deficiency observable to some degree in all previous building on the campus...a failure to correlate the utilitarian with the monumental parts of the design.... Every building presents portions where it is as undesirable as it is impossible to exceed a minimum of expenditure. In such places one exacts simplicity of treatment rather than lack of treatment."

This criticism applies especially to the north elevation of Wheeler Hall, which lies along Campanile Way. Although the fact that the building

View of Hilgard Hall from the northeast.

would be viewed from Sather Gate dictated that the south facade be the most embellished, the utilitarian treatment of the north elevation, which faced the celebrated campus axis to the Golden Gate, seems inappropriate. The south elevation of Doe Library on Campanile Way also suffers from a conspicuous lack of "treatment," giving it a utilitarian quality that its use over time for delivery services has only reinforced. On the other hand, Hilgard Hall, which is about half the size of Wheeler and cost about half as much, has a better correlation between the design of its principal facade and the more utilitarian courtyard elevation to the northeast.

Gilman Hall, also finished in 1917, was the third building to benefit from the 1914 bond issue. Named for Daniel Coit Gilman, second president of the university, the building was the third home for the College of Chemistry. Because the Organic Act of 1868, the founding legislation for the university, made no provision for a college of chemistry, President Gilman secured legislation to establish one in 1872. The next year, more than half of the newly constructed South Hall was occupied by a chemical laboratory. The double brick walls were a means of fireproofing the structure.

In 1890 a dedicated chemistry building was erected. Under William B. Rising, first dean of the college, the main activity of chemists in the University of California was the analysis of minerals, drugs, and agricultural products; Rising was also the state analyst. During his thirty-six

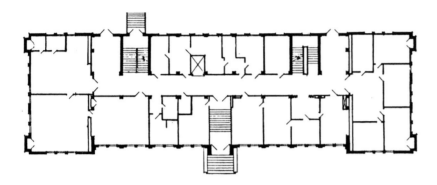

First-floor plan of Gilman Hall. The facade differs from that of Le Conte Hall in having two entrances; otherwise the composition is the same.

years as dean, the number of graduates from the college rose, but only four doctoral degrees were awarded. In 1912 Gilbert Lewis came from the Massachusetts Institute of Technology to succeed Rising and build up the graduate and research programs. Under his direction the college began a long period of expansion.

The 44,700-square-foot Gilman Hall, built of concrete for $205,053, housed administrative offices, classrooms for instruction in physical chemistry and chemical engineering, and the chemistry library. Its lackluster appearance suggests a budget that encouraged little expenditure of design time or talent in the supervising architect's office. Still, Howard and his staff must have enjoyed creating the variation on the traditional Ionic column capital used on the colonnade.

14 World War I and Postwar Changes at the University

1917–1924

On September 6, 1916, Howard wrote to President Wheeler requesting a sabbatical leave for 1917. His last sabbatical had been in 1910–11; the years in between had been strenuous, particularly 1915. He also observed that the buildings then under way, Hilgard, Wheeler, and Gilman, would be nearly finished by the summer of 1917.

That fall, too, Howard traveled to New York, mainly to see his son, Robert, who was attending the Art Students League in New York.[52] Unlike many parents, who were more concerned with how their children would earn their way in the world, the Howards took a keen interest in the artistic pursuits of their children. As Janette Howard Wallace recalls, "There was not always money for new shoes, but there was always money for books." Money for travel and cultural events—opera, ballet, theater, concerts—was considered money well spent.

Howard spent part of his sabbatical leave in Carmel, where he had built additions to their home there. A letter of August 26, 1917, to Rob describes "the little old place snuggled away among the trees, with peek-hole glimpses here and there through the branches, of the lovely bay and lagoon and meadows and mountains. We have kept all the additions in the same character as the original cabin, perfectly charming and not at all 'architectural.' Your mother started the place and fixed its character." John had a new workroom where he was no doubt writing the next volume of his trilogy of epic poems. The work was titled "Pheidias," and would treat the Athenian sculptor as emblematic of the classical spirit.

Howard's idyllic retreats in Carmel were offset by the effects of World War I. His eldest son, Henry, who graduated from the University of California with a degree in architecture in 1916, had volunteered in February 1917 to serve in a unit of the French army ambulance corps in France. Rob also enlisted that spring. Student and faculty opinion was divided on issues surrounding the war. Rob later recalled in an interview that the regular Thursday teas for architecture students that the Howards hosted at Rose Leroy often erupted in emotional discussions that revealed both anti- and pro-German viewpoints.

Wheeler's position was particularly difficult. His studies at the universities of Leipzig, Berlin, and finally Heidelberg, where he received his Ph.D. summa cum laude in 1885, had made him deeply sympathetic to German culture. Kaiser Wilhelm was a personal friend, and his large photograph occupied a place of honor on the mantel in the president's house.

Howard was increasingly moved by patriotic sentiments and wrote stirring letters on the subject to Henry, who was commissioned a lieutenant in the army in February 1918. By now Howard knew many people who were involved in the war. Even his former office manager William Raiguel had enrolled in aviation school. In June, Howard joined the Red Cross, with the intention of working in France for that organization. Although Mary did not like the idea of his going overseas in wartime, he left California in early August, sailed from New York on August 28, and arrived in Paris on September 8. He was sent to Bordeaux, where he worked with French refugees, officials, and private citizens in what he described as "one of the greatest opportunities and privileges of my life." After three months in Bordeaux, he was ordered to report to Paris, where he was transferred from the Department of General Relief to the Department of Personnel. The official tone of the report he submitted to the Red Cross on his year of service masked a highly critical view of the efficiency of the organization. Writing to Mary in May 1919, he compared working for the Red Cross to "carrying water in a sieve."

In Paris he met some officers in the American Expeditionary Force (AEF), who were engaged in organizing educational services for an AEF university. They asked Howard to work with them. His request to be assigned to that work was granted, and during the months of March and April he was on loan from the Red Cross to the university, where he delivered two series of illustrated lectures on the history of architecture, one in Beaune and the other at Bellevue, near Paris. After his loan period ended on May 1, 1919, he enjoyed a sixteen-day leave in the south of France, where he studied Cézanne's life and work for the third volume of his trilogy of epic poems. The title, "Cezaronet," was a composite of Cézanne, Renoir, and Monet, whom Howard considered the only painters worthy of bearing the mantle of the age. At the end of May he returned to Paris and obtained a release from the Red Cross.

Despite the hardships of war, Howard had dedicated himself to his refugee work and teaching, both of which were rewarding. He had also managed to join Henry and Robert in Paris, where they enjoyed a camaraderie intensified by the war and their distance from home. When the exhilaration of the armistice celebrations in Paris wore off, Howard reported that he and others were all "keyed up" and wondered if they could ever settle down.

The immediate postwar years were not a time for optimism in Howard's practice. While he was in Europe in the service of the Red Cross he received news of Phoebe Hearst's death on April 13, 1919. He wrote Mary that "she seemed so fixed an institution that it never seemed as if she could die—in a real sense she never can. She will always be a gracious presence, none the less potent for her bodily absence."

Wheeler retired from the presidency on July 15, 1919. David P. Bar-rows succeeded him, taking office in December. Spiraling enrollments and rising costs of all kinds caused the university to adopt a deficit budget until 1921, when the biennial appropriation for the university maintenance was increased from $4 to $9 million. A crisis in faculty relations arose in the months between Wheeler's retirement and Barrows's instatement. The so-called faculty revolution was resolved by an agreement between the faculty and the regents early in 1920, whereby the faculty gained increased powers of self-government that had been blocked during Wheeler's auto-cratic administration. The faculty gained direct access to the regents through authorized committees, a provision Barrows did not wholly sup-port because it excluded him from some communications between the faculty and the regents. Wary of the development of the Los Angeles campus, Barrows expressed concern that competition between the two campuses for funds and faculty would lower the standing of both.

In this climate of uncertainty, Howard's prospects for campus work dimmed. He conveyed his pessimism in a letter of January 28, 1920, to Mary, then in Europe with Janette and Beth Gregory visiting Henry and Rob, who were studying in Paris and sopping up French culture in travels and visits to museums. "None of the university work on which I have been working since I came home has developed yet," he wrote. "Prices are so high and conditions so uncertain that the architecture scene is even more than commonly insecure." The office in San Francisco, now in the First National Bank Building, had so little work that Raiguel, Howard's office manager of many years, left to take another job. Commenting on one of the office projects, a school in Susanville, California, Howard wrote: "A job is a job these days." Another project, a laboratory building for the Union Oil Company, took him to Los Angeles, which he had not visited for many years. The city mystified him; he found it "a strange place, unlike any other I know. No head or tail to it. It just seems to straggle aimlessly and in fact endlessly."

Howard's letters from this period also contain commentary on the political issues of the postwar period, reflecting a staunchly Democratic, liberal perspective. An ardent supporter of Woodrow Wilson and the League of Nations, he was infuriated by the bias against Wilson and the French that he detected in an article by John Maynard Keynes titled "The Economic Consequences of the Peace." He also wrote a letter to his friend Herbert Croly protesting the *New Republic*'s objections to the peace treaty and the League. On April 15, 1916, he wrote to Emma Goldman

saying that he had "attended many [of her] addresses with interest, profit, and pleasure." Because he had heard that she was to be jailed for speaking about birth control, he was, as a believer in free speech, sending a "small contribution for her defense fund."

There was one piece of good news. In March 1920 Howard wrote Mary that he had submitted *Pheidias* to the University of California Press. Although the policy of the press was to publish only scientific works, Howard argued that years of research in architectural history had preceded the poem and justified its consideration. On May 4 he wrote that the press had offered to publish the poem if Howard would pay the cost. He thought he might do that at a later date.

One campus project that was not developing the way Howard wished was the California Memorial Stadium. The logical location for the stadium, he thought, was in the so-called Oxford block in the southwest corner of the campus, near California Field in the area designated on the general plan for athletic activities. When planning for the stadium began in 1922, however, the university had not yet acquired the property, and the consulting engineers instead recommended a site in a canyon southeast of the Greek Theater. Howard opposed this site both because it departed from the general plan and because it was a nature preserve prized by bird and wildflower enthusiasts. Prominent faculty members such as Charles Mills Gayley, head of the English department since 1889, also opposed locating the stadium in the canyon.

On June 20, 1922, Howard wrote Mary that the decision for the canyon site was "apparently beyond reversal…. It seems that they [the regents] all feel under obligation to the engineers who steered them up the canyon and they want me to be in control of the work; so the problem is to establish a modus operandi in our relations. Rather a difficult situation, but there should be some basis for agreement—it remains to be seen." A separate agreement had to be negotiated because although Howard's contract as supervising architect stipulated that he was to get 6 percent of the university work west of Piedmont Avenue, the canyon site was east of the avenue. In the end Howard's office did the work, but he was not happy with the situation.

Howard expressed other complaints in a letter to the comptroller, Robert Gordon Sproul, on August 17, 1922:

> It has come to my attention that several pieces of architectural work are proposed or underway on the campus which have not been taken up with me by your office, or, if taken up at an earlier state are proceeding without notifying me…. The contract specifies that my duties as Supervising Architect shall be "to render full architectural services…in the design of all buildings," etc. This was made to include temporary buildings because, although I should have preferred to be relieved of such work, it was necessary to have the permanent work safeguarded as it could only be by giving the Supervising Architect charge of all buildings.

He then reiterated a point he had made many times before: economically, the office could do the work only on a regular basis, not an occasional one. Although a somewhat informal arrangement had worked in the past, "Of late the tendency not to call me in seems to be growing, and as I have certain responsibilities and your office certain others, I think we should be careful to safeguard the University and each other." Otherwise, he observed, the university might blame him for something he knew nothing about, or blame Sproul for not having contacted him. It was not that he wanted to work on temporary campus buildings for reasons of profit, Howard stated. His interest was only in relation to the campus as a whole or to specific buildings that he had designed.

Present cases in point are the proposed roads…and the alteration work in the library. In the latter case I had been making sketches and studying proposed schemes for years, at a good deal of expense to myself, yet when the work goes ahead, I am simply ignored. If such work is not to be looked after by me the contract provides that it may be withdrawn by mutual consent of the Regents and the Supervising Architect…the mutuality being an important thing for both sides. Another instance, which it seems to me is open to question is the handling of the women's athletic interests since the burning of Hearst Hall [in 1922]. Though I have heard nothing from you of this matter, I understand from the papers that Mr. Hearst wishes Mr. Maybeck to be the architect for the reconstruction. I have no desire to interfere with such an arrangement; on the contrary I should be very glad to cooperate in every possible way, but here again I have assumed certain responsibilities, and if I am to carry them properly I must be cognizant of affairs as they develop and have an opportunity to advise regarding them. I think you will agree that all this is not quite as it should be. Where does the fault lie? And can it not be eliminated?

More letters to Sproul complaining of work planned or under way without Howard's approval followed. Construction work on temporary buildings west of Harmon Gymnasium was the subject of a November 14 letter. The issue of control of campus landscaping arose once more in a letter of January 23, 1923. A Mr. Flint had prepared a plan for planting around East Hall, and the work had been carried out without Howard's knowledge. "Such procedure treads on my toes," Howard wrote. "You may recall the disagreeable, absurd and ineffectual conditions which used to exist in the whole realm of planting on campus….[There were] so many cooks that all the broth was spoiled and everybody was out of sorts with indigestion…. I offered to look after such work without remuneration." No expenditure was contemplated unless funds were made available. In most cases planting plans were prepared by John Gregg or someone in his department and submitted to Howard for approval. The only reimbursements to the supervising architect's office were for draftsman's services; fees were to be paid only for the design of walls, balustrades, and grading when part of a proposed building. Howard reminded Sproul that as of May 11, 1915, his agreement with the regents was that he was constituted the university landscape architect and engineer. Finally, Howard asked Sproul if he would "bring about agreement with all parties interested in campus landscape work."

No evidence exists that Sproul acted on Howard's request, if indeed the request was formally submitted. Howard's state of mind as projected by these letters is not a hopeful one. Throughout their marriage his wife had tried, with little success, to dissuade him from brooding over reversals of fortune. Now he had less private work, and the erosion of his influence on university development was particularly frustrating. Although these letters may merely represent attempts to externalize his brooding, cumulatively they probably worked to his disadvantage. With his close allies now gone or near retirement, the regents and the administration were no longer attentive to his rights and opinions. In the end Howard's grievances appear to have made him a nuisance to those in power.

In July 1923 William Wallace Campbell, an astronomer who had served as director of the Lick Observatory since 1901, succeeded David Barrows as president of the university. Campbell was Howard's contemporary and also a client, since Howard had done work for the observatory, most recently the design of two cottages in the fall of 1922. Knowing of Campbell's appointment in advance, Howard wrote him a letter on June 4, 1923:

> In view of your entering upon the presidency of the University of California, I feel that you should have an absolutely free hand for your great task. I beg, therefore, to tender my resignation of all my various duties in connection with the University, to take effect on July 1st next, or, in the case of certain architectural undertakings, as soon thereafter as will be in accordance with my specific engagements with the Regents.
>
> With most cordial good wishes for the success of your administration.

Campbell replied with surprise that a professor should resign in such circumstances. Howard responded on June 13 that his only thought in writing was to clear the atmosphere because his relation to the university was not the usual one. "Many things have happened within the last year or two which have given me grave concern as to the tenableness of my position," he wrote. He had come to think that some adjustment of his position must be made and had spoken about this to Regent Britton, chair of the buildings and grounds committee. Howard felt that if he was to continue as supervising architect, he must have assurance that the regents wanted him and would support him. Britton had told him that this was the case, but he wanted clarification.

Campbell's reply to this letter stated that he was willing to remove causes of friction to the extent possible. Howard then wrote on July 27, after Campbell had assumed the presidency, that "I will continue in my work at the University as Supervising Architect, Professor of Architecture, and Director of the School of Architecture. My tender of resignation dated June 4th is therefore withdrawn." He added that "there should be no difficulty in reaching a mutually satisfactory understanding with regard to points which have given rise to difficulties in the past without modifying the agreement between the Regents and myself." He would continue in his positions with the School of Architecture for the year ending June 30, 1924, at a salary of $6,000.

PRELIMINARY SKETCH FOR STUDENTS' UNION
UNIVERSITY OF CALIFORNIA
JOHN GALEN HOWARD ARCHITECT

STUDY FOR STUDENTS' UNION, U.C.

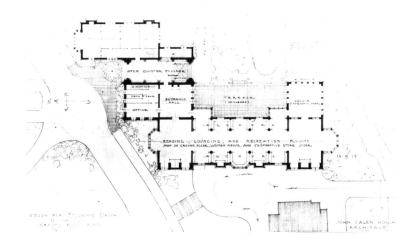

STUDY FOR STUDENTS' UNION
U OF C
GROUND FLOOR PLAN

JOHN GALEN HOWARD
ARCHITECT

SKETCH FOR STUDENTS' UNION
UNIVERSITY OF CALIFORNIA
JOHN GALEN HOWARD · ARCHITECT.

Three buildings were completed in 1923: Henry Morse Stephens Memorial Hall (the campus's first student union), the Women's Faculty Club, and Le Conte Hall; of these, the student union was conceptually most interesting. Dedicated on March 16, the building was built with $225,000 subscribed by students, alumni, and faculty members and $175,000 appropriated from the funds of the Associated Students of the University of California. Henry Morse Stephens had come to head the history department in 1902, the year the Howards moved to Berkeley; he remained in that position until his death in April 1919. The naming of the student union in his honor was a tribute to his great popularity, as well as to his varied and rich learning, productive scholarship, wisdom, vision, and creative force. (Indeed, Stephens was judged such a powerful presence on the campus that his ghost was said to haunt the faculty club tower where he had lived for many years.)

Like the other nonacademic buildings on campus—the faculty clubs and the Senior Men's Hall—the student union was located south of Strawberry Creek. Howard's use of a simplified Tudor revival style instead of a classic revival mode signaled its nonacademic status. Nor was it set, like the buildings in the main part of the campus, on a leveled platform. Instead, the structure fit into the slope of its creekside site. Its terraces on the east side overlooked the creek and its wooded environs—an informal character appropriate to its use. One of the few distinguished interiors that Howard's typically straitened building budgets permitted is the graduate students common on the second floor of the east section of the building. The tall, rectangular room's shallow, polygonal bays filled with windows at either end provide a generous amount of daylight to offset the dark, stenciled, beamed ceiling and wood-paneled walls. Above the fireplace a scrolled, wooden mantelpiece frames a large portrait of Henry Morse Stephens.

The Women's Faculty Club, also completed in 1923, was located east of the Senior Men's Hall near the first Faculty Club (for men) and, again, south of Strawberry Creek. Although clad in brown shingles, the two-story Women's Faculty Club, with its simplified Georgian revival style, is more formal in appearance than the rambling building that the Men's Faculty Club had become after additions in 1903 and 1904 of new wings to the original structure.

Le Conte Hall, which was dedicated in March 1924, honored the brothers John and Joseph Le Conte, born in 1818 and 1823, respectively, on a plantation near Liberty, Georgia. In addition to a chemical laboratory and a botanical garden, their father had a scientific library that enabled him to train his children in natural history and science. Both John and Joseph attended Franklin College (later the University of Georgia), and both became physicians after gaining their M.D. degrees from the College

OPPOSITE, TOP
The main floor plan for Stephens Memorial Hall reveals the building's openness to the meander of Strawberry Creek, which runs along the south side at a lower level than the north side. The main terrace facing east was a popular student gathering place opening off the "Tap Room" and men's club rooms. A smaller terrace on the floor above provided an outdoor space for the women's club room. The five-story west wing housed the student cooperative store on the ground and mezzanine levels. It opened onto a court where an octagonal kiosk called the "Ink Well" contained a mechanism that dispensed free ink for fountain pens for thirty years. The projecting bay window on the tower's north side marks the location of the Stephens Memorial Room.

BOTTOM
The final design shows the tower buttressed by octagonal corner turrets and a greater role given to the fenestration in defining the horizontal lines of the composition.

of Physicians and Surgeons in New York City. They served in the Confederate army and ended the war in Columbia, South Carolina. With their property destroyed and their postwar prospects dim, the brothers decided to go to California, where sympathy for the Confederate cause still lingered. John became a professor of physics at the University of California and served as its third president from 1876 to 1881; Joseph was professor of geology and natural science. Both men brought fame to the university through their various scientific interests. John died in 1891, and Joseph in 1901.

Le Conte Hall stands opposite Gilman Hall; together they defined the beginning of a north-south axis from what was then South Drive to the Hearst Memorial Mining Building. The facades of the two reinforced-concrete buildings are nearly identical and have the same ornamental detail. Major additions made in the 1950s and 1960s have minimized the visual importance of both buildings, such that today as works of architecture they seem uninspired. Although it is tempting to interpret their lack

SKETCH FOR PHYSICS BUILDING
UNIVERSITY OF CALIFORNIA
JOHN GALEN HOWARD, ARCHITECT

of invention to Howard's declining influence on campus plans, it is also true that the portion of the budget allocated for equipping scientific buildings far exceeded that for design.

Howard's last buildings on the campus were Haviland and Hesse Halls. Haviland was dedicated on March 25, 1924, and occupied by the School of Education. The design strongly resembles drawings Howard made some years earlier for a replacement for North Hall that was never built. A concrete building somewhat smaller than California Hall, Haviland is also a rectangular block with a tiled hip roof capped by a

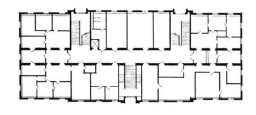

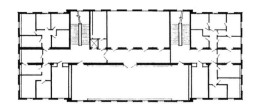

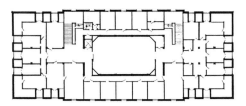

SKETCH FOR NEW NORTH HALL
UNIVERSITY OF CALIFORNIA
— JOHN GALEN HOWARD, ARCHITECT

copper-framed skylight. As with Hilgard Hall, Howard devised ways to enrich the concrete surface, a variety of ornamental detail calling attention to such important parts of the building as entrance doors and windows, corners, and cornices. On the upper floor indirectly illuminated by the skylight is a fine, Adamsesque interior, which housed the School of Education's Lange Library.

Hesse Hall, built for the College of Mechanics, was also completed in 1924. Designed as a heat and power laboratory, it was a rectangular concrete block with few openings. It is now so bracketed by subsequent large additions that only its north and south walls are visible to passersby. These walls are scored with a linear pattern around the windows and doors that mimics blocks of stone in low relief; a stringcourse of dentils underscores a simple molded cornice. Hesse's minimal classicism looks forward, if unintentionally, to the postmodern use of classical detail as a kind of shorthand in the 1970s and 1980s.

Dismissal as Supervising Architect and a Career as Educator

15

1923–1931

September 1923, Janette Howard Wallace recalls, was very hot and dry. For days a strong north wind had swept down over the sparsely built hills above Rose Leroy. On the afternoon of September 17 Janette, now a student at the university, had gone down to the campus to attend a class. Her mother Mary was in bed with the flu. When heavy smoke was observed pouring over the northern hills, classes were canceled.[53] Janette returned home to find her mother outside with a hose trying unsuccessfully to wet down the area around the house. Fire engines called to a fire at Mills College in Oakland that morning had lowered the water pressure such that there was very little water to be had in north Berkeley that afternoon. Janette and Mary watched as the houses near them burst into flames; one burned to the ground in twenty minutes. As the fire approached their house, they packed what valuables they could and fled to the campus. Taking refuge in the architecture building, the "Ark," at the edge of the campus on Hearst Avenue, they waited for John, who was at his San Francisco office.[54] Students were loading up books from Howard's architecture library and moving them out because the wooden Ark was considered likely to burn. Henry and Rob went to the campus and recruited other students to go up to Rose Leroy, where they stayed through the night using hoses and buckets of water to douse sparks carried on the wind.

Farther up the hill on Greenwood Terrace, Sadie Gregory stayed on the roof of their wood-shingled house playing the hose over it to ward off the fire. At sunset the wind suddenly dropped, and the worst was over. The campus was spared. Although a few houses around Rose Leroy and Greenwood Terrace survived the fire, the Howards' first house on Ridge

Road burned to the ground. As for Rose Leroy, the top floor burned completely, and water damaged the ground floor, making it uninhabitable.

Soon after the fire John and Mary moved to San Francisco. On December 10, 1923, Howard wrote to his poet friend John Neihardt in Iowa thanking him for his letter of sympathy for their sufferings during the fire: "Our losses were considerable, but were mostly confined to things that didn't mean very much to us and we were fairly well insured.... We have taken a little house in San Francisco and are enjoying the adven-

John Galen Howard photographed ca. 1923.

ture heartily, especially since we have our two oldest sons near at hand."

Since the Gregorys owned Rose Leroy, Howard did not have the responsibility of restoring it. He and Mary were now free to live where they wished. San Francisco with its rich cultural life attracted them, and because their family had shrunk (Henry and Rob were living on their own in San Francisco, Janette lived at her sorority house in Berkeley, and Charles and Langley were in New York), a smaller house was possible. John and Mary moved into Castle Court, a group of small attached houses on Russian Hill.

In a letter to President Campbell of March 13, 1924, Howard called attention to a temporary building that was being planned outside the supervising architect's office, and expressed his objection to being removed from supervision work (though in what context he does not say). Then at the end of June, having planned a sabbatical with two-thirds pay from July 1 to December 31, 1924, and a leave without pay from January to June 1925, he departed alone for Europe. He was traveling in the Middle East when the news reached him that the regents, on November 22, 1924, had canceled his contract as supervising architect, though his position as director of the School of Architecture remained secure. Henry, who was at the time working in his father's office, wrote to Warren Gregory in December saying it was regrettable that the regents took action when his father was

John and Mary Howard in a light-hearted moment on a vacation.

absent. Apparently "skirmishes" over campus projects had taken place that Henry considered responsible for "the break." He was concerned that his father would magnify the causes of his dismissal unnecessarily.

Howard left no account of his reaction to his dismissal. However, a letter of January 18, 1926, to Edwin Bergstrom in Los Angeles gives some indication of his continuing frustration with his situation in Berkeley: "I have been seriously considering withdrawing from the University in Berkeley…. Circumstances have conspired to make me feel rather useless and helpless, just at the time when I think I ought to be able to render my best service…. Might there be any chance in the South for me to use whatever faculties I have to the limit?" Howard noted on the draft of the letter that he had received a friendly reply, but did not refer to the matter again.

During his leave of absence in 1925 John and Mary lived in Cassis, a small fishing town in the south of France. There Howard worked on "Cezaronet," the epic poem he had begun in France in 1919, and they enjoyed trips around the countryside. Janette Howard Wallace recalls that when they returned to California, "Pop was sporting a huge beard down over his chest and a fisherman's cape and beret, which caused much amusement among the students at the Ark." He soon reverted to his usual formal attire. He continued as director of the School of Architecture and as a full professor and seems to have spent much of his time at the Ark.

The Howards now began a seminomadic life, moving several times during the next few years. They left Castle Court and returned to Berkeley in 1925, but in 1926 they lived at 1017 Vallejo Street in San Francisco. Willis Polk had designed this double residence on Russian Hill in 1892 for Mrs. Virgil Williams, a painter and an active member of the local community of artists and writers; her husband had founded the California Institute of Design. Apparently, Polk performed the work without pay in exchange for being able to live in one section of the house with his family.[55] The house was opposite the cottage once occupied by their dear friend Joseph Worcester, who had died in June 1913, and held many memories for the Howards.

In a letter to Janette from Berkeley written on November 5, 1927, Mary described a visit to the site of their old friends the Gregorys' new house at "the Farm," near Santa Cruz, California. Warren Gregory had begun to acquire the property—ultimately 200 acres—in 1916. Before he died in 1926, he and Sadie had started to plan their house and hired Henry Howard to design it. Henry had drawn up many plans, but Sadie Gregory was so difficult to please that before she settled on one Henry had decided to move to New York, where architectural offices had more work than San Francisco. William W. Wurster, a young graduate of the Ark and friend of the Gregorys, was then engaged to design the house; he had already made five schemes for it. Toward the letter's end, Mary expressed her reactions to Howard's treatment by the university:

> Some days I feel so bitter it seems as if I could not endure living here, and then I hear your father speak of the "infinite relief" he has not to have to struggle with all sorts of people and problems, and he seems so serene and well that I realize he has already left an imprint of his ability and worth greater than most men of his age, and that he is free—free now to live as he will and where he will. He is planning to keep his room at the faculty club as a study, peaceful and quiet and just for himself, and after Christmas vacation, I will find a small apartment where we can live together.

Although Howard's role as an educator at the University of California was a result of his appointment as supervising architect for the Hearst Architectural Plan and not a priority that he had set for himself, he took the responsibility seriously. The scarcity of competent people to hire for his university work was an added incentive. President Wheeler had supported Howard's educational goals. In his 1899 inaugural address Wheeler stated: "When the University shall have once begun to teach the art of architecture by good example, it may also and must undertake to teach by good doctrine as well."

At the time of Howard's appointment, the West, while attractive for its resources, was considered by many to be a cultural desert. Warren Perry, who would succeed Howard as director of the school in 1927, published an article in 1923 in which he observed that although the region

Members of the architectural fraternity, Tau Sigma Delta, photographed in May 1920. In the front row from left to right are Warren Perry, John Galen Howard, and William C. Hays.

was "gloriously endowed by nature, blessed with those rare advantages of climate and with the faint aroma of adventure,... its contribution to building, painting, sculpturing, was at its most unhappy time in our history. Never was art so dead as when California was, for the most part, settled. In the face of the mass accumulation of dreadfulness that housed the Californian at the end of the eighteen hundreds, reaction was painfully slow, for thoughtless habit had taken the place of conscious and regulated design."

Perry believed that the "tradition of a more distant and better past" in the eastern part of the country had produced "endowed and cultivated men" in the field of architecture. A few of them (doubtless he had Howard in mind), attracted by among other things the "lingering romance and freedom of the new country," had come west bringing "the true spark of architectural fire, never quite extinguished on earth—though sometimes perilously smothered with ashes and slag."

As the first school of architecture established in the West and only the thirteenth in the nation, the importance of initiating a curriculum that would rank with the country's best was clear. Not surprisingly, Howard's personal success at the École des Beaux-Arts in Paris and his allegiance to its program assured its use as a model for the Berkeley program.

Ark students talked about their work in a jargon that used French words but gave them a meaning intelligible only to those familiar with the culture of the école. Design problems were "projets"; "esquisses" were

Architecture students moving their float made for the Ark Jinks down Hearst Avenue to the campus northside entrance. Howard's 1912 apartment building for faculty members at the corner of Euclid and Hearst Avenues, is shown in the background on the left.

the preliminary sketches, executed in the "atelier," or studio, on which the final solutions had to be based. When the "projet" was due, a small cart, a "charrette," was wheeled around the studio to receive the boards on which the finished designs were rendered. The students wore berets and smocks like those worn at the école. They also held annual costume balls, or "Ark Jinks," for which elaborate sets and props were made. At the earliest such affairs, students dressed as animals while John and Mary Howard came as Mr. and Mrs. Noah.

Howard taught the main courses in the school: elements of architecture; planning; history of ancient and classic architecture; and architectural theory. The three other members of the faculty were William C. Hays, assistant in architecture; H. W. Seawell, instructor in watercoloring and pen-and-ink drawing; and M. Earl Cummings, instructor in modeling. These men also worked in Howard's office.

In 1912, four years after the first addition to the Ark was completed, Howard wrote President Wheeler to request still more space:

> The need is now so great for a practical doubling of the size of
> the building that students have to wait their turn at table. We have
> had to get along the best we could without either an exhibition

room or a lecture hall, borrowing from our neighbors the space and apparatus for giving some of the courses for which we have no space in the building.

In one respect the Department has to complain of too great success for its students have alluring opportunities to enter offices before we feel that they are rightly out from under our wing. It is our hope as time goes on the custom will be established for all the students to continue their work with us for two years of graduate study

This view of the Architecture Building from the southeast shows the 1912 addition on the east end that housed an exhibition hall with a skylight. The adjoining lecture hall had a seating capacity of two hundred and a raised stage on the south end. The plaster cast of a Greek temple frieze reflected the veneration for classical antiquity that Howard and his faculty shared.

or continue their studies at Eastern schools or abroad. For five or six years we have been represented (and most admirably) by students at the Ecole des Beaux-Arts in Paris.

In answer to Howard's plea, 8,500 square feet of space was added to the Ark in 1912, at a cost of $10,000. This addition contained a thirty-by-seventy-foot exhibition hall on the east end of the building and an adjacent lecture hall to the south with seating for up to two hundred people. New drafting rooms were added to the north side, and a wooden pergola open to the courtyard sheltered students circulating from the drafting rooms to the lecture and exhibition halls. The following year Howard designed a simple brown-shingled building, with 10,900 square feet of space, for drawing instruction on a site east of the Ark. The building had a two-story section on the west side and a three-story section on the east side. It provided overflow space for the architecture studios until 1924, when the newly formed Department of Art moved in.[56]

Also in 1913, the department was awarded the status of a professional school and was thereby allowed to award bachelor degrees in architecture at the end of two years of postgraduate studies. Thus the instruction in design—the main focus of the school's curriculum—which took place in the third and fourth years of the undergraduate program, was intensified during two more years of professional studies. In 1915 Howard instituted a system, modeled on that of the école, of advancement by gaining points, or "values." During their last four years, students moved through the five required stages by entering competitions (called *concours* at the école). The competition programs were not, however, always tied to those of the national Beaux-Arts Institute of Design, and the submissions were not sent to the institute's headquarters in New York City for judgment, as was usually the case when schools made use of the institute's program. Instead School of Architecture faculty members made up the juries, often holding lengthy deliberations about student work in the exhibition hall.

Although training in the use of the classical vocabulary of form was a strong feature of the program, classical styles were not decreed. By the same token, while modernism—which was assuming ever greater influence, particularly following the 1925 Exposition des Arts Decoratifs in Paris—was neither encouraged nor ruled out, none of the faculty was a modernist during Howard's tenure.

Life in the Ark absorbed more of Howard's time after his work as supervising architect ended in 1924. He had always enjoyed the company of young people and relished teaching the history courses that were also popular with students outside the school. Although his lecture style was not dramatic—he was soft-spoken and formal in his bearing—his delivery had the strength of his convictions. He was also highly regarded as a critic. E. Geoffrey Bangs, Howard's last partner and a former student, recalled that Howard didn't tell students what to do. "He made you do everything you could do and pushed you and pushed you. He wasn't particularly interested in whether you did it in this style or that...because he was teaching you to be yourself."[57]

Although Howard retired from the directorship of the School of Architecture in 1927, he agreed to stay on the faculty for two more years, at which time he would be eligible for a Carnegie pension. Warren Perry, Howard's loyal protégé and associate, was appointed his successor. Mary wrote Janette that the alumni of the Ark had given Howard a grand dinner with 125 people in attendance from all over the state. Howard gave a great talk, she wrote, and was cheered by the audience.

The architecture building—still considered temporary—seems to have gained a more permanent place in Howard's affections. In an article in the 1927 university yearbook, *Blue and Gold,* he wrote: "There seems to be some sort of magnet that brings the students round at night and at odd hours when perhaps it would be better for them if they were getting exercise in the open air. There's a homelikeness in the old shack that makes for deep and lasting friendships, rouses high ideals."

In 1928 the Howards settled in an apartment at 2631 Durant Avenue in Berkeley. Mary reported to Janette that she had installed the Bokhara rugs, her desk, the mahogany table, black teakwood stands, the oval mirror, and a William Keith painting "to make the place look Howardlike."[58]

After years spent in search of a publisher for his book-length poem *Pheidias,* Howard finally reached an agreement with the Macmillan Company in New York in June 1928. Although he had to pay $1,400 toward its publication, approximately the sum he had paid to publish *Brunelleschi* thirteen years earlier, he was pleased with the contract. Many letters passed between him and the associate editor, L.H. Titterton, about revisions of the manuscript and the design of the book. Howard wanted *Brunelleschi* used as a model; when Macmillan provided him with a sample, however, the typography and book and cover designs did not suit him. In the end, Robert Howard designed the book jacket, which featured a frieze taken from a Greek black-figured vase against a terra cotta color. By March 1929 John Galen had reviewed galley proofs, whereupon he

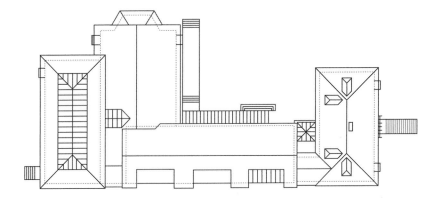

The Ark as it was in 1912; the building had expanded to six times its original size in the six years of its existence.

departed to join Mary and Janette for travel in Spain and France.

Although *Pheidias* was not released until August, Macmillan sent out copies for review before that date. In April, Howard wrote to John Whitton, a reviewer who had asked for a précis:

> I set out to make a sculptor real. That idea was at the heart of my purpose 20 years ago before I chose the sculptor. I fixed on Pheidias as the outstanding representative of one of the great art periods, as an artist riding the crest of his time... a figure sufficiently in evidence to be of interest yet personally so much of a shadow as to give opportunity for free imaginative treatment in a psychological close-up.... I tried to make the time and place real too, read practically all the Greek literature and modern works relating to the subject, vis-

ited the sites, made pilgrimages to the museums where the sculptures, or the better copies of them, are available for study. It did not interest me to write an argued discussion; it did interest me, immensely, to put into the sculptor's mouth the results of the discussions which took place inside my own mind regarding him.

A letter of October 17, 1929, to a Mr. Garfield in Cleveland, Ohio, stated that Howard had written the entire poem in nine months in Carmel during his sabbatical of 1917–18. "But it took a weary time to get it into print," he added. "The publishers are disheartened by the sales. I am not surprised, though I like to think the book has a public if it could only find it."

On their return from Europe in 1929, the Howards went to Bridgewater, Massachusetts, where they researched his ancestor John Howard. The New England Historical Genealogical Society informed Howard that his ancestor had been a carpenter-builder in Bridgewater. Although Howard had never been much interested in his genealogy, he enjoyed discovering the gray shingled barns, spreading buildings with Z courts, and many houses that his forebear had built. The buildings seemed to anticipate his own choice of a profession.

In 1930 John developed health problems that curtailed his physical activities. Among them were shingles, kidney problems, and angina pectoris, all of which were painful and required a great deal of rest. The doctors prescribed ten hours of rest in bed every night and one hour in the afternoons. Although leisurely strolling on level ground was permitted, there was to be no sudden exertion, no climbing stairs unnecessarily, and no weight gain. He was not to take either a very cold or very hot bath. The last prohibition was difficult for Howard, who, as a tense man, was accustomed to taking steam baths for relaxation.

Although the year passed without undue restrictions on cultural events, fate intervened on June 17, 1931, when, after attending a concert in San Francisco, Howard went for a steam bath and succumbed to a fatal heart attack.

Letters and telegrams of condolence poured in from all over the country and Europe. Mary bore her loss with characteristic strength and was gratified by the outpouring of praise and sadness over John's sudden death. William Wurster, who remembered with great pleasure attending the "teas" hosted by the Howards at their home, wrote Mary about the university's intention to place a bench in Howard's memory on the campanile esplanade. Instead, a plaque memorializing Howard's career was set in the pavement near the entrance to Sather Tower.

One of Howard's last writings, composed on June 9, 1930, for an American Institute of Architects convention, set down his philosophy of architecture, tying it to his avocation of poetry:

Architecture is a language, a means of expression.... Our native language, whether or not it be the best language that ever was, or could be, runs far back into the past, and we couldn't, if we desired, alienate it from its past. We speak English words, but what is the ancestry of those words? Many are Saxon, some are Grecian...yet it is the English language—a living tongue because it incorporates in itself the new means of expression characteristic of each successive age. Is that not what we are trying to do in architecture? We can't throw away the materials with which we build. We can't throw away the way in which we put things together. We can't throw away tradition in any thoroughgoing sense except as we substitute for it something that fits the new case better—something that is indefinable in advance since it is a thing of the future, a mystery we are seeking to give advanced form to. The important thing is the spirit in which the design is produced. The great design is certainly not going to be made in an archaeological frame of mind.... The great design, the creative design, is the product of an open mind, free from prejudice against either old or new.... Let us use tradition for what it has to offer us, that fits the case, without setting it up as superior merely because it is tradition. When traditional forms no longer fit...find new forms for the new problem.

Howard's graphic signature, which appears on many of his drawings and personal documents.

John Galen Howard's life offers us a window on the wide-open world of California and its state university in the period from the end of the nineteenth century to the Great Depression. His buildings, standing as solid evidence of his contribution to that world, remain the crowning jewels of the university campus. The buildings are mute, but when perceived in the light of Howard's words in his letters and published writings, they reveal the effect of that world on this at once reserved and passionate man.

Appendix
Buildings by John Galen Howard

University of California Buildings, 1903–24

Existing

 Hearst Greek Theater, 1902–3

 Hearst Memorial Mining Building, 1902–7

 Faculty Club additions, 1903–4

 California Hall, 1903–5

 Power House, 1904

 Architecture Building, or the "Ark" (present North Gate Hall),
  1906–12?

 Senior Men's Hall (Order of the Golden Bear Club), 1906

 Doe Memorial Library, 1907–11, 1914–17

 Sather Gate and Bridge, 1908–10

 Boalt Hall (present Durant Hall), 1908–11

 Agriculture Hall (present Wellman Hall), 1910–12

 South Hall Annex (originally a shop building for the Department
  of Physics; now the Center for Studies in Higher Education), 1913

 Drawing Building (present Naval Architecture building), 1913–14

 Sather Tower, or the Campanile, 1913–14

 Wheeler Hall, 1915–17

 Hilgard Hall, 1916–17

 Gilman Hall, 1917

 Military Science Building (present Dwinelle Annex), 1920

 California Memorial Stadium, 1922–23

 Stephens Hall, 1923

 Women's Faculty Club, 1923

 Le Conte Hall, 1923

 Haviland Hall, 1924

 Hesse Hall, 1924

Demolished

A number of buildings designed in the office of the supervising architect by Howard and his staff were subsequently razed for a variety of reasons. A list of these buildings is included because their number gives an indication of the volume of campus work Howard produced during his tenure and of the changes in the physical development of the campus.

Anthropology Building (1904), a corrugated iron structure that housed the Hearst collection; it was razed in 1953 to clear the site for Hertz Hall.

Printing office at 2 Barrow Lane (1917), a concrete building razed in 1964 to widen the Bancroft Way entrance at Telegraph Avenue.

California Field (1904), the university's first enclosed football field with bleachers, razed in 1925 to clear the site for the Hearst Gymnasium for Women and playing fields. A running track (1915) immediately west of California Field was removed after the completion of Edwards Field (1932).

Chemistry auditorium (1913), a concrete lecture hall addition to the 1891 chemistry building by Clinton Day, razed in 1959 to clear the site for Latimer Hall. Chemistry annex (1915), a wooden building razed in 1963 to clear the site for Hildebrand Hall.

Freshman chemistry laboratory (1915), a concrete structure razed in 1962 to clear the site for the physical sciences lecture hall.

Decorative art building and decorative art annex (1909), a wooden building and a corrugated iron structure south of faculty glade, both razed in 1964 to improve campus landscaping.

Hearst range greenhouses (1925), 22 structures that formed a research area for the College of Agriculture, razed 1959–62 to clear sites for Tolman Hall and the biochemistry building.

Home economics building (1917), a wooden building located north of the mechanics building, razed 1930 as a fire hazard.

Hygiene and pathology laboratory (1908), razed 1930 as a fire hazard.

Spreckels physiological laboratory (later Spreckels art building; 1903), a wooden building razed in 1955 to clear the site for Morrison Hall.

Veterinary science buildings (1924), wooden laboratories east of California Memorial Stadium, razed in 1959 to clear the site for the Strawberry Canyon recreational facilities.

Selected Buildings Not Designed for the University of California

* indicates that the building has been demolished.

Massachusetts

Majestic Theatre, Boston (designed for James M. Wood), 1901–2

New Jersey

Clark residence, Newark (condition unknown), ca. 1896

Newark High School (condition unknown), 1897–98

Howard residence, Upper Montclair (location and condition
    unknown), ca. 1898

Montclair Library (condition unknown), 1901

New York

*The Electric Tower, Pan-American Exposition, Buffalo, 1901

Long Island College Hospital (condition unknown)
    (Howard & Waid), 1903–4

A.D. Julliard residence (location and condition unknown), ca. 1896

*Essex Hotel, New York City (Howard, Cauldwell & Morgan),
    1896–98

Hotel Renaissance (Howard, Cauldwell & Morgan), 1897–98?
    4 West 43d Street, New York City

Freylinghusen and Gillespie residences, Tuxedo Park
    (locations and condition unknown), ca. 1899

California

Berkeley

*First National Bank building, ca. 1901
    southwest corner of Shattuck Avenue and Center Street

*McLaughlin residence, ca. 1902
    1629 Euclid Street

*John Galen Howard residence, 1902–3
    2421 Ridge Road
    (destroyed in the 1923 fire)

Adolph Miller residence (coop housing), 1902–3
    2420 Ridge Road
    (major alterations and additions; the western part of the building
    is the original residence that survived the 1923 fire)

Warren Gregory residence, 1903, 1908
    1459 Greenwood Terrace

Cloyne Court, 1904
    2600 Ridge Road

Claremont Court Entrance Gates, 1905
    Claremont Avenue and the Uplands

*Public Library
(site of the present main branch of the Berkeley
Public Library), ca. 1905
*Lucy Sprague residence, 1906
Ridge Road
(next to Howard residence; destroyed in the 1923 fire)
South Berkeley Bank, 1906
3290 Adeline Street
*John D. Galloway residence, 1908
1500 Euclid Avenue
*Berkeley National Bank, 1908
northeast corner Shattuck Avenue and Center Street
Duncan MacDuffie residence and outbuildings, 1910–11
Tunnel Road
Arlington Circle fountain
(part of the Northbrae tract designed for the Mason
MacDuffie real estate company), 1911; restored 1998
Rose Leroy (Howard residence), 1912
1401 Leroy Avenue
George B. Noyes residence, 1912
1486 Greenwood Terrace
Shepard residences, 1912
2422 and 2428 Hillside Avenue
Euclid Apartments, 1912
1865 Euclid Street
Stewart Edward White residence (location unknown), 1916
Charles and Mary Roeth residence, 1923
2548 Cedar Street

Oakland
Lake Merritt Boathouse, pumping station section, 1909
Emerson Elementary School, 1923
4803 Lawton Avenue
First Congregational Church, 1929
2501 Harrison Street

San Francisco
Levi Strauss building (Howard & Galloway), 1907
98 Battery Street
Italian American Bank building (Howard & Galloway), 1908
460 Montgomery Street

Adam Grant building (Howard & Galloway), 1908–10
    114 Sansome Street
San Francisco General Hospital (with Frederic Meyers
    and John Reid Jr.), 1909–15
    1001 Potrero Avenue
Fremont Empress Theater (Howard & Galloway), 1910
    949–961 Market Street
St. Francis Wood: planned by the Olmsted Brothers for the
    Mason MacDuffie Company with a central boulevard, a land-
    scaped median strip, and tree-lined streets separated by planting
    from sidewalks. The gates, terraces and two fountains were
    designed by Howard and Henry Gutterson and installed in
    1912–13. Howard also designed the north entrance to this
    prestigious housing tract.
Residence (with Mark White), 1912
    864 Francisco Street
Civic Center Auditorium (with Frederic Meyers and
    John Reid Jr.), 1913
    Grove Street between Larkin and Polk Streets
Pierce Arrow building, 1915
    1101 Polk Street

Colma
    Tevis memorial in the Cypress Lawn Cemetery, 1912

Washington
    University of Washington, Seattle: classroom building (original art
    museum for the Alaska-Yukon Exposition; Howard & Galloway,
    supervising architects), 1909

Notes

1   The process of admission to the École des Beaux-Arts might take
    several months or more. First, the candidate enrolled in an atelier
    associated with the school and after some preparatory study
    obtained a letter from the *patron*, or from another recognized artist,
    recommending that he take the entrance examination. The examina-
    tions were given semiannually, and those who took them were called
    "aspirants." The aspirants were allowed to prepare themselves by
    using the school library and attending lectures on such subjects as
    the theory and history of architecture, construction, and perspec-
    tive. The oral and written examinations included the subjects of
    mathematics, descriptive geometry, architectural history, drawing—
    usually of ornament from a cast—and architectural design. A more
    detailed account of the process may be found in Arthur Drexler, ed.,
    The Architecture of the Ecole des Beaux-Arts (New York: Museum of
    Modern Art, 1977); and Donald D. Egbert, *The Beaux-Arts Tradition in
    French Architecture: Illustrated by the Grands Prix de Rome,* ed. David
    Van Zanten (Princeton: Princeton University Press, 1980).

2   "Reminiscences of Janette Howard Wallace, daughter of John Galen
    Howard and Mary Robertson Bradbury Howard" (1987), 8.

3   Even in the 1880s, French students had complained that the école's
    facilities were being usurped by foreigners. See Egbert, *Beaux-Arts
    Tradition,* a revealing history of the evolution of the Beaux-Arts tra-
    dition in French architecture and its principles and methods. On
    page 68, the author cites an 1886 pamphlet of protest written by
    French students, "De l'envahissement de l'École des beaux-arts
    par les étrangers" (On the invasion of the École des Beaux-Arts
    by foreigners).

4   Enthusiasm for the école's training waned after the turn of the cen-
    tury. Irving Morrow, a student of Howard's in the School of Archi-
    tecture who had consulted him about the école, wrote him from
    Paris in the summer of 1908 that he had not chosen Laloux's atelier,
    as Howard had advised, and that he was disappointed in the school

and felt neglected. "It is decidedly the fashion in the school to neglect all practical considerations as deliberately as possible." Among his fellow students were many who said, "We are not here to do *architecture;* we are here to do the *school.* We shall have plenty of time to be practical when we get out." Morrow felt that a good building was one that served its purpose. Here, he said, "people pronounce plans beautiful without knowing anything of the programme." Having completed the first twelve-hour sketch problem, he remarked: "I was really quite gratified at the amount of irrelevant ornament I could think of in 12 hours." Morrow returned to the San Francisco Bay Area, where he practiced architecture and was well known for his critical writing about buildings. He was the architectural consultant for the Golden Gate Bridge and chose its famous color.

5   Reinstein's article on the architectural contest may be found in the *San Francisco Chronicle* of December 23, 1895. The statement was also published on page 2 of the January 1896 issue of the *California Architect and Building News.* His reference to Maybeck as "a freak" is in Richard Longstreth, *On the Edge of the World: Four Architects in San Francisco at the Turn of the Century* (Berkeley: University of California Press, 1998), 245.

6   Mrs. Hearst signed her letter "Phebe," which was also the spelling in an article by H. S. Allen, "The Hearst Architectural Competition," published in the *American Monthly Review of Reviews* in October 1899. The article includes a brief biography that gives her maiden name as "Phebe Elizabeth Appersin." Hearsay has it that it was President Benjamin Ide Wheeler, a classical philologist, who called Mrs. Hearst's attention to the spelling of her name and suggested that she might change it to conform to the Greek.

7   Trustees of the Phoebe Apperson Hearst Architectural Plan for the University of California, *The International Competition for the Phoebe A. Hearst Architectural Plan for the University of California* (San Francisco: H. S. Crocker Co., [ca. 1899]), 8–10.

8   For information on the Grand Prix de Rome, see Drexler, *Architecture of the Ecole des Beaux-Arts;* and Egbert, *Beaux-Arts Tradition.*

9   These quotations can be found in William Warren Ferrier, *Origin and Development of the University of California* (Berkeley: Sather Gate Bookshop, 1930), 477–78.

10 See Trustees of the Hearst Architectural Plan, *International Competition*, 24–25.

11 A detailed description of the university's financial affairs in the last decades of the nineteenth century is given in Ferrier, *Origin and Development of the University of California*, chap. 23: "The Quarter Century from 1875 to 1900," 382–90.

12 All comments by the jury in what follows are from Trustees of the Hearst Architectural Plan, *International Competition*, 28–36.

13 By all accounts, Worcester was a creative thinker. He had built two homes for himself that influenced young architects such as Bernard Maybeck, Willis Polk, and A. C. Schweinfurth. The second, a cottage on the crest of Russian Hill, was in an enclave of shingled, redwood houses that belonged to artists, writers, and their friends, who exemplified the city's counterculture. For a more detailed description of the area and its residents, as well as of the work of Maybeck, Polk, Schweinfurth, and Coxhead, among others, see Longstreth, *On the Edge of the World*.

14 Charles Keeler, "Friends Bearing Torches," exists in handwritten form and typed transcription in the Keeler Papers, Bancroft Library.

15 In a tribute to Wheeler written for the April 1908 issue of the *University Chronicle*, his friend of thirteen years, Henry Morse Stephens, recalled, "The first thing that struck me about Benjamin Ide Wheeler was the intensity of his Americanism.... Though primarily a philologist and a student of Greek, the thing that attracted his colleagues and his students was his...humanity." In 1907 Wheeler was offered the presidency of the Massachusetts Institute of Technology, causing the University of California consternation. On June 11, 1907, the board of regents adopted a body of resolutions concerning Wheeler and stated, "the regents realize that President Wheeler's work for the University has not been accomplished without criticism, but the regents hereby go on record as endorsing his work." The criticism referred to was not explained; the resolution simply noted insufficient knowledge of the facts.

16 According to hearsay, Ben Weed, a member of the class of 1894, had discovered the hollow in the hills and taken his classmates there for a class pageant. Thereafter the site was used informally for the "mystic rites" of fraternities and, according to President Wheeler, as a "temenos of Dionysos." See Ferrier, *Origin and Development of the University of California*, 485.

17   The early history of the campus may be found in Ferrier, *Origin and Development of the University of California;* and Loren W. Partridge, *John Galen Howard and the Berkeley Campus: Beaux-Arts Architecture in the "Athens of the West"* (Berkeley: Berkeley Architectural Heritage Association, 1978).

18   Of the twelve buildings constructed from 1873 to 1900, eight were designed by Clinton Day, a native son and graduate of the university. His father, Sherman Day, was a trustee of the College of California and the son of Jeremiah Day, a president of Yale. For a detailed history of the campus plans, see Partridge, *Howard and the Berkeley Campus.*

19   Howard's partnership with Waid lasted from 1901 to 1904 and was located at 156 5th Avenue in New York City. Waid functioned as the office's general manager; his responsibilities included the preparation of specifications, contracts, and drawings and the supervision of the work of the contractors for various projects. This business arrangement applied to the "California work" at hand, which entailed the execution of all preliminary sketches and drawings as well as working drawings for the mining building.

20   The facade of the Craftsman house that Howard designed for the Millers was incorporated into the much enlarged building at 2420 Ridge Road that is now a student housing cooperative. The major addition, designed by Ratcliff, Slama & Cadwalder, was built in the 1960s.

21   John Galen Howard, "California Hall," *University Chronicle* 8 (1905): 44–48.

22   Croly's effusive praise for Howard's work—influenced by Howard's words as well as by what he saw—was not untypical of the architectural journalism of the time. But his dismissal of Stanford University's architecture was based on opinions that were somewhat idiosyncratic. For although Leland Stanford had requested a design that would reflect early California, ultimately the Stanford buildings had more in common with the Romanesque revival style that Shepley, Rutan & Coolidge had inherited from H. H. Richardson than with the straitened classical mode of the California missions.

23   In 1948, when the applied mining courses were discontinued, the mining laboratory was remodeled almost beyond recognition and given over to administrative and other uses.

24   The rudimentary character of the mission buildings, constructed in the last decades of Spain's New World empire, was not a priority

of the monks in charge of the building program. The missions were frontier efforts; they lacked the wealth and skill that made many of the missions in Mexico opulent examples of ecclesiastical power. Another example on the UC campus of a building designed—according to its architect, Bernard Maybeck—with the California missions in mind is the original part of the faculty club, built in 1902. Yet even though the faculty club is more modest and plain than the mining building, its appearance does not readily recall the primitive buildings of California's colonial period.

25   Rafael Guastavino y Moreno first exhibited his vaulting system at the Centennial Exhibition held in Philadelphia in 1876. He and his son introduced their system to architects and engineers in the United States in 1881. In 1889 they established a company that subsequently provided domes and vaults for over a thousand buildings in the United States. The vaulting technique used thin bricks in laminated shell structures assembled with an extremely adhesive and fast drying mortar. The vaults' stability came from fusing bricks and mortar into a homogeneous material that could absorb both compression and tension. The multiple layers increased the area of mutually mortared joints. The thin, curved surfaces gained additional strength from the distribution of loads both to the sides of the vaults and downward, with minimal lateral thrust. The process was carried out without scaffolding by trained workers; it was less expensive, easier to install, and much lighter than most other vaulting systems. Rafael called his system Catalan or timbrel vaulting or cohesive construction; more recently it has been called "masonry plywood." An 1893 book by Guastavino Sr. titled *Cohesive Construction* became a handbook on the subject. When the company went out of business in 1962, the Guastavino system was largely forgotten. George R. Collins acquired the company records, now housed in Columbia's Avery Library, and wrote a seminal article for the October 1968 issue of the *Journal of the Society of Architectural Historians*.

26   On August 22, 1906—by which date the memorial vestibule design had been completed—Victor H. Henderson, secretary to the Board of Regents, wrote Howard that William Randolph Hearst had expressed regrets that the memorial vestibule was not finished in marble instead of brick. Two days later Howard answered Henderson's letter saying that it was "not too late to finish the Memorial Vestibule in marble throughout,—a proposition to which I would accede with enthusiasm" (Regents Records, Bancroft Library). However, Hearst did not respond to Howard's letter, and the matter was dropped.

27   The three drawings, one ink drawing on linen and two pencil drawings on tracing paper, are in the Guastavino Fireproof Construction Company/George Collins architectural records and drawings archive in the Architectural Drawings collection of the Avery Library at Columbia University. One of the pencil drawings has Howard's signature. The factory order card lists 10,000 unglazed corrugated tiles, which were shipped via the New Jersey Central Railroad around May 7, 1906. No records of the construction crew have been found.

28   Caches of unused tiles with "Guastavino" stamped on the back were found during the work for the seismic retrofitting of the mining building in 1999–2002. The Hearst Memorial Mining Building Seismic and Program Improvements Project was directed by UC Berkeley's Office of Capital Projects, Rob Gayle, project manager. NBBJ was the executive architect, with Brendan Kelly as project architect. Rutherford & Chekene was the structural engineer of record, with Doug Robertson as project engineer. Wm. Kreysler and Associates designed and constructed the reinforcement to the Guastavino tilework in the memorial vestibule, and Page & Turnbull acted as consulting architects for the preservation of the building's historic character.

Base isolation was the process used to retrofit the building. In this process the building's base is separated from the surrounding terrain so that in an earthquake the structure responds more slowly and therefore less violently than the ground around it. In the case of the mining building, an unreinforced masonry building, the entire foundation had to be replaced to make room for the isolation system below the first-floor level. The new foundation was typically 5.5 feet below the original foundation, and in some areas 20 feet. During the initial construction over 700 drilled piers were installed next to the old foundation. Temporary beams supported the existing structure while the old foundation was replaced with a new series of seismic isolators and concrete beams. Thus the building experienced minimal structural impact during the retrofit, and the new foundation enables it to move almost two feet in any horizontal direction during an earthquake. The seismic isolators resemble large spools about three feet in diameter and two feet tall; they are made of many layers of alternating rubber and steel sandwiched between thick metal plates on the top and bottom. Twenty-four viscous-fluid dampers akin to shock absorbers on large vehicles are incorporated into the isolation system to control the horizontal movement. On January 11, 2002, the process of transferring the building from the piers to the new foundation was completed.

As part of the restoration of the mining building much of the former laboratory's interior shell was restored to its original appearance. However, the original furnishings and equipment were replaced with state-of-the-art research equipment. The building's main tenant is the College of Engineering's Department of Materials Science and Engineering. The project was completed in 2002.

29   Loren W. Partridge, *John Galen Howard and the Berkeley Campus: Beaux-Arts Architecture and "The Athens of the West"* (Berkeley Architectural Heritage Association, 1978), 23.

30   The West Gate, located at the campus entrance across from Center Street and funded by the class of 1953, features a marble slab framed by ornamental grillwork with the inscription "University of California." Although the gate, installed in 2000, was not designed by Howard, its presence testifies to the endurance of his plans.

31   A transcript of this interview with William Gray Purcell, which took place December 23, 1950, was given to the author by architectural historian David Gebhard.

32   John Debbo Galloway was an outstanding structural engineer; his expertise contributed to the success of many of Howard's buildings, notably Doe Library.

33   A new power plant was constructed in 1931, and the old building was converted by W. P. Stephenson for use as the University Art Gallery. In 1968 a new building, designed by Mario J. Ciampi, was constructed on Bancroft Way across from the main campus to house the University Art Museum.

34   Even though Howard was on leave during the spring and summer of 1907, much of the work in progress in the supervising architect's office required his attention. Projects included contour maps and profiles of building sites for the general plan, grading, planting trees, and a plan of the north-south campus axis from Euclid Street to Dana Street and Telegraph Avenue. The grading and macadamizing of Hearst Avenue east of Euclid Street to the edge of the campus was under way. Ongoing work also included the stairs, skylights, and installation of lab equipment for the Hearst Memorial Mining Building and the inscription and carved marble chairs for the Greek Theater donated by William Randolph Hearst. These tasks dragged on until October. Off-campus work for the university included buildings for the School of Agriculture at the University Farm in Davisville (later named Davis), a plant pathology research laboratory at Whittier in southern California, and a vault building at the James Lick Observatory on Mount Hamilton east of San Jose.

35 The combined salary from Howard's two university positions of $10,000 equaled that of President Wheeler and was a cause of envy in the architectural community. However, Howard plowed much of his supervising architect's salary into his practice, which was not always profitable. For example, William C. Hays, in an oral history from 1969 (located in the Bancroft Library), noted some non-university commissions for residences that, exceeding their budgets, were canceled by the clients. According to Hays, Howard often "had his head in the clouds."

36 All comments attributed to Howard in 1903 in this chapter are from "Architectural Plans for the University."

37 Hubert Howe Bancroft (1832–1918) began his long career as a bibliophile in 1856 in San Francisco, where he opened a stationery and book store. Over time this enterprise expanded into a publishing business that he referred to as a "history factory." In 1905 Bancroft's library was sold to the University of California and moved to the campus in Berkeley, where it was eventually housed in its own building, designed by Arthur Brown Jr. and constructed in 1949. The collection, which focuses on Bancroft's own fields of interest, is an unmatched source of published and unpublished materials on the western part of North America, with emphasis on California, Mexico, and Central America. The University Archives are housed in the Bancroft Library as well.

38 The present configuration of the raised terrace and stairway opposite the main entrance is the result of new underground stacks constructed to meet seismic code requirements.

39 Hays related this anecdote in an interview for his oral history, "Order, Taste, and Grace in Architecture," in 1959. The manuscript is in the Bancroft Library.

40 Howard's comments on the library's design can be found in "The Doe Library." *Californian Journal of Technology* 10 (Nov. 1907): 8–10.

41 The San Francisco firm of Esherick Homsey Dodge & Davis was in charge of Doe Library's north addition and seismic improvements project. The first phase was completed in 1996; as of fall 2001, the final phase is still in progress.

42 In 1949 the library annex—now the Bancroft Library—was built on the site of North Hall. Since the Bancroft building rises to the same height as Doe Library, the commanding effect of the pyramidal

skylight capping the stacks can no longer be appreciated. Ironically, the original stacks have now been removed for seismic reasons, leaving a very high, rather ghostly cavity in their place.

43 The very next day Howard wrote Mary disavowing his loathing of the idea of work in California. He certainly wanted to work, but sometimes he couldn't help getting angry. His anger, he said, had caused him to write "a terrible letter."

44 Efforts to enlist the support of the national chapter had begun earlier in the year. In a letter dated March 7, 1913, from Howard to Walter Cook, president of the national chapter, Howard acknowledged Cook's telegram and letter of February 24, saying that "we are very much gratified that the Institute is going to take this whole matter up. I foresee that there will have to be a radical reconstruction [of the chapter]…and we need every bit of help from the Institute which it can give us; by 'we' in this connection, I mean all self-respecting professional architects." A letter from Howard to Cook dated March 15, 1913, addressed the issue of the chapter reorganization: "A precipitate and ill-considered reorganization is as much to be feared as no reorganization at all. Necessarily for the moment our new organization is outside of the Chapter though we still retain our membership in the Chapter. If the reorganization can be brought about within the present shell—well and good; if not we shall be in a position to ask for a new charter."

45 On May 8 Howard wrote Cook, "You will be interested to know that a strong and harmonious group of architects met last evening and organized as the San Francisco Society of Architects. We have got just the men we want for the first group. Those who were present last evening are: John Bakewell, Jr., John Baur, J.H. Blohme, Arthur Brown, Jr., E.A. Coxhead, John J. Donovan, Lewis P. Hobart, J.G. Howard F.A.I.A., George W. Kelham, F.H. Meyer, L.C. Mullgardt F.A.I.A., Albert Pissis F.A.I.A., Willis Polk, W.O. Raiguel, John Reid, Jr., Houghton Sawyer, Clarence R. Ward, C.P. Weeks." L.B. Dutton, W.C. Hays, and H.H. Meyers accepted the invitation to join but could not attend. "Our idea is to apply for a charter from the Institute at the earliest practical moment…. I am, of course, writing in a purely informal and personal manner."

46 On April 17, 1916, Howard noted that of the 480 copies of *Brunelleschi* printed, 90 had been sold, 183 sent to libraries and reviewers, 64 were on consignment, and 143 were still on hand.

47   Howard never wrote about the circumstances of his meeting Nei-
      hardt, the well-known author of *Black Elk Speaks.* Presumably, Howard
      began their correspondence by sending Neihardt a fan letter.

48   Harry R. Wellman was an agricultural economist whose long career
      in this field led to his appointment in 1952 as vice president of
      agricultural sciences and in 1958 as vice president of the university.
      He was named acting president in 1967 after the regents dismissed
      Clark Kerr.

49   South Hall, constructed in 1873, was originally intended for use
      by the agriculture department, as the sheaves of cereal and wheat
      on the cast stone panels that adorn the building's upper story attest.
      Because of intense demand for space by several other departments,
      however, the domain of agriculture remained confined to South
      Hall's basement until 1888, when the first agriculture building
      was built.

50   For a detailed description of the evolution of the design, see
      Partridge, *John Galen Howard and the Berkeley Campus,* 29–31.

51   A 1965 oral history with John Gregg, edited by Suzanne Riess
      and titled "Half a Century of Landscape Architecture," is in the
      Bancroft Library.

52   Robert, now twenty years old, had been a problem student, rarely
      earning passing grades in the Berkeley public schools he attended.
      Howard had arranged for Arthur Upham Pope, an English scholar
      living nearby, to tutor Robert. This arrangement worked well as far
      as whetting Robert's interest in the culture of far-off places such
      as Egypt, which he visited on seven different trips. But Robert's
      strength was in working with his hands in a variety of materials.
      From 1913 to 1916 he attended the School of the California Guild of
      Arts and Crafts in Berkeley (later absorbed into the California Col-
      lege of Arts and Crafts in Oakland), where he studied painting and
      drawing with such well-known California artists as Perham Nahl,
      Xavier Martinez, and Worth Ryder. Charles, who was three years
      younger than Robert, was more inclined toward the scholarly life.
      He graduated from the University of California in 1922 with a major
      in journalism and pursued graduate studies in English at Harvard
      and Columbia. During a trip to Europe he fell under the spell of a
      painting by Giorgione in the town of Castelfranco north of Venice
      and took up painting, ultimately becoming one of the noted painters
      in the avant-garde movements of the 1930s and 1940s. Henry
      received a diploma from the École des Beaux-Arts in Paris, where he
      studied from 1919 to 1921. His career in architecture began in his

father's office and in the office of Bakewell & Brown; later he moved to New York City, where he worked for several offices. For more biographical information on the second generation of Howards, see the catalogue for the exhibition *The Howards: First Family of Bay Area Modernism,* ed. Stacey Moss (Oakland: Oakland Museum, 1988).

53   A high-voltage wire that had fallen in the hills beyond Wildcat Canyon caused the fire, which burned in the grassland for some time unnoticed. The fire swept through several square miles in north Berkeley, destroying some 584 buildings and damaging 100 more.

54   From 1923 to 1927 the firm was John Galen Howard and Associates; the letterhead listed E. Geoffrey Bangs, Henry C. Collins, Henry Temple Howard, and Charles F.B. Roeth.

55   Polk moved out of the house in 1900, probably due to bankruptcy, which hit him in the late 1890s. Although he recovered and enjoyed renewed prominence during his association with Daniel Burnham from 1901 to around 1910, erratic behavior seems to have prevented him from continuing this success. Longstreth, *On the Edge of the World,* has the most complete account of Polk's work.

56   The eastern section of the drawing building was demolished in 1930 to make room for the engineering materials laboratory. The remaining section served as a technical training center for engineers and architects until 1950, when it became the first home of the recently founded Department of City and Regional Planning. Since 1964, when the planning department moved to Wurster Hall, the drawing building has housed the School of Naval Architecture.

57   Walter Steilberg (1886–1974) graduated from the University of California in 1910 and worked in the offices of Irving Gill, Myron Hunt, John Galen Howard, and Julia Morgan before opening his own office in 1921. In an interview with the author in 1972, Steilberg stated that Howard was a perfectionist and would destroy nearly finished drawings that did not meet his standards. Steilberg actually witnessed Howard's destruction of a drawing of the reading room elevation of Doe Library, which he thought another architect would probably have kept.

58   Over the years of their friendship Howard had purchased a number of Keith's paintings; most were sold during the course of their many moves.

Selected Bibliography

Archival Material

The John Galen Howard Correspondence and Papers, The Bancroft Library, University of California at Berkeley, is an archive of letters, diaries, graphic material, and fragments of manuscripts given to the Bancroft Library by the Howard family in August 1966. This is the principal collection of Howard's letters and those of his family, and the source of the quotations from their letters in this book.

The University Archives, the main source of materials relating to the history of the University of California, are also housed in The Bancroft Library. Quotations in this book from Phoebe Apperson Hearst, President Benjamin Ide Wheeler, Regent Jacob B. Reinstein, and other university representatives are from the Correspondence and Papers of Phoebe Apperson Hearst (72/204c), Records of the Office of the President (CU-5, Series 1), and the Regents Records (CU-1).

The Environmental Design Archives, College of Environmental Design, University of California at Berkeley, houses the John Galen Howard Collection, with records, drawings, and photographs relating to Howard's architectural career. The collection includes examples of Howard's student work at the École des Beaux-Arts, personal and professional papers, office records consisting of scrapbooks and clipbooks, Phoebe A. Hearst Architectural Plan competition drawings, and files and drawings for many campus buildings.

Books and Related Manuscripts

Cardwell, Kenneth H. *Bernard Maybeck: Artisan, Architect, Artist.* Salt Lake City: Gibbs M. Smith, [1977] 1983.

Draper, Joan. "John Galen Howard." Chapter 3 in *Toward a Simpler Way of Life: The Arts and Crafts Architects of California,* ed. Robert Winter. Berkeley: University of California Press, 1997.

———. "John Galen Howard and the Beaux-Arts Movement in the United States." Master's thesis, University of California, Berkeley, 1972.

———. "The Ecole des Beaux-Arts and the Architectural Profession in the United States: The Case of John Galen Howard." In *The Architect: Chapters in the History of the Profession,* ed. Spiro Kostof. New ed., with foreword by Dana Cuff. Berkeley: University of California Press, 2000.

Drexler, Arthur, ed. *The Architecture of the Ecole des Beaux-Arts.* New York: Museum of Modern Art, 1977.

Egbert, Donald Drew. *The Beaux-Arts Tradition in French Architecture: Illustrated by the Grands Prix de Rome.* Ed. David Van Zanten. Princeton: Princeton University Press, 1980.

Ferrier, William Warren. *Origin and Development of the University of California.* Berkeley: Sather Gate Bookshop, 1930. (The quotations on pages 29–30, 61, and 108 above are from pages 477–78, 484, and 489, respectively.)

Freudenheim, Leslie Mandelson, and Elisabeth Sussman. *Building with Nature: Roots of the San Francisco Bay Region Tradition.* Santa Barbara: Peregrine Smith, 1974.

Howard, John Galen. *Pheidias,* New York: Macmillan, 1929.

Keeler, Charles. *The Simple Home.* 1904; Santa Barbara: Peregrine Smith, 1979.

Longstreth, Richard. *On the Edge of the World: Four Architects in San Francisco at the Turn of the Century.* 2d ed. Berkeley: University of California Press, 1998.

Moss, Stacey. *The Howards: First Family of Bay Area Modernism* (catalogue). Oakland: Oakland Museum, 1988.

Partridge, Loren W. *John Galen Howard and the Berkeley Campus: Beaux-Arts Architecture in the "Athens of the West."* Berkeley: Berkeley Architectural Heritage Association, 1978.

Scott, Mel. *The San Francisco Bay Area: A Metropolis in Perspective.* Berkeley and Los Angeles: University of California Press, 1959.

Stadtman, Verne A., ed. *The Centennial Record of the University of California, 1868–1968.* Berkeley: University of California Printing Department, 1967.

Trustees of the Phoebe Apperson Hearst Architectural Plan for the University of California. *The International Competition for the Phoebe A. Hearst Architectural Plan for the University of California.* San Francisco: H. S. Crocker Co., [ca. 1899].

Woodbridge, Sally B., ed. *Bay Area Houses.* 2d ed. Salt Lake City: Peregrine Smith, 1988.

——. *Bernard Maybeck, Visionary Architect.* New York: Abbeville Press, 1992.

Periodicals

Allen, H. C. "Appreciation." *California Arts and Architecture* 40 (Aug. 1931): 13.

Bach, Richard F. "Hilgard Hall, University of California, John Galen Howard, Architect." *Architectural Record* 46 (July/Dec. 1919): 203–10.

Cahill, B. J. S. "A Description of the First Prize Plans Drawn by Mons. E. Bénard of Paris." *California Architect and Building News* 20 (Sept. 1898): 99–106.

——. "A Description of the Second Prize Plans Drawn by Messrs. Howells, Stoke and Hornbostel of New York." *California Architect and Building News* 20 (Nov. 1898): 122–27.

——. "A Description of the Third and Fourth Prize Plans Drawn by Messrs. Despradelles and Codman of Boston, and Messrs. Howard and Cauldwell of New York." *California Architect and Building News* 20 (Dec. 1898): 136–38.

Collins, George R. "The Transfer of Thin Masonry Vaulting from Spain to America." *Journal of the Society of Architectural Historians* 27 (Oct. 1968): 176–201.

Croly, Herbert. "The New University of California." *Architectural Record* 23 (April 4, 1908): 271–93.

Hays, William Charles. "The Home of a California Architect, J. Galen Howard, Esq." *Indoors and Out* 3 (Feb. 1907): 217–21.

———. "Some Architectural Works of John Galen Howard." *Architect and Engineer* 40 (Jan. 1915): 46–82.

Howard, John Galen. "The Paris Training." *Architectural Review* 5 (1898): 4–7.

———. "The Spirit of Design at the Ecole des Beaux-Arts." *Architectural Review* 5 (1898): 25–27.

———. "The Hearst Memorial Mining Building for the College of Mining." *University of California Magazine* 8 (Oct. 1902): 285–91.

———. "The Architectural Plans for the Greater University of California." *University Chronicle* 5 (1903): 273–291.

———. "The Greek Theater Architecturally Considered." *Daily Californian*, Sept. 25, 1903.

———. "California Hall." *University Chronicle* 8 (1905): 44–48.

———. "The Doe Library." *California Journal of Technology* 10 (Nov. 1907): 8–10.

———. "The Library." *University Chronicle* 14 (1912): 332–340.

———. "The Campanile." *California Journal of Technology* 17 (Nov. 1913): 51–56.

———. "The Outlook and Inlook Architecturally." *Architectural Record* 34 (Dec. 1913): 531–43.

———. "Country House Architecture on the Pacific Coast." *Architectural Record* 40 (Oct. 1916): 323–55.

———. "Benjamin Ide Wheeler Hall." *Blue and Gold* 45 (1917): 12.

———. "Completion of the University Library." *Blue and Gold* 45 (1917): 13.

———. "The New Wing of the Agricultural Building." *Blue and Gold* 45 (1917): 13–14.

———. "The Chemistry Building." *Blue and Gold* 45 (1917): 14–15.

———. "Ensemble View." *Blue and Gold* 45 (1917): 15.

———. "The School of Architecture." *Blue and Gold* 55 (1927): 24.

———. "The Future of Architecture on the Pacific Coast." *Pacific Coast Architect* 31 (Feb. 1927): 9–10, 23.

Howard, John Galen, S.B. Christy, Thomas S. Rickard, and William Randolph Hearst. "Dedication of the Hearst Memorial Mining Building." *University Chronicle* 9 (1907): 3–10.

Kelham, George W. "The University of California." *Architect* 14 (Aug. 1917): 81–120, 133.

"Laying the Corner-Stone of the Hearst Memorial Mining Building." *University Chronicle* 5 (1903): 292–300.

London, Jack. "Simple Impressive Rite at Corner-Stone Emplacement of Hearst Memorial Mining Building." *San Francisco Examiner*, Nov. 19, 1902.

Maybeck, Bernard. "The Planning of a University." *Blue and Gold* 7 (1900): 17–20.

"Model of the New University." *University Chronicle* 7 (1904–5): 233–35.

Morrow, Irving F. "Recent Work at the University of California." *Architect and Engineer of California* 50 (July 1917): 39–49.

"Obituary [of John Galen Howard]." *Architectural Record* 70 (Oct. 1931): 278.

O'Toole, M.C. "Dedication of the Hearst Memorial Mining Building." *California Journal of Technology* 10 (Sept. 1907): 23–26.

Perry, Warren Charles. "John Galen Howard: Architect, Teacher and Poet." *Architect and Engineer* 106 (Aug. 1931): 60.

——. "Arkana." *California Engineer* 1, no. 4 (April 1923).

"The Phebe Hearst Architectural Plan." *University Chronicle* 1 (1898): 61–65.

Polk, Willis. "The University Competition." *Wave*, Nov. 7, 1896, 3.

——. "The University Competition." *Wave*, Jan. 29, 1898, 2–3.

Robertson, Doug. "Seismic Considerations for Guastavino Ceiling, Vault, and Dome Construction." *APT Bulletin* 30, no. 4 (1999): 51–58.

"Some Interesting Facts about the Campanile." *California Journal of Technology* 17 (Feb. 1914): 132.

Wheeler, Benjamin Ide. "Outlook of the University." *Sunset* 9 (Oct. 1902): 359–64.

Willey, the Rev. S.H. "The Selection of the Site of the University and Its Name." *University Chronicle* 4 (1901).

Oral Histories, Interviews, and Unpublished Manuscripts

A.I.A. "Proceedings of the San Francisco Chapter of the American Institute of Architects in the Matter of the Trial of John Galen Howard, Frederick H. Meyer, and John Reid, Jr." San Francisco, 1913.

Bangs, E. Geoffrey. Interview by Sally B. Woodbridge, May 1972.

Hays, William Charles. "Order, Taste, and Grace in Architecture." Regional Oral History Office, Bancroft Library, University of California, Berkeley, 1969. (Interviews completed in 1959.)

Howard, Robert, Janette Howard Wallace, and members of the Gregory family. Interviews during the mid-1980s by Sally B. Woodbridge.

Laurie, Michael, with David C. Streatfield. "Seventy-five Years of Landscape Architecture at Berkeley: An Informal History." Part 1: "The First 50 Years." Berkeley, 1988. Environmental Design Library, Wurster Hall, UC Berkeley.

Perry, Warren. Interview by Sally B. Woodbridge, April 5, 1972.

Wallace, Janette Howard. "Reminiscences of Janette Howard Wallace, daughter of John Galen Howard and Mary Robertson Bradbury Howard." Santa Cruz, "The Farm," 1987. Bancroft Library, UC Berkeley.

Illustration Credits

Plates (following page 120)

Plate number

1   Howard's proposal for the Phoebe Apperson Hearst Plan, 1917.
    John Galen Howard Collection (1955-4), Environmental Design Archives,
    University of California, Berkeley.

2   South facade of Boalt Hall, now called Durant Hall.
    Photo © 2002 by Chuck Byrne.

3   North elevation of California Hall.
    Photo © 2002 by Chuck Byrne.

4   South facade of Hearst Memorial Mining Building.
    Photo © Rob Super; author's collection.

5   South facade of Hearst Memorial Mining Building, detail.
    Photo © 2002 by Chuck Byrne.

6   View of Hearst Memorial Mining Building from the southeast.
    Photo © 2002 by Harvey Helfand.

7   Main entrance doors to Doe Memorial Library, detail.
    Photo © 2002 by Chuck Byrne.

8   Main facade of Doe Memorial Library from the northeast.
    Photo © 2002 by Harvey Helfand.

9   West end of the reading room block.
    Photo © 2002 by Chuck Byrne.

10 West elevation of reading room block, detail.
    Photo © 2002 by Chuck Byrne.

11 View of Agriculture Hall, now called Wellman Hall, from the southwest.
    Photo © 2002 by Chuck Byrne.

12 View of Sather Tower from the west.
    Photo © 2002 by Chuck Byrne.

13 West facade of Hilgard Hall, detail.
    Photo © 2002 by Chuck Byrne.

14 View of Hilgard Hall from the southwest.
    Photo © 2002 by Chuck Byrne.

15 Main entrance of Hilgard Hall, detail.
    Photo © 2002 by Chuck Byrne.

16 South facade of Wheeler Hall, detail.
    Photo © 2002 by Chuck Byrne.

17 View of Wheeler Hall from the southwest.
    Photo © 2002 by Chuck Byrne.

18 End bays of Wheeler Hall, detail.
    Photo © 2002 by Chuck Byrne.

Figures

Page number

5   California houses drawn by Howard in 1888.
American Architect and Building News, March 16, 1889.

6   Howard's pen-and-ink sketch of Santa Barbara Mission, summer 1888.
American Architect and Building News, March 16, 1889.

9   Drawing of All Saints' Episcopal Church in Pasadena.
American Architect, March 30, 1889.

12   John Galen Howard at age 26.
Portrait Collection, The Bancroft Library.

18   Mary Robertson Bradbury in 1886 with family and friends.
Robert B. Howard Photographic Collection.

20   Rendering of Hotel Renaissance, New York City.
Architect and Engineer 130 (June 1937): 42.

23   View of University of California campus from the east, ca. 1890.
University Archives, The Bancroft Library.

24   View of central campus from the north, ca. 1885.
University Archives, The Bancroft Library.

27   Portrait of Phoebe Apperson Hearst.
Trustees of the Phoebe Apperson Hearst Architectural Plan for the University of
California, *The International Competition for the Phoebe A. Hearst Architectural Plan for
the University of California* (San Francisco: H. S. Crocker Co., [ca. 1899]).

32   Émile Bénard's first-prize entry and Howard and Cauldwell's fourth-prize
entry in the 1899 competition.
Trustees of the Phoebe Apperson Hearst Architectural Plan for the University of
California, *The International Competition for the Phoebe A. Hearst Architectural Plan for
the University of California* (San Francisco: H. S. Crocker Co., [ca. 1899]).

35   Rendering of auditorium building from Howard and Cauldwell's submission
to the 1899 competition.
Trustees of the Phoebe Apperson Hearst Architectural Plan for the University of
California, *The International Competition for the Phoebe A. Hearst Architectural Plan for
the University of California* (San Francisco: H. S. Crocker Co., [ca. 1899]).

36   Émile Bénard's rendering of a longitudinal section of the gymnasium.
John Galen Howard Collection (1955-4), Environmental Design Archives, University
of California, Berkeley.

38   View of the exhibition of the international competition entries, San Francisco, 1899.
Trustees of the Phoebe Apperson Hearst Architectural Plan for the University of
California, *The International Competition for the Phoebe A. Hearst Architectural Plan for
the University of California* (San Francisco: H. S. Crocker Co., [ca. 1899]).

41   Plan of Bénard's winning scheme.
Trustees of the Phoebe Apperson Hearst Architectural Plan for the University of
California, *The International Competition for the Phoebe A. Hearst Architectural Plan for
the University of California* (San Francisco: H. S. Crocker Co., [ca. 1899]).

44   Bénard's revised plan, 1900.
University Archives, The Bancroft Library.

49   President Benjamin Ide Wheeler on horseback, ca. 1917.
University Archives, The Bancroft Library.

51   Floor plans and elevations for Howard and Cauldwell's second-prize entry in
the 1896 competition for the New York Public Library.
Architect and Engineer 113 (May 1933) and 130 (May 1937).

53   Howard's design for Electric Tower, 1901 Pan-American Exposition, Buffalo, New York.
American Architect and Building News 72 (June 1901): plate 1327.

58 Map of campus, 1897.
   John Galen Howard Collection (1955-4), Environmental Design Archives, University
   of California, Berkeley.

60 Bird's-eye view drawing of proposed design for Greek Theater, ca. 1901–2.
   University Archives, The Bancroft Library.

61 Photograph of Greek Theater, 1960s.
   University Archives, The Bancroft Library.

65 West elevation of South Hall, ca. 1880.
   University Archives, The Bancroft Library.

69 Howard and Gregory families on a Thanksgiving Day picnic, Berkeley Hills, 1902.
   Robert B. Howard Photographic Collection.

70 Photograph and first-floor plan of Howard family's home at 2421 Ridge Road, Berkeley.
   Indoors and Out, March 1907.

71 Photographs of the terrace and garden path at 2421 Ridge Road, Berkeley.
   Indoors and Out, March 1907.

72 Two views of the main living room at 2421 Ridge Road, Berkeley.
   Indoors and Out, March 1907.

75 President's house, ca. 1915.
   University Archives, The Bancroft Library.

76 First- and second-floor plans of California Hall.
   Capital Projects, © The Regents of the University of California.

76 Aerial view of California Hall, 1945.
   University Archives, The Bancroft Library.

79 Howard's proposed design for buildings flanking the Golden Gate
   axis of campus, ca. 1911.
   University Archives, The Bancroft Library.

81 Formal presentation of Hearst Memorial Mining Building, drawn in 1901–2,
   and two photographs of the building, taken ca. 1914.
   University Archives, The Bancroft Library.

82 Second- and third-floor plans of Hearst Memorial Mining Building.
   Capital Projects, © The Regents of the University of California.

82 View of Hearst Memorial Mining Building from the southeast.
   Author's collection; photographer unknown.

83 Longitudinal section of the mining building.
   Capital Projects, © The Regents of the University of California.

86 Partial view of memorial vestibule interior, 1970s.
   Photo by author.

87 Memorial vestibule under construction, 1905.
   University Archives, The Bancroft Library.

91 Architecture Building photographed from the west, ca. 1910.
   John Galen Howard Collection (1955-4), Environmental Design Archives, University
   of California, Berkeley.

93 Architecture Building photographed from the northwest, with
   recently completed 1908 addition.
   John Galen Howard Collection (1955-4), Environmental Design Archives, University
   of California, Berkeley.

95 Senior Men's Hall, from Students' Co-operative Society, University of California
   (Berkeley: Students' Co-operative Society, [1907]).

96 Plan for 1909 Alaska-Yukon-Pacific Exposition.
   Architect and Engineer 130 (July 1937): 24.

99 Rendering of north elevation of Doe Memorial Library, ca. 1907.
   University Archives, The Bancroft Library.

101   Floor plans for the first, second, and fourth floors of Doe Memorial Library.
        Capital Projects, © The Regents of the University of California.

101   Photograph of Doe Memorial Library from the northeast, ca. 1917.
        University Archives, The Bancroft Library.

102   Rendering of west elevation of Doe Memorial Library, ca. 1917.
        University Archives, The Bancroft Library.

103   Photograph of Doe Memorial Library reading room interior, 1978.
        Author's collection; photographer unknown.

104   Rendering of Doe Memorial Library from the northwest, ca. 1917.
        University Archives, The Bancroft Library.

105   Proposed museum of art, natural history, and ethnology.
        University Archives, The Bancroft Library.

107   First-floor plan of Boalt Hall.
        Capital Projects, © The Regents of the University of California.

107   Boalt Hall in 1912.
        University Archives, The Bancroft Library.

108   Section drawing of Boalt Hall.
        Capital Projects, © The Regents of the University of California.

109   Photograph of Boalt Hall reading room.
        University Archives, The Bancroft Library.

111   Howard's study for Sather Gate, 1908, and photograph, ca. 1914.
        University Archives, The Bancroft Library.

113   Photograph of John Galen Howard, ca. 1910.
        Portrait Collection, The Bancroft Library.

116   Phoebe Apperson Hearst Plan for the University of California, January 1914.
        University Archives, The Bancroft Library.

122   Proposed plan for San Francisco Civic Center, 1913, and bird's-eye view
        of the complex of civic buildings.
        Architect and Engineer of California, January 1915.

126   Rendering of San Francisco Civic Auditorium, 1915.
        Author's collection.

130   Rose Leroy, the Howard family's second Berkeley home,
        viewed from the northwest, 1970.
        Author's collection.

131   First- and second-floor plans Rose Leroy.
        Author's collection.

131   The Howards' living room.
        Robert B. Howard Photographic Collection.

132   Photograph of Mary Howard and her daughter Janette, 1913.
        Robert B. Howard Photographic Collection.

135   Rendering of College of Agriculture buildings, 1914.
        John Galen Howard Collection (1955-4), Environmental Design Archives, University
        of California, Berkeley.

136   First- and second-floor plans of Agriculture Hall.
        Capital Projects, © The Regents of the University of California.

136   South facade of Agriculture Hall.
        University Archives, The Bancroft Library.

137   North elevation of Agriculture Hall, ca. 1915.
        University Archives, The Bancroft Library.

138   Howard's proposed landscaping for the agriculture complex, ca. 1912.
        University Archives, The Bancroft Library.

140   Presentation rendering of Sather Tower by Stafford Jory.
       John Galen Howard Collection (1955-4), Environmental Design Archives, University
       of California, Berkeley.

141   Rendering of design for Sather Tower Esplanade by Stafford Jory.
       University Archives, The Bancroft Library.

142   Howard's study for Sather Tower, 1911; postcard of Sather Tower, 1917;
       drawing of Campanile Way, 1914; drawing of Sather Tower with oval
       at east end of central esplanade, 1914.
       University Archives, The Bancroft Library.

144   View of walk through botanical garden, 1917.
       University Archives, The Bancroft Library.

145   View of Hilgard Hall from the west, 1917, and detail of balcony
       above doorway on courtyard elevation.
       University Archives, The Bancroft Library.

147   First- and third-floor plans of Wheeler Hall.
       Capital Projects, © The Regents of the University of California.

147   Wheeler Hall from the southwest, ca. 1919.
       University Archives, The Bancroft Library.

148   Rendering of Wheeler Hall, n.d.
       John Galen Howard Collection (1955-4), Environmental Design Archives, University
       of California, Berkeley.

150   View of Hilgard Hall from the northeast.
       University Archives, The Bancroft Library.

151   First-floor plan of Gilman Hall.
       Capital Projects, © The Regents of the University of California.

155   Rendering of Howard's design for the California Memorial Stadium, 1921.
       University Archives, The Bancroft Library.

159   Two studies by Howard for Stephens Memorial Hall, ca. 1919.
       University Archives, The Bancroft Library.

160   Main floor plan for Stephens Memorial Hall and rendering of final design.
       University Archives, The Bancroft Library.

162   Howard's drawing of Le Conte Hall, ca. 1920.
       University Archives, The Bancroft Library.

163   First-, second-, and third-floor plans of Haviland Hall.
       Capital Projects, © The Regents of the University of California.

163   Howard's sketch of proposed North Hall, 1921.
       University Archives, The Bancroft Library.

166   John Galen Howard, ca. 1923.
       Portrait Collection, The Bancroft Library.

167   John and Mary Howard on a vacation.
       Robert B. Howard Photographic Collection.

169   Members of the architectural fraternity, Tau Sigma Delta, 1920.
       John Galen Howard Collection (1955-4), Environmental Design Archives, University
       of California, Berkeley.

170   Architecture students moving their float made for the Ark Jinks down Hearst Avenue.
       John Galen Howard Collection (1955-4), Environmental Design Archives, University
       of California, Berkeley.

171   Architecture Building photographed from the southeast, with 1912 addition.
       University Archives, The Bancroft Library.

173   Rooftop plan of Architecture Building as it was in 1912.
       Drawing by Chuck Byrne.

175   Howard's graphic signature.
       University Archives, The Bancroft Library.

Index

Italic page numbers refer to illustrations and their captions.

Adobe houses, *4, 5, 6*
Agricultural, Mining, and Mechanic Arts College, in Berkeley, 25, 27
Agriculture Hall (Berkeley campus), *116,* 134, *136–38, 137,* 139, 143, 146, *plate 11*
Aitken, Robert, 85
Alaska-Yukon-Pacific Exposition, in Seattle, 26, 95–96, *96,* 112, 118
All Saints' Episcopal Church, in Pasadena, 8, *9*
American Institute of Architects (AIA), 52, 97, 115, 120, 191n44;
    San Francisco chapter of, 123–28
Angels Flight, in Los Angeles, 4
Antwerp, 29, 30
Architectural League of New York, 14
Arch Street, in Berkeley, 68
Ark, the (architecture department building, Berkeley campus), *91, 93,*
    93–95, 165, 168, 170–72, *171, 173*
Arts and Crafts movement, 8, 69
Art Students League, in New York, 13, 17, 152
Associated Students of the University of California, 161
Association for the Improvement and Adornment of San Francisco, 117
"Athens of the West," 26, 50, 78, 102, 105
Atterbury, Grosvenor, 120
Axis, of Berkeley campus architectural plan, *41,* 48, 55–56, *57,* 62, 64–66,
    79, 89–90, 98–99, 150, 162

Bacon Hall (Berkeley campus), 24, 62, 89, 98
Bakewell, John, 191n45
Bakewell & Brown architectural firm, 112, 123, 125, 193n52
Bancroft, Hubert Howe, 99, 190n37
Bancroft Library (Berkeley campus), 99, 106, 190n37, 190–91n42
Bancroft Way, in Berkeley, 109, 110, 189n33
Bangs, E. Geoffrey, 172, 193n54
Baroque style, 12
Barrows, David P., 154, 158
Baur, John, 191n45
Beaux-Arts Institute of Design, 172
Belcher, John, 34
Bénard, Émile: and designs for Hearst Architectural Plan, 33, 34, 36, 39–40, *41,* 42–43, *44,*
    45, 47–48, 52, 55–56, 63, 65, 66, 98; and disagreements with plan's sponsors, 39–40,
    42–43, 45–48, 52, 54–56; JGH's revision of designs by, 47–48, 57, 59, 63–67, 78, 79,
    89, 98, *116;* and relations with JGH, 54–56
Bennett, Edward, 121
Bergstrom, Edwin, 167
Berkeley, city of, 22, 25, 30–31, 62, 92–93; fire of 1923 in, 165–66, 193n53; residential architec-
    ture in, 69, *70–72, 71–73, 75,* 186n20. *See also* University of California at Berkeley
Berkeley, George, 25
Bibliothèque Nationale, in Paris, 20, 86
Bibliothèque Sainte Geneviève, in Paris, 25
Billings, Frederick, 23, 25

Blohme, J. H., 191n45
Boalt, Elizabeth, 106
Boalt Hall (Berkeley campus), 79, 106, *106–9*, 108–9, *116*, 143, 149, *plate 2*
Boese, Henry A., 92
Bohemian Club, 30, 46, 73
Bolton, A. L., 143
Boston, 1, 2, 12, 21, 63; public library in, 17, 25, 86
Botanical garden (Berkeley campus), 98, 100, *100–101*, 139, 141, *144*
Bouguereau, William Adolphe, 11
Boyle Heights, in Los Angeles, 4, 8
Bradbury, Mary Robertson. *See* Howard, Mary
Bradbury Building, in Los Angeles, 4
Brown, A. Page, 37
Brown, Arthur, 190n37, 191n45
Brunelleschi (poem by JGH), 119–20, 173–74, 191n46
Budd, James H., 27
Budd Hall (Berkeley campus), 134
Buffalo Electric Tower, 52, *53*
Bunker Hill, in Los Angeles, 4, 7, 8
Burnham, Daniel, 117, 118, 119, 121, 193n55
Bushnell, Horace, 22
Butler, Nicholas Murray, 120

Cahill, B. J. S., 30
California College of Arts and Crafts, 192n52
California Hall (Berkeley campus), 63, 74, *76*, 77, 78, 79, 89, 99, 100, *104*, *106*, 108, 110, *116*, 143, *plate 3*
California Institute of Design, 168
California Memorial Stadium (Berkeley campus), *155*, 155–56
Campanile. *See* Sather Tower
Campanile Way (Berkeley campus), 138, 141, *142*, 150
Campbell, William Wallace, 158
Carmel, 73, 152, 174
Carr, Jeanne C., 4
Carrère, John, 50
Carrère & Hastings architectural firm, 21, 30, 50, *51*
Caukin & Haas architectural firm, 6–7
Cauldwell, Samuel M., 21, 35, *51*
Centennial Exhibition, in Philadelphia, 187n25
Center Street, in Berkeley, 66, 89, 90, 189n30
Cézanne, Paul, 153
"Cezaronet" (poem by JGH), 153, 167
Champney, Edward Frere, 95
Christy, Samuel B., 54, 80
Ciampi, Mario J., 189n33
Civic Center, in San Francisco, 120, 121, 122, 123–28, *126*
Classic style. *See* Neoclassic style
Cliff House, in San Francisco, 30
Cloyne Court, in Berkeley, 73
Codman, Stephen, 35
College Avenue, in Berkeley, 66, 89
College Homestead Association district, in Berkeley, 62
College of California, 23, 25, 62
Collins, Henry C., 193n54
Columbian Exposition, in Chicago, 26, 38
Columbia University, 9, 29, 35, 120
Committee for Reconstruction (Committee of Forty), in San Francisco, 117
Competition for Hearst Architectural Plan. *See* Hearst Architectural Plan, competition for
Congregational Association of California, 23
Contra Costa College, 23
Cook, Walter, 29, 34, 190–91nn44–45
Coolidge, Charles, 3
Coxhead, Ernest, 1, 2, 8, 9, 31, 46, 73, 191n45
Coxhead & Coxhead architectural firm, 30

Cram, Ralph Adams, 19–20
Croly, Herbert, 77–79, 84, 85, 88, 155, 186n22
Cummings, Melvin Earl, *61, 110,* 170, *plate 7*

Daley's Scenic Park, in Berkeley, 69
Day, Clinton, 134, 186n18
Day, Jeremiah, 186n18
Day, Sherman, 186n18
Delano & Aldrich architectural firm, 112
Denneville, Paul E., 146
Derleth, Charles, *143*
Despradelle, Constant Désiré, 35, 43
Doe, Charles Franklin, 99
Doe Memorial Library (Berkeley campus), 76–77, 97, 98–100, *99, 101–4,* 102–6, 110,
        116, 142–43, 149, 150, 189n32, 190nn41–42, *plates 7–10*
Donovan, John J., 191n45
Duban, Félix, 20
Durant, Henry, 23, 25
Durant Avenue, in Berkeley, 173
Durant Hall (Berkeley campus). *See* Boalt Hall
Dutton, L. B., 191n45
Dwinelle, John W., 23

Earthquake: of 1906, 92–93, 112, 117. *See also* Seismic retrofitting
East Hall (Berkeley campus), 62
École des Beaux-Arts, in Paris, 13, 14–20, 183nn1,3, 183–84n4, 192n52; American architects
        influenced by, 14, 19, 20, 29, 31, 34, 36–37, 43, 127, 128, 143, 170, 171, 172;
        JGH's education at, 14–19
Elmslie, George Grant, 90
Essex Hotel, in New York City, 21
Euclid Avenue, in Berkeley, 69, 73, 130, *170*
Exposition des Arts Decoratifs, in Paris, 172

Faculty Club. *See* Men's Faculty Club; Women's Faculty Club
Farquharson, David, 62
Farquharson & Kenitzer architectural firm, 62
Faville, William B., 121, 123
Ferry Building, in San Francisco, 37, 38, *38*
Fire: and earthquake of 1906, in San Francisco, 92, 112, 117; of 1923, in Berkeley, 165–66, 192n53
Founders' Rock, 23, 25

Galloway, John Debbo, 94, 95, 96, 112, 189n32
Gayle, Rob, 188n28
Gayley, Charles Mills, 100, 156
Geary, John B., 23
Giannini Hall (Berkeley campus), 137, 146
Gilbert, Cass, 112, 133
Gill, Irving, 118, 119, 193n57
Gilman, Daniel Coit, 150–51
Gilman Hall (Berkeley campus), 150–51, *151,* 152, 162
Ginain, Paul-René-Leon, 15
Golden Gate Bridge, 184n4
Goldman, Emma, 155
Goodhue, Bertram Grosvenor, 119
Grand Prix de Rome, 29, 34, 45
Greek architecture, 59, 102–3, 105, 106, 109, 146, *171*
Greek Theater (Berkeley campus). *See* Hearst Greek Theater
Green, Charles Sumner, 73
Greenwood Terrace, in Berkeley, 165
Gregg, John W., 143, 145–46, 157
Gregory, Sadie, 68, 73, 129, 130, 165, 166, 168
Gregory, Warren, 68, 73, 119, 128, 129, 130, 166, 167, 168
Guadet, Julien, 29
Guastavino, Rafael, 86, 187n25; tiles manufactured by, 85–87, *86,* 188n28;
        vaulting system of, 86, 187n25

Haight, H. H., 25

Hale, Ruben, 117

Harmon Gymnasium (Berkeley campus), 62, 89

Harris, Harvey, 90

Hastings, Thomas, 50

Haviland Hall (Berkeley campus), 162–63, *163*

Hays, William C., 69, 71, 90, 102–3, 113, 123, *169*, 170, 190n35, 191n45

Hearst, George R., 27

Hearst, Phoebe Apperson, 27, *27*, 69, 73, 93, 154, 184n6; Berkeley architectural plan sponsored by, 27, 30, 33, 39–40, 42–43, 45, 48, 50, 52, 62, 63, 74, 80, 97, 114; and relations with Émile Bénard, 39–40, 42–43, 45, 48, 52; and relations with JGH, 45, 57, 59, 80, 114, 119

Hearst, William Randolph, 59, 61

Hearst Architectural Plan, competition for, 27–31, 32, 33–38, *35*, *36*, *38*; and Bénard's design, 33, 34, 36, 38, 63, 66, 98; and JGH's design, 33, 35, 35–36, *44*; Maybeck's involvement in, 27–29

Hearst Architectural Plan, postcompetition phase of: and Bénard's difficult temperament, 39–40, 42–43; and Bénard's revised design, 40, *41*, 42, 45, 63, 65; importance of main axis in, *41*, 48, 55–56, 57, 62, 64–66, 79, 89–90, 98–99, 150, 162; JGH's recruitment for, 43, 45–50, 52–56; and JGH's revision of Bénard's design, 47–48, 57, 59, 63–67, 78, 79, 89, 98, *116*, 141, *plate 1*; JGH as supervising architect of, 47, 50, 52, 54, 57, 63, 69, 89   90, 92, 96–97, 112–15, *116*, 120, 156–58, 166–67, 189n34, 190n35; Maybeck's involvement in, 40, 42, 43; and Pascal's defense of Bénard, 43, 45, 52, 55–56

Hearst Avenue, in Berkeley, *41*, 98, 165, *170*

Hearst Greek Theater (Berkeley campus), 59, *60*, 61, *61*, 63, 89

Hearst Hall (Berkeley campus), 62

Hearst Memorial Mining Building (Berkeley campus), 27, 45, 56, 59, 63, 79–80, *81–83*, 83–88, *86–87*, 89, 106, *116*, 149, 188n28, *plates 4–6*

Henderson, H. V., 96–97, 143

Hesse Hall (Berkeley campus), 162, 164

Highland Place, in Berkeley, 73

Hilgard Hall (Berkeley campus), 137, *144–45*, 146, 150, 151, 164, *plates 13–15*

Hillegass tract, in Berkeley, 66, *116*

Hobart, Lewis P., 191n45

Hoover, Ira Wilson, 90

Hotel Renaissance, in New York City, 20, 21, 68

Howard, Amasa (JGH's brother), 2

Howard, Charles Houghton (JGH's son), 21, 68, 166, 192n52

Howard, Edwin (JGH's brother), 2

Howard, Henry Temple (JGH's son), 21, 68, 152–53, 154, 165, 166, 167, 168, 192–93n52, 192n54

Howard, Janette (JGH's daughter). *See* Wallace, Janette Howard

Howard, John Galen: awards and prizes received by, 14, 17, 52; charged with unprofessional conduct, 123–28; death of, 174; drawings by, *4*, *5*, *6*, 6, 11, 13, 15, *110*, *111*, *142*, *143*, *158*, *159*, *162*, *163*, *175*; and education at Académie Julian (Paris), 11; and education at Art Students League (New York), 13; and education at Boston Latin School, 2; and education at École des Beaux-Arts (Paris), 14–19; and education at Massachusetts Institute of Technology (MIT), 1, 2–3; and employment by Caukin & Haas, 6–7; and employment by McKim, Mead & White, 12–14, 52, 54; and employment by Henry Hobson Richardson, 1, 3; and employment by University of California, 47, 50, 52, 54, 57, 63, 69, 89–90, 92–94, 96–97, 112–15, *116*, 120, 156–58, 166–72, 189n34, 190n35; and employment by James M. Wood, 8, 9–10; and engagement to Mary Robertson Bradbury, 17–18; and family relations, 2–3, 18–19, 21, 68, 69, 73, 115, 152, 154, 166, 174; genealogical research by, 174; graphic signature of, *175*; income of, 52, 97, 112–13, 114, 115, 120, 158, 190n35; on iron construction, 20; on landscape architecture, 143, 145; leisure activities enjoyed by, 69, 72, 73; and partnership with Samuel M. Cauldwell, 21, 30, 35, *51*; and partnership with John Debbo Galloway, 92, 94, 112, 189n32; and partnership with William C. Hays, 90; and partnership with Arthur Markwart, 90; and partnership with Dan Everett Waid, 63, 186n19; physical appearance of, *12*, 49, 92, *113*, *166*, 168, *169*; poetry by, 72, 119–20, 130, 133, 152, 153, 155, 167, 173–74, 191n46; political views of, 155; private practice launched by, 21; and professorship at University of California, 52, 63, 69, 93–94, 114, 168–72; and Red Cross service, 153, 154; and relations with Émile Bénard, 54–56; and relations with Ernest Coxhead, 1, 2, 8, 31, 46; and relations with Gregory family, 68, 73, 119, 128, 129, 130, 166, 168; and relations with Phoebe Apperson Hearst, 45, 57, 59, 80, 114, 119, 154; and relations with Willis Polk, 1, 2, 8–9, 31, 37, 123; and relations with Benjamin Ide Wheeler, 45–50, 52, 59, 102–3, 168–69; and relations with Joseph Worcester, 37–38, 46–47, 68, 168; and residence in Berkeley, 68–69, 70–72, 71–73, 129–30, *130–31*, 132, 165–66, 168, 173; and residence in Boston, 1, 2; and residence in Carmel, 73, 152; and residence in Los Angeles, 1–2, 3–4, 6–7, 8, 10, 71; and residence in New Jersey, 21; and residence in New York, 12–14; and residence in Paris, 14–19; and residence in San Francisco, 166, 168; and sabbaticals, 115, 152, 167, 174; San Francisco Society of Architects formed by, 127–28, 191n45; Society of Beaux-Arts Architects cofounded by, 19; speeches given by, 48–49, 61, 80, 85; and travels in Europe, 11–12, 54–55, 115, 118, 137, 153–54, 167, 173; and visits to Berkeley, 30–31, 45–49, 59; and visits to San Francisco, 10, 30–31, 46–47, 57, 59; watercolor by, 14; and World War I, 153–54; writings by, 20, 63–67, 72, 78, 83–84, 98, 106, 113–15, 119–20, 133, 152, 153, 155, 167, 172–75, 191n46

Howard, John Galen, architectural designs by, 177–81; Agriculture Hall (Berkeley), 116, 134, *136–38*, 137, 139, 146; Alaska-Yukon-Pacific exposition (Seattle), 95–96, *96*, 112, 118; "Ark" (architecture department building, Berkeley), *91*, *93*, 93–95; Berkeley residences, 69, 70–72, 71–73, *75*, 129–30, *130–31*, 132, 186n20; Boalt Hall (Berkeley), 79, 106, *106–9*, 108–9, *116*; California Hall (Berkeley), 63, 74, *76*, *77*, 78, 79, *116*; California Memorial Stadium (Berkeley), *155*, 155–56; Civic Center (San Francisco), 120, *121*, 122, 123–28, *126*; Cloyne Court (Berkeley), 73; Doe Memorial Library (Berkeley), *76–77*, 97, 98–100, *99*, *101–4*, 102–3, 105–6, *116*, 193n57; Essex Hotel (New York City), 21; Gilman Hall (Berkeley), 150–51, *151*; Haviland Hall (Berkeley), 162–63, *163*; Hearst Architectural Plan competition entry, *33*, *35*, 35–36; Hearst Greek Theater (Berkeley), 59, *60*, 61, *61*, 63; Hearst Memorial Mining Building (Berkeley), 45, 54, 56, 59, 63, 79–80, *81–83*, 83–88, *86–87*, 106, *116*; Hesse Hall (Berkeley), 162, 164; Hilgard Hall (Berkeley), 146, 164; Hotel Renaissance (New York City), 20, 21, 68; Italian American Bank (San Francisco), 90; Julliard townhouse (New York), 21; Le Conte Hall (Berkeley), *143*, *151*, 161–62, *162*; Long Island City Hospital, 63; Madison Square Garden building (New York City), 13, 52; Majestic Theater (Boston), 21, 63; miscellaneous postwar projects, 154; Montclair Library (New Jersey), 63; Newark High School (New Jersey), 21; New York Public Library, 21, 50, *51*; Pan-American Exposition tower (Buffalo), 52, *53*, 118; Philosophy Hall (Berkeley), *79*; power plant (Berkeley), 95; Sather Gate (Berkeley), 109–10, *110–11*, *116*; Sather Tower (Berkeley), *116*, 139, *140–42*, 141; Senior Men's Hall (Berkeley), 95, 161; Stephens Memorial Hall (Berkeley), *159–60*, 161; student union (Berkeley), *160*, 161; Wheeler Hall (Berkeley), 65, 146, *147–48*, 149–50; Women's Faculty Club (Berkeley), 161. *See also names of specific buildings*

Howard, John Langley (JGH's son), 68, 166
Howard, Levi (JGH's father), 2
Howard, Mary (née Bradbury; JGH's wife), 17–18, *18*, 68, 69, 130, *132*, 133, 153, 154, 165, 166, 167, *167*, 168, 172–74
Howard, Robert Boardman (JGH's son), 21, 68, 152, 154, 165, 166, 173, 192n52
Howard & Cauldwell architectural firm, 21, 30, 35
Howard & Galloway architectural firm, 92, 94, 95–96, 112
Howell, John, 113, 133
Howells, Stokes & Hornbostel architectural firm, 35
Howison, George H., 31
Hunt, Myron, 90, 193n57
Hunt, Richard Morris, 14
Hunt, Thomas Forsyth, 145–46

Iron construction, 19–20
Italian American Bank, in San Francisco, 92
Italian Renaissance, 25, 106, 137

Jackson, Frank, 57
Jones, William Carey, 27, 29, 39, 40, 45, 100
Jory, Stafford, *141*
Julliard, A. D., 21

Keeler, Charles, 46–47
Keith, William, 37, 93, 173, 193n58
Kelham, George, 126–27, 191n45
Kellogg, Martin, 27, 88
Kelly, Brendan, 188n28
Kerr, Clark, 192n48
Keynes, John Maynard, 155
Kreysler, William, 188n28

Labrouste, Henri, 25, 86
Laloux, Victor-Alexandre-Frédéric, 15
Landscape architecture, 139, 141, 143, 145–46
Latin heritage, in California, 78–79
Lawson, Andrew, 100
League of Nations, 155
Le Conte, John, 161–62
Le Conte, Joseph, 161–62
Le Conte Avenue, in Berkeley, 69, 73
Le Conte Hall (Berkeley campus), *143*, *151*, 161–62, *162*
Legislature, California state, 22, 25, 33, 61, 74
Lempke, Max, 90
Le Nôtre, André, 143
Leroy Avenue, in Berkeley, 129. *See also* "Rose Leroy"
Lescher, Theodore A., 39, 45
Leuschner, Armin O., 149
Leuschner Observatory (Berkeley campus), 62
Lewis, Gilbert, 151
Library (Berkeley campus). *See* Doe Memorial Library
Licensing of architects, 19
Log cabins, 95
Long Island City Hospital, 63
Lord, Hewlett & Hull, 35
Los Angeles, 1–2, 3–4, 6–7, 8, 10, 71, 154
Louisiana Purchase Exposition, in St. Louis, 26

Majestic Theater, in Boston, 21, 63
Markwart, Arthur, 90
Marsten, George, 118, 119
Massachusetts Institute of Technology (MIT), 1, 2–3, 9, 14
Matthews, Edgar A., 73, 123, 126–28
Maybeck, Bernard, 26–29, 31, 37, 40, 42, 43, 46, 62, 73, 157, 185n13, 187n24
McClaren, John, 30
McDougall, George B., 126, 127
McKim, Charles Follen, 13, 15, 17, 25, 52, 54
McKim, Mead & White architectural firm, 12–14, 17, 25, 30, 35, 86
Mechanics and Mining building (Berkeley campus), 62
Mediterranean style, 74, 85, 137
Men's Faculty Club (Berkeley campus), 161, 187n24
Meyer, Frederick H., 123, 125, 127, 128, 191n45
Meyers, H. H., 123, 125, 127, 128, 191n45
Michelangelo, 11
Miller, Adolph C., 72
Mining Building (Berkeley campus). *See* Hearst Memorial Mining Building
Mission Revival style, 78
Missions, colonial, 6, *6*, 8, 10, 70, 71, 78, 85, 186n22, 186–87n24
Moffitt, James K., 73
Monet, Claude, 153
Mooser, William, 123, 126, 128
Morgan, Julia, 90, 193n57
Morrill Act, 25
Morrison Room (Berkeley campus), 99
Morrow, Irving F., 149–50, 183–84n4
Muir, John, 4, 93
Mullgardt, L. C., 191n45

Neihardt, John G., 133, 192n47
Neoclassic style, 11, 74, 77, 78, 83–85, 102–3, 105, 106, 137
New York City, 12–14, 19, 20, 21, 68; public library in, 21, 50, *51*, 103
North Hall (Berkeley campus), 24, 62, 66, 98, 99, *100–101*, *104*, 106, 149, 162, *163*

Oakey, Alexander, 30
Oakland, 22, 23, 25, 62, 112
Olmsted, Frederick Law, 62
Olmsted Brothers, 95, 118, 119

Order of the Golden Bear, 95
Oxford Street, in Berkeley, 65, 90, 98

Page & Turnbull architectural firm, 188n28
Palace Hotel, in San Francisco, 10
Palmer & Hornbostel architectural firm, 112
Panama-California International Exposition, in San Diego, 26, 118–19
Panama Canal, opening of, 115, 117, 118
Panama-Pacific International Exposition, in San Francisco, 26, 117, 118, 119, 121, 125, 146
Pan-American Exposition, in Buffalo, 26, 52, 53, 118
Paris, 11, 14–19, 20, 25, 29, 153–54. *See also* École des Beaux-Arts
Partridge, Loren, 88
Pasadena, 4, 8, 9, 73
Pascal, Jean-Louis, 29, 34, 39, 42, 43, 45, 52, 54–56, 62
Perry, Warren, 169, 172
Pheidias (poem by JGH), 152
Phelan, James Duval, 117
Philosophy Hall (Berkeley campus), 79, 108
Piedmont Avenue, in Berkeley, 156
Pissis, Albert, 45, 74, 112, 191n45
Plowman, George T., 90
Poetry, by JGH, 72, 119–20, 130, 133, 152, 153, 155, 167, 173–74, 191n46
Polk, Willis, 1, 2, 8–9, 119, 168, 185n13, 191n45, 193n55; and Hearst Architectural Plan, 31, 36–37, 38; and San Francisco AIA chapter, 126–27; and San Francisco Civic Center, 121, 123
W. W. Polk & Son architectural firm, 9
Porter, Bruce, 37, 46
Power plant, on Berkeley campus, 89, 95
Prairie School style, 90
Presbytery of San Francisco, 23
President's house (Berkeley campus), 45, 74, 75, 89, 137
Professionalization of architectural practice, 19
Purcell, William Gray, 90
Puvis de Chavannes, Pierre-Cécile, 17

Raiguel, William, 118–19, 153, 154, 191n45
Ratcliff, Slama & Cadwalder architectural firm, 186n20
Ratcliff, Walter, 90
Raymond Hotel, in Pasadena, 4
Red Cross, JGH's service in, 153
Reid, John, 112, 123, 125, 127, 128, 191n45
Reinstein, Jacob B., 26, 27, 29, 30, 31, 39, 40, 42, 43, 47, 57, 59
Renaissance style, 105, 106
Renoir, Pierre-Auguste, 153
Richardson, Henry Hobson, 1, 3, 10, 13, 14, 186n20
Ridge Road, in Berkeley, 69, 70, 72, 73, 92, 94, 129, 165–66, 186n20
Rising, William B., 151
Rococo style, 12
Roeth, Charles F. B., 193n54
Rolph, James, 123, 124
Roman architecture, 11, 74, 102–3, 109, *109*, 146. *See also* Neoclassic style
Rome, 11–12
Roosevelt, Theodore, 61
"Rose Leroy" (JGH's residence), 129–30, *130–31*, 132, 153, 165–66
Rose Street, in Berkeley, 129
Royal Museum of Fine Arts, in Antwerp, 30
Rubens, Peter Paul, 11
Ruef, Abe, 118
Ruskin, John, 20
Rutherford & Chekene engineering firm, 188n28

San Diego, 26, 118–19
San Francisco, 10, 26, 30–31, 37, 38, 90; American Institute of Architects chapter in, 123–28, 191n44; Civic Center in, 120, 121, *122*, 123–28, *126*; earthquake of 1906 in, 92–93, 112, 117; Panama-Pacific International Exposition in, 26, 117, 118, 119, 121, 125; Society of Architects formed in, 127, 191n45

San Juan Capistrano, 10

Santa Barbara, *6, 8*, 10

Santa Cruz, 168

Santa Fe railroad company, 4, 7

Sather, Jane K., 73, 109, 139

Sather, Peder, 109

Sather Gate (Berkeley campus), 109–10, *110–11, 116*, 150

Sather Tower (Berkeley campus), *76–77, 110–11, 116*, 139, *140–42, 141*, 174, *plate 12*

Sawyer, Houghton, 191n45

Scenic Avenue, in Berkeley, 69, 73

Schmitz, Eugene, 117, 118

Schultze, Henry A., 127

Schweinfurth, A. C., 37, 185n13

Scott, W. F., 90

Sculptures, on Berkeley campus, 85, 105, 110, *plates 7, 13, 15–16, 18*

Seattle, 26, 95–96, 112

Seawell, H. W., 170

Second Empire style, 62

Seismic retrofitting: of Doe Memorial Library, 190n41, 191n42; of Hearst Memorial Mining Building, 188n28

Senior Men's Hall (Berkeley campus), 95, *95*, 161

Shattuck Avenue, in Berkeley, 62, 90

Shaw, Norman, 29

Shepley, George, 3

Shepley, Rutan & Coolidge architectural firm, 78, 186n22

Sistine Chapel, 11

Society of Beaux-Arts Architects, 19

South Drive (Berkeley campus), 89, 162

Southern Pacific railroad company, 4, 62

South Hall (Berkeley campus), 24, 62, *65*, 66, 106, 149, 192n49

Sprague, Lucy, 72

Sprague, Mary, 72

Sproul, Robert Gordon, 156–57

Sproul Hall (Berkeley campus), 110

Stanford, Leland, 3, 26, 30, 186n22

Stanford University, 26, 30, 78, 186n22

State funding, for Berkeley campus construction, 33, 61, 74, 99, 134, 146, 149

Steel construction, 77, 86, 92, 100, 134, *143*

Steilberg, Walter, 193n57

Stephens, Henry Morse, 100, 161, 185n15

Stephens Memorial Hall (Berkeley campus), *159–60*, 161

Stephenson, W. P., 189n33

Strawberry Creek, in Berkeley, 33, 66, 109, 110, 141, 161

Streetcars, in Berkeley, 62

Student union (Berkeley campus), *160*, 161

Swedenborgian Church, in San Francisco, 37, 46

Taxation, in California, 22, 33

Telegraph Avenue, in Berkeley, 62, 66, 109, 110

Tharp, Newton J., 112

Thomas, John Hudson, 90

Tietjens, Eunice, 133

Titterton, L. H., 173

Toepke, William H., 123

Topography, of Berkeley campus, 29, 31, 66, 73, 110

Tudor style, 161

University Art Museum (Berkeley campus), 189n33

University Avenue, in Berkeley, *44*, 64–65, 66, 89, 90

University Land and Improvement Company, 73

University of California at Berkeley: architecture department at, 93–94, 143, 145, 169–72; College of Agriculture at, 134, 145; College of Chemistry at, 150–51; division of landscape architecture at, 143, 145–46; early map of, *58*; enrollment in, 25, 79–80, 94, 149, 154; fac-

ulty relations at, 154; founding of, 22–23, 25; regents of, 27, 40, 42, 56, 57, 61, 90, 94, 96, 114, 115, 154, 158, 167, 185n15, 192n48; topography of, 29, 31, 66, 73, 110. *See also* Hearst Architectural Plan; *names of specific buildings*
University of Washington at Seattle, 96

Van Brunt & Howe architectural firm, 9
Vaulting system, Guastavino's, 86, 187n25
Vaux, Calvert, 62
Veblen, Thorstein, 130
Vickery, Atkins & Torrey firm and gallery, *109*, 113

Waid, Dan Everett, 63, 186n19
Wallace, Janette Howard (JGH's daughter), 18, 72, 73, 92, 129, 130, *132*, 152, 154, 165, 166, 167, 168, 172, 173
Wallot, Paul, 29, 34, 54
Ward, Clarence R., 121, 191n45
Ware, William Robert, 3, 9, 14, 29
Washington University, in St. Louis, 113
Ben Weed's amphitheater, 59, 185n16
Weeks, Charles Peter, 57, 191n45
Wellman, Harry R., 192n48
Wellman Hall (Berkeley campus). *See* Agriculture Hall
West Gate (Berkeley campus), 189n30
Wheeler, Benjamin Ide, 33, 43, 49, 52, 55, 56, 73, 74, 93–94, 117, 149, 153, 154, 184n6, 185nn15–16, 190n35; academic career of, 50; donors solicited by, 61, 77, 106; Greek Theater promoted by, 59; and plans for Doe Memorial Library, 100, 102–3; and relations with JGH, 45–50, 52, 59, 102–3, 168–69
Wheeler, Charles, 57
Wheeler Hall (Berkeley campus), 65, 146, *147–48*, 149–50, 152, *plates 16–18*
White, Stanford, 13, 14
Whitton, John, 174
Willey, Samuel H., 22
Williams, Virgil, 168
Willingale, Peter, 54
Wilson, Frank, 69, 113
Wilson, Woodrow, 155
Women's Faculty Club (Berkeley campus), 161
Wood, James M., 8, 9–10, 21
Worcester, Joseph, 37–38, 46–47, 68, 168, 185n13
World's Columbian Exposition, in Chicago, 26, 38
World War I, 152–54
Wurster, William W., 168
Wurster Hall (Berkeley campus), 95, 193n56

Young, Harriet, 90

Design, Composition and
Digital Photo Restoration: Chuck Byrne/Design
Type Family: Stone Cycles
Index: Andrew Joron
Printer/Binder: Friesens Corporation